P9-DMY-214

THE PUBLIC OPTION

THE PUBLIC OPTION

How to Expand Freedom, Increase Opportunity, and Promote Equality

Ganesh Sitaraman *and* Anne L. Alstott

Harvard University Press

Cambridge, Massachusetts
London, England
2019

Printed in the United States of America

First printing

Library of Congress Cataloging-in-Publication Data

Names: Sitaraman, Ganesh, author. | Alstott, Anne, 1963– author.
Title: The public option : how to expand freedom, increase opportunity, and promote equality / Ganesh Sitaraman and Anne L. Alstott.
Description: Cambridge, Massachusetts : Harvard University Press, 2019. | Includes bibliographical references and index.
Identifiers: LCCN 2018040631 | ISBN 9780674987333 (alk. paper)
Subjects: LCSH: Public administration—United States. | Government ownership—United States. | Government property—United States. | Public interest—United States. | United States—Politics and government. | United States—Economic policy.
Classification: LCC HD3885 .S58 2019 | DDC 338.6/20973—dc23
LC record available at https://lccn.loc.gov/2018040631

Contents

Part Three
THE PUBLIC OPTION AND PUBLIC POLICY

THE PUBLIC OPTION

Introduction

The role of public institutions in our lives is so familiar that we mostly don't give them much thought. We stop by the local post office to mail a letter, without reflecting on the public support that makes it possible to send that letter anywhere in the country for less than a dollar. We drop off our kids at the public school and take the subway, train, or highway to work. Many of us have attended state universities, and many more have vacationed at a national park or cooled off at a public swimming pool. And we count on Social Security and Medicare to provide security for us after we retire.

Since the founding of our country, Americans have drawn on the power of public action to lay the foundations of the freedom and equality that we prize. These foundations are, in large measure, made up of the very institutions that we take so much for granted.

It's not a radical idea to acknowledge that public institutions, funded by the public and voted on by the public, play an essential role in our everyday lives. What is new, and what we focus on in this book, is that many beloved American institutions take a distinctive form that we call the *public option.* The public option refers to a government program with two features: it provides an important service at a reasonable cost, and it coexists, quite peaceably, with one or more private options offering the same service. You can mail a package via the U.S. Postal Service, or you can pay Federal Express to deliver it more quickly. You can vacation in Yosemite National Park for a moderate fee, or (if you can afford it) pay for fancier digs in a private resort. You can check out a book for free from the public library, or you can buy your own private copy at a bookstore or online.

As these examples suggest, the public option is often attractive because it offers a high-quality service for a reasonable price. But it is an option, competing directly with other options provided by the private market—a form of competition that can be beneficial to both the public and the private realm. This aspect of the public option makes it a very American institution; it leverages public resources without preempting private provision.

We believe that the public option has the potential to do even more. We show in this book that new public options could transform many different spheres of life, from child care to college, from banking to retirement, and beyond.

The idea of the public option has recently been in the news thanks to the debate about health care coverage. In the lead-up to the passage of the Affordable Care Act in 2010, policy makers struggled with how to guarantee universal coverage at a reasonable price. One promising proposal, though it was not enacted, was called the "public option"—a government health insurance program that would be offered alongside private plans and would ensure that anyone could buy coverage at a fixed, affordable price.

The public option in health care has three big advantages. First, it's public: the government (unlike a private company) can guarantee access to health care at a fixed price. Two, it's an option: no one has to use it. If the public insurance plan is a good deal, well, then snap it up. But if you like the terms offered by Aetna or Blue Cross better, then sign up with them. Finally, because the public option exists alongside the private option, the private option has to compete to make a better product—something especially important in highly concentrated sectors like health care.

The public option didn't make it into the Affordable Care Act, but it is a feature of many other institutions that are central to American life. The public school movement opened up the possibility of education to the American masses—an option previously available only to families that could afford private tutors or schools. The Postal Service offers a public option in every neighborhood by providing a public mail service that exists alongside—and competes with—private options like Federal Express and UPS. Public universities are public options, often providing excellent education at a price far below that of private schools. But families can choose the route that suits them.

Public options are everywhere, and they are some of the most celebrated, beloved, important, and effective parts of our society. Public libraries and national parks are obvious treasures, but the list goes on and on: public swimming pools, public golf courses, public housing, public broadcasting like NPR, public defenders in the courts, public highways and transit systems, public museums like the Smithsonian. Not to mention the humble neighborhood playground: you can take your child to play on the swing set at the public park down the street—or, if you prefer, you can choose to buy your own and put it in your private backyard.

The two of us were talking about how pervasive these public options are when we had our lightbulb moment: "Why not try public options in other areas?" we wondered. Our thoughts turned first to retirement. Both of us had been federal employees early in our careers, and so we knew firsthand that the government has an excellent retirement plan for its workers, providing safe investment options with low fees. Some policy wonks have proposed extending this program to all Americans, and we realized that this would amount to a public option for retirement funding.

The possibilities mushroomed as we brainstormed and began our research. Postal banking—that is, a basic bank account offered via the postal service—exists in many countries and actually existed in the United States for a big chunk of the twentieth century. Such a service could help address the precarious financial position of many low- and moderate-income families, who are not well served by private banks. And on we went. We knew we'd have to think hard and put the idea through its paces, but it seemed incredibly promising then, and it seems even more so now that we have worked out our ideas in more detail.

But we also noticed a puzzle. The public option is thoroughly familiar, and yet it hasn't—outside the specialized arena of health care—formed part of the national conversation about the challenges facing the United States in the twenty-first century. The reason, we have come to believe, is that many Americans have lost faith both in government and in private markets.

The anti-government script is part and parcel of American politics these days, and we all know it by heart. Government is bloated; government is wasteful; government is run by bureaucrats who are lazy and incompetent. Markets, in contrast, are said to be efficient and effective: they discipline any bad actors on their own, and they save money while providing excellent services. On this view, it follows that the best—and only—course is to privatize government functions and starve the government Leviathan.

This romance with the private marketplace took a big hit during the global financial crisis of 2008, when financial markets imploded, largely as a result of speculation, fraud, and illegal behavior. The Great Recession threw millions of Americans out of work, and they learned (or relearned) the lesson that private firms and markets, too, can be bloated, wasteful, and incompetent. In the years since, company after company has been in the news for getting hacked (Equifax), engaging in widespread fraud (Wells Fargo), or scooping up data without our full consent (Facebook).

The experience of the Great Recession and the scandals of the years since could leave us mired in cynicism. We could conclude that nothing works—that government and private firms are equally corrupt and incompetent.

But the two of us reject this cynical view. We don't think that government or markets are perfect, but neither do we see them as hopelessly incompetent. We think it's not only possible but critical to take a pragmatic look at what government can do well. All around us are public options—schools, universities, parks, Social Security—that function really well. We should sit up and take notice of the big role that public options already play in everyday life. And we should ask what more they might do.

The United States has navigated disruptive social and economic change over and over throughout its history. Now, as then, we can join together to ensure that every American, young, middle-aged, or old, has access to the social infrastructure necessary for a flourishing life. It turns out that public options can help reconstruct that foundation. They could improve access to affordable education, affordable child care, and secure retirement—just to name a few possibilities—and thus expand freedom, increase opportunity, and promote equality, all at the same time.

In the last fifty years, one of the most popular public policy solutions to virtually any problem was the market subsidy. A market subsidy drops government money into the marketplace, usually by means of tax subsidies or vouchers. The idea is that the invisible hand of competition will operate to allocate goods like health care, college education, and retirement savings in the most beneficial way. But market subsidies have failed, often spectacularly. Prices for health care, college, and child care are higher than ever, and increasingly out of reach for ordinary families. Rather than lowering costs to consumers, subsidies have too often ended up in the pockets of insurance companies and business managers.

Public options, by contrast, use direct government provision to ensure universal access. At the same time, they make markets work better. Instead of tossing government dollars into the marketplace, public options provide citizens with services at a guaranteed price and quality. And when they operate alongside private options, they can actually make markets work better simultaneously. We understand the virtue of markets in promoting consumer choice and allocating resources, and we believe that private markets should be allowed to do their work—when they can do it well. What public options do is to provide a reliable starting point for consumers and an anchor for market competition.

To understand the potential of public options, however, we must also confront their limitations. Public education is a prime example. Free public education is an important foundation for college and life success, and it has served generations of Americans well. But public schools in poor districts face an array of challenges. Public housing, to take another example, has provided safe and affordable shelter for generations of working-class families. But some housing developments have been badly run or have become havens for crime. Our optimism is not naive. We realize that public options cannot magically solve the economic, social, and political problems of poverty or structural racism. While we mean to restore your faith in such programs, we do not intend to do so by asking you to take anything on faith alone.

In Part 1, we make a general case for public options. We show why and how they can help shore up the social infrastructure of America, ensuring that every citizen has the opportunity to enjoy a productive and healthy life. Chapter 1 tours the dominant approaches to public policy from the end of World War II to the present—the era that saw the expansion of employer-based benefits, followed by deregulation and tax cuts imposed by neoliberals. In Chapter 2, we provide a basic definition of public options and make the case for how they expand freedom and opportunity, improve market competition, are good for businesses, and strengthen our democracy. We then dig deeper in Chapter 3, where we explore how public options relate to alternative—market and regulatory—approaches to addressing public policy problems. Chapter 4 tackles some counterarguments and discusses the limits of public options.

In Part 2, we explain how public options have worked across a variety of sectors. Chapter 5 looks at some prominent successes, ranging from the post office, public libraries, and public swimming pools to Social Security. In Chapter 6, we discuss some of the areas where public options have had serious challenges, including public education and public housing. We investigate what went wrong and why subsidies are not the answer.

In Part 3, we consider how a public option could help address critically important sectors of our social infrastructure. Chapters 7 through 12 look in detail at five of these sectors, retirement, higher education, banking, child care, and health care, and suggest some additional areas from broadband internet to credit reporting.

Americans have long understood the power of collective action to promote the essential values of freedom and equality. Public options are evidence of our common civic faith; restoring our confidence in them, and expanding their reach, will ensure that the twenty-first century is a time of security and prosperity for all.

Part One

UNDERSTANDING THE PUBLIC OPTION

1

The Limits of Private Action

Since the end of World War II, two big ideas have animated American public policy. Employer-sponsored social benefits dominated from the late 1940s through the 1970s. Neoliberalism, prominent from the 1980s through the 2000s, turned to markets and private actors to achieve social goods.

Both of these models have now failed, albeit for different reasons. Sea changes in work and family life mean that virtually no one anymore has a lifetime job with union protections and secure benefits. And the financial turmoil of the early 2000s, culminating in the Great Recession, taught us hard lessons about the dangers of relying on unregulated markets. The financial crash triggered mass unemployment and mass foreclosures that ruined lives and still echo today, a decade later. No longer can anyone suppose that the unregulated market will provide a secure platform on which ordinary people can build their lives. Knowing something about the intentions behind both efforts, and how and why they came undone, is essential before we turn to the promise of public options.

The End of the Treaty of Detroit

In the spring of 1950, Walter Reuther, the head of the United Auto Workers, and Charlie Wilson, the head of General Motors (GM), came to a historic agreement. GM would give its workers a monthly $125 pension, cover half the cost of health care, and increase pay in step with increases in the cost of living and rising productivity. *Businessweek* called it a moment of "industrial statesmanship." *Fortune* dubbed the agreement the "Treaty of Detroit."[1]

The Treaty of Detroit established the paradigm for American social policy in the post–World War II era. Many people incorrectly think that the mid-twentieth century was defined by "big-government liberalism," a system in which the federal government provides a robust welfare state to the American people. But this was not the model for public policy in mid-twentieth-century in America. In fact, American public policy rarely took on the mantle of government-provided social goods. There were a few big-government programs—most notably Social Security and Medicare—but these were exceptions, not the rule. As proof, just compare our efforts to those of European countries. European governments provided socialized health care, free college education, and robust social welfare benefits to their citizens regardless of their wealth. The American government did none of those things. Under the Treaty of Detroit, it was General Motors, not Uncle Sam, that provided workers with a pension and health care. In the decades after 1950 this model spread, and it became the norm for much of the industrial and corporate sectors, whether or not they were unionized. We want to be clear that the employer-based approach was a model, a framework. Not everyone was included in it, and it didn't fully succeed even on its own terms. But it served as a powerful vision for how social policy was supposed to work.

The employer-benefits approach was based on a number of assumptions. The first was that people would have the same employer for their entire working life, starting at age eighteen or twenty-two and continuing until retirement at age sixty-five. Employees were expected to be hardworking and responsible; in return for their loyalty, employers paid them a decent wage, and their jobs were secure.[2] Retirement meant a big party with friends and family and a gold watch from the employer, as a token of appreciation.

The second assumption was that employers would provide workers with critical social benefits. Employees would get health care and pensions, and eventually even educational, child care, housing, transportation, and other benefits, from their employers, not from the government. Employer-based benefits had been around since the late nineteenth century, but they took off during the 1940s. Between 1940 and 1945, health insurance coverage expanded from 1.3 million American workers to 32 million workers.[3] After the war, the country continued along the employer-based benefits path instead of creating national programs, as many European countries did. In America, government programs existed largely as a safety net for those who fell through the cracks of the employer-based system. The extremely poor received health care through Medicaid. The elderly and retirees got their health care through Medicare and a minimal pension through Social Security's old age provisions. The disabled, orphans, and widows received a basic income through Social Security. But these were exceptions. As a general approach to public policy, ordinary Americans would not get their benefits from the government.

The third assumption underlying the Treaty of Detroit was that employers would provide a "family wage." Families were thought of as a male breadwinner, a stay-at-home wife, and children.[4] When Reuther and Wilson negotiated the Treaty of Detroit, the idea of wages rising with the cost of living and with productivity improvements was partly a function of the need for workers to provide for their families. Indeed, between 1948 and 1978, the median man's income kept pace pretty well with productivity. Productivity rose 108 percent during this period; hourly compensation increased 96 percent.[5]

Starting in the 1970s, however, companies increasingly began withdrawing from the Treaty of Detroit. Oil shocks, stagflation, increasing competition from abroad, and an ideological shift that emphasized shareholder profits instead of stakeholder well-being all contributed to corporations shedding the view that they were "in it together" with their workers. Employers instead increasingly shifted risk onto their workers.[6] One of the best examples of what Jacob Hacker calls the "great risk shift" was the move from providing defined-benefit pension plans to offering defined-contribution pension plans. Defined-benefit plans give retirees a fixed amount in their yearly pension, which means the risk of market fluctuations is borne by the employer sponsoring the pension. Defined-contribution plans, in contrast, involve employees putting money into pension funds and investing that money; the retiree, not the company, bears the risks of market fluctuations. In 1980, there were 30 million defined-benefit plan participants, compared to only 19 million defined-contribution participants. By 2006, there were only 20 million defined-benefit participants, compared to 66 million defined-contribution participants.[7] Today companies rarely, if ever, offer new defined benefit pension plans to their employees. Workers bear the risks of the market.

The trouble with the Treaty of Detroit model is that the assumptions undergirding the system of employer-based benefits are no longer reasonable, if they ever were. Americans don't stay in the same job or career for decades. According to a 2016 Gallup study, 21 percent of millennials reported changing jobs within the past year.[8] This isn't unique to millennials. Even past generations of workers went through multiple job transitions throughout their lifetimes.[9]

When people do work for companies, they increasingly are not actually employees of the company. The most prominent example is Uber and the "gig economy." Uber claims that drivers are just using their mobile platform, and they are therefore not employees of the tech company. On this understanding of the gig economy, because workers are not employees, the company doesn't have to provide benefits—no retirement package, no health insurance, no unemployment insurance.

The gig economy might get the most attention, but technology companies aren't the only—or even the most common—cases of this phenomenon. Consider a housekeeper working at the San Francisco Marriott. Even though its name is prominently displayed outside, Marriott doesn't own the property—a company called Host Hotels and Resorts does. Nor does Marriott employ the housekeeper or manage her hours or payroll—that's the job of

Crestline Hotels and Resorts, a hotel management company. Marriott does establish guidelines for how the housekeeping staff is supposed to maintain the hotel rooms. But this is a far cry from the old days, in which Marriott would have owned the property, managed the hotel, and employed the people working there. This example, taken from David Weil's *The Fissured Workplace,* shows just how far the employer-employee relationship has changed in the last generation.[10] Today, Weil argues, workplaces across a variety of sectors have been fractured, leading to complex employment relationships. Employees are now often working for contractors or subcontractors. Sometimes they are independent contractors who have no direct relationship with a company at all. Whether you call it the "gig economy," the "1099 economy," or the "patchwork economy," the common theme is that workers are increasingly cobbling together different forms of employment—part-time, gig, independent contracting, and self-employment.[11] They aren't working for a single employer.

The decline of the lifetime employer idea and the fissuring of American workplaces strike at the very core of the Treaty of Detroit's employer-based benefits model. It makes little sense for employers to pay expansive pensions to a worker whose tenure is only a few years. And for workers who switch jobs frequently, it is a hassle to change retirement plans and health care providers every time they move to a new company. When companies use independent contractors or gig workers, the situation is even more problematic. These individuals don't get any benefits. The legacy of the Treaty of Detroit leaves them out in the cold.

The basic idea behind the family wage hasn't fared well, either. Almost every assumption behind the imagined ideal of a 1950sstyle family, where Dad comes home from work to a stay-at-home mom and a couple of kids, is out of date. While wages and productivity grew together in the Treaty of Detroit era, the ordinary male worker's wages have been stagnant since the 1970s.[12] True, household incomes continued to rise through the 1970s and 1980s until about 2000.[13] But this was partly because women entered the workforce in increasing numbers. In May 1950, when the Treaty of Detroit was signed, 33 percent of women were in the workforce. Fifty years later, in May 2000, that number was 60 percent.[14] Women's income buoyed households that were already struggling under the model of breadwinner liberalism.

Whether or not the Treaty of Detroit paradigm suited the age of managerial corporations, it is certainly out of sync with employment and families today. Adhering to the approach of employer-based benefits makes little sense given contemporary conditions. While some people might be nostalgic for the America of the 1950s, nostalgia is rarely a good guide to public policy.

The Perils of Neoliberalism

As companies withdrew from the Treaty of Detroit, a second paradigm for public policy took hold. Neoliberalism was defined by its desire to use markets as the means to achieve social goals and by its view that markets were an end in themselves.[15] Ideologically, neoliberalism grew out of a conservative intellectual movement that was powered by anti-government Austrian economic theorists who fled Europe in the mid-twentieth century, and it was buoyed by the Cold War and the fear of communism.[16] It gained political dominance with the elections of Ronald

Reagan in the United States and Margaret Thatcher in the United Kingdom and became virtually universal when liberals turned to neoliberal policies in the 1990s and 2000s.[17]

When it came to public policy, neoliberals thought that markets—rooted in strong private property and contract rights—were the best way to achieve the well-being of society and to preserve and advance freedom for all. On their theory, government would do little more than enforce contract and property rights. If government was going to act to advance broader social goals (like health or education), it would do so through private markets. Privatization involved outsourcing government functions to profit-seeking companies. Deregulation became central to neoliberalism because it freed markets to act without constraints. Vouchers, state-provided coupons to purchase private services, became the dominant approach for how government could advance social goals by market means.[18]

When we look back from beyond the 2008 crash, neoliberalism seems woefully naive. But Reagan-era policy makers were facing their own age of anxiety and were searching for an alternative to old institutions that no longer seemed viable. The economic chaos of the late 1970s, with high inflation and economic stagnation, called for desperate measures. The old Treaty of Detroit model was already moribund. Modern economics had resurrected Adam Smith and the promise that an unregulated, laissez-faire market could do a far better job than any command-and-control government intervention.

And we cannot forget the role of the Cold War. Neoliberalism equated markets with freedom and big government with Soviet-style planned economies. Unfettered capitalism, the Reaganites believed, could pull the United States out of the economic doldrums of the late 1970s and provide the fuel needed to win a decisive economic, political, and ideological victory against the Soviets.

But in retrospect, we know that neoliberalism had a number of failings, including an almost religious faith in markets even in the face of empirical evidence of their failings and flaws. Unquestioning acceptance of market efficiency often led proponents to ignore fundamental problems with the neoliberal approach: that profit-seeking actors would try to use fraud, force, and deception to cheat people for their own gain; that markets can lead to the concentration of economic power and, as a result, undermine the very functioning of competitive markets; and that profit-seeking actors would seek to use government to benefit themselves, at the expense of taxpayers, consumers, and a competitive market. All of these neoliberal problems came home to roost at one time or another, and sometimes all at the same time.[19]

Consider the neoliberal turn in higher education, for-profit colleges. Instead of the government funding public universities and community colleges directly and allowing people to attend private non-profit colleges if they desire, the neoliberal approach urged two things. First, private, profit-seeking actors should run institutions of higher education; second, the government should give students a voucher to go to whatever school they wanted. The vouchers in this case are Pell Grants, federal grants given to students directly for use at any college or university, and federal student loans, some of which the government subsidizes by not requiring students to pay interest while in school. On the neoliberal model, students can use Pell Grants and federal student loans at any school in the market—public, nonprofit, or for-profit. The hope was that the market would create new and better options for students.

So how did the experiment turn out? The neoliberal higher education model turned into a way for shareholders and CEOs to make boatloads of money off taxpayers by deceiving prospective students, saddling them with unconscionable levels of debt, and leaving them without a decent education or any reasonable job prospects.

According to a report from the U.S. Senate Committee on Health, Education, Labor, and Pensions, in 2009, 86 percent of the revenues for the fifteen publicly traded for-profit colleges came from taxpayer dollars.[20] Think about what that means. For every $100 of revenue that for-profits earned, $86 came from taxpayers and only $14 came from other sources. And the absolute dollars at stake are large. In the 2009–2010 school year alone, the U.S. government invested $32 billion in for-profits, or a whopping 25 percent of the Department of Education's budget for student aid programs. Pell Grants alone amounted to $7.5 billion (up from only $1.1 billion in 2000–2001).[21]

Neoliberalism's faults are sometimes more subtle. One example is basic banking services. Most of the time we don't notice that dollar bills say on them "legal tender." What that means is that the government has mandated that bills can be used to pay for goods and services. For a variety of reasons, including security and technology, most employers don't pay their employees in legal tender—in cash. Instead, they pay either with a check or with direct deposit. For many people, that isn't a big deal; it's convenient. You just go to the bank and deposit the check, or if you have direct deposit, the money automatically appears in your account. But 7 percent of American households—15.6 million adults and 7.6 million children—don't have a bank account.[22] As a result, just to get access to the money that they are owed for their work, they have to use check-cashing establishments that charge exorbitant fees.

Neoliberalism's faith in markets also too often ignores the consequences of concentrated economic power. In this case, a lesson from history went ignored. In the late nineteenth and early twentieth centuries, industrialization led to massive consolidation of industry. During the "great merger movement" of 1895 to 1904, more than 1,800 firms disappeared. By 1904, 40 percent of American industry was under the control of only 300 corporations.[23] Concentrated economic power had a variety of detrimental consequences. It meant that employers had more power over their workers, it meant that monopolies could raise prices on customers, and it meant that corporations and their wealthy leadership had more resources to influence public policy. In response, Progressive Era reformers passed antitrust laws and public utilities regulations in order to break up or regulate concentrated economic power. They did so not just for economic reasons of efficiency but also for constitutional reasons. They understood that America could not remain a republic—it could not have political freedom—if power was concentrated in a small number of corporations that would try to rig the political system to serve their interests.[24]

Three generations later, during the ascendency of neoliberalism, Robert Bork, then a professor and later a judge, penned a famous tract, *The Antitrust Paradox,* arguing that antitrust policy should not take into account political factors, the market ecosystem, or anything except economic efficiency. As Bork's ideas took hold, antitrust prosecutions languished. Today we are in the midst of what the *Economist* calls the "great merger wave."[25] Looking at 900 sectors of the economy, the magazine found that two-thirds had become more concentrated between 1997 and 2012.[26] Concentrated power once again means less competition, higher prices, and the increasing political power of big monopolies that control virtually every aspect of Americans' lives.

Of course, the 2008 economic crash was one of the consequences of the long neoliberal moment. Deregulation meant deceptive and fraudulent practices in a variety of sectors, including the housing and financial markets. The neoliberal preference to facilitate social goals through government-supported vouchers, subsidies, and incentives only deepened this pathology. Federally supported housing finance allowed financial institutions to capture the benefits of their bets without bearing the risks when those bets went bad. And consolidation and concentration in the financial sector produced Wall Street banks that were "too big to fail," leading to government bailouts.

Despite its many problems, fondness for (if not necessarily robust faith in) neoliberalism remains strong. Many people remain nostalgic for this easy-to-understand approach to public policy. But the financial debacle of 2008–2009 and its continuing aftershocks should leave Americans in no doubt. Nostalgia for neoliberalism is perilous. We need better options.

Beyond Privatization: The Possibilities of Public Options

The public option challenges the privatization agenda by turning it on its head. Privatizers begin with the assumptions, often undefended, that government programs are always and everywhere ineffective and corrupt and that private markets work perfectly. It's no surprise, then, that they propose to turn over public functions—ranging from prisons to roads to welfare programs—to private firms that are motivated by profits.

The case for public options, by contrast, doesn't rest on black-and-white assumptions about either government or the private sector. We don't assume that government always works well, or that government should muscle out private provision. Instead, we think that public options can add social value when the power of government is needed to guarantee universal access to the basics of modern life. So public options aren't socialist-style big government—they don't aim to replace markets. Instead, public options exist alongside market options. Citizens can rely on the public option but also can turn to the marketplace for additional choices, combining public and private options in ways that work best for them.

2

Why Public Options?

The social contract evolves as society changes. In its time, the Treaty of Detroit supported an idea of the social contract that had wide appeal: a lifetime job at a wage that enabled workers to support their families by buying necessities and having the middle-class dream of a house, a car, an annual vacation, and a secure retirement. So the values behind the social contract in that era were something like, "If you are willing to work hard, you can have a good life." In that era, with or without a high school diploma (let alone a college degree), Americans could expect to participate in the good life as long as they were willing to work (or to marry a worker, in the case of many women).

The Treaty of Detroit was a market system, since workers paid for all of this out of their wages. But it wasn't laissez-faire by any stretch of the imagination: government rules supported labor unions and subsidized employer-provided benefits. This system, as Chapter 1 described, fell apart as economic and social conditions changed. Without economic growth and a robust demand for unskilled labor, the Treaty could no longer guarantee profits to firms along with plentiful jobs for workers of all backgrounds.

The neoliberal market subsidies that gained prominence between the 1980s and the early 2000s, by contrast, expressed a very different social contract. Its values were something like, "Everyone has to look out for themselves in the marketplace, but the government will provide a few extra dollars to buy important goods for people who have extremely bad luck in the market." That market ideal answered the access and accountability questions in a characteristic way: citizens should buy whatever education they needed to succeed in the marketplace. As savvy consumers, they should vet providers (like colleges and employers) for themselves. Market subsidies would help poorer students take out loans, but students had to figure out for themselves what jobs would pay the most and how much student debt was too much. So those who picked the wrong majors or were bilked by for-profit schools—well, they had only themselves to blame.

The logic of neoliberalism spread well beyond college and employment, of course. Retirees were told to save for their own retirement, with (or, often, without) government subsidies. Workers were left to choose their own investments and their own advisors. And savers who lost money in the stock market crash or who paid outrageous fees to unscrupulous banks—well, they should have made better choices.

The Great Recession dampened Washington's enthusiasm for the neoliberal social contract. After the crash of 2008, it became much harder to ignore the failures of the marketplace. Big banks' predatory and risky practices came to light, as did profiteering in the student loan market by financial institutions and for-profit colleges. No longer was it tenable to suppose that market subsidies alone would give everyone a fair shake.

But policy makers and citizens alike are struggling to find a new mode of policy making that expresses an appealing social contract for our time. This is where public options can contribute to a national conversation about what we owe each other, as well as to a wonkier discussion about policy tools. Public options express a collective commitment to freedom, to opportunity, and to markets that distribute resources fairly amid the realities of globalization, the gig economy, and modern family life.

What Is a Public Option?

Many people may have encountered the public option during debates over health care. In that context, a public option is a government-provided health insurance policy (think Medicare) that is universally available to every American. But it is also an option. If you don't want to use Medicare for your health insurance, you don't have to. You can buy private health insurance instead. The key is that under a public option, the provision of health care doesn't depend on an employer (as in the Treaty of Detroit model) or on profit-seeking corporations (as under the neoliberal model). Of course, while the public option was discussed in health policy circles in the 1990s and 2000s, it was never enacted.

We can now begin to specify what distinguishes the public option from other policy approaches. A public option is a government program that provides some important good or service, like health insurance, at a controlled price. Libraries, post offices, and public schools are classic public options, and it is important that they be recognized as such. In each case, the government provides an important resource (books, mail service, and education) and makes it available to everyone, either for free or for a low price. Of course, nothing in life is really free, so taxpayers foot the bill for free and below-cost items. But the important point is that we pay nothing extra to borrow a book at the library or have our kids learn arithmetic, and we pay only a few cents to mail a letter.

A public option, then, isn't simply any activity in which government plays a part. Instead, we mean a government program that has two essential elements:

- First, the program guarantees access to important services at a controlled price.
- Second, the program coexists (or could coexist) with private provision of the same service.

When we say that public options operate alongside private options, we have in mind two possibilities. One is what we call a *baseline public option,* which provides a universal, basic level of service. People who want more (either in quantity or quality) can pay for additional, private services, but everyone receives the baseline. In this sense, Social Security is a baseline public option, because nearly all workers participate. You can save more for retirement, if you like, but paying FICA taxes is mandatory. And although you can refuse to claim Social Security benefits, you don't get a refund if you do.[1]

Some public options, though, compete on an equal footing with private services. These *competitive public options* offer higher quality or lower pricing, but participation is optional. So, for example, public libraries provide a competitive public option. Anyone can go to the library, check out a book, and read it at home for free. But the book might not be available right away, and you can't keep it forever. For people who want the book faster or want to read it repeatedly over the years, there's also a private option: purchasing the book.

Implicitly, then, baseline public options enroll everyone, with few or no exceptions. Policy analysts call this an "opt-in default," because people are automatically included and must take affirmative steps to exit (and only some may be permitted to do so). For instance, almost all workers must pay Social Security payroll taxes, with limited exceptions for state employees and students. By contrast, competitive public options generally adopt an "opt-out" default, so people do not participate unless they choose to do so. When you go to the public library and check out a book, you're choosing to do so.

Both competitive and baseline public options share the non-exclusivity that is a core feature of the public option. Both are public programs, run by public officials with public funding, but they aren't the exclusive means by which citizens may gain access to a given good or service. Thus, the U.S. Postal Service is a public option (one can send mail by other means), and public schools are a public option (one can utilize private schools).

Now, it may at first seem that a baseline public option isn't an option at all but rather a mandatory public program. What's optional about Social Security? Answering that question requires a distinction between the benefits side and the funding side of baseline public options. First is the benefits side. A baseline public option offers everyone a base level of goods or services but is not the exclusive means of acquiring the good. Individuals may reject the public option entirely or may accept it and "top up" by buying a private supplement. Social Security is a baseline public option in just this way. Recipients can refuse to claim the pension and fund their retirement without it (as the Amish and some other groups do). More commonly, people supplement the public pension system with private pension savings and programs. By contrast, exclusive government provision (admittedly rare in the United States but not as rare in other countries) makes the government the sole provider and forecloses the private option. National defense is an example, and so are state-owned exclusive liquor stores.

Second is the funding side. A baseline public option often is funded through universal taxes that cannot be avoided. Thus, Social Security imposes payroll taxes, as does Medicare. These baseline public options employ universal taxation in order to secure stable funding and wide participation. Some competitive public options adopt the same strategy: in most places in the United States, everyone pays the taxes that fund the public schools, even if they choose to send their kids to private schools.

In Chapter 3, we offer a few words on how public options might be funded. For now, our point is that the key characteristic of the public option is that it is non-exclusive on the benefits side, even if it may be mandatory on the funding side.

These ideas raise a host of questions, both principled and practical. In the remainder of this chapter, we sketch the notions of fairness that motivate public options, and we illustrate how they extend values already embedded in American society and history. As we will show, the justifications for public options often resonate in a familiar range. We will argue that the government should act to secure important goods for its citizens and to address market failures. So our innovation does not lie in our rationale for public action in some form. Rather, our contribution is to help delineate the array of ways in which the government may act—and demonstrate when the public option may be preferable to other modes.

Freedom and Opportunity

Since the founding of the country, the government has acted to secure the preconditions of freedom for all Americans. In the earliest years, land promised opportunity, but land in the East was scarce and expensive. Without inherited wealth, ordinary workers couldn't hope to step into the middle class. Thomas Jefferson and his successors responded by purchasing land in the West from other countries. The government also funded armies that battled Native Americans (often unjustly and viciously) to secure the land for white settlers. The government passed homestead acts, enabling farmers to get a plot of land for themselves at an affordable price, and it funded and built roads, canals, railways, and other infrastructure to support development in the West. In their time, these public options were the social prerequisites for a version of freedom that entailed land ownership and self-sufficiency.

Public options also supported opportunity in twentieth-century America. Industrial work promised new opportunities but also presented new risks. Workers leaving the farm for the city could earn higher wages and enjoy the luxuries of urban life, but they left behind their social support system. Parents could no longer combine farm work with child-rearing, and so the gendered division of labor sent men into the workforce, leaving wives at home. And the prospect of aging brought new anxieties, since workers no longer had a farm—or an extended farm family—to support them if they outlived their ability to work. Social Security—one of the most successful public options—responded to these anxieties. The program guarantees that workers and their dependents can live decently despite the loss of a paycheck in the case of disability, early death, and retirement.

But our public policies have not kept pace with social change. In twenty-first-century America, the foundations of economic opportunity have shifted again. Some post-high-school training or education is increasingly a minimum credential for good jobs. Even elite workers now participate in the gig economy. Many people switch jobs to take advantage of new opportunities to earn and to gain skills. Working parents and single parents are the new norm.

One of the most important features of public options is that they increase equality, and equality of opportunity in particular. Politicians and commentators often talk about equality of opportunity as something that exists in any free society. But in the last few decades, it has been increasingly clear that there isn't equal opportunity for everyone in America. Studies show that intergenerational economic mobility is much rarer than the American dream promises. A kid in Charlotte, North Carolina, whose family is in the lowest 20 percent of incomes in America has only a 4.4 percent chance of making it into the top 20 percent. In San Jose, California, the kid would have a 12.9 percent chance—much higher, but still not the 20 percent chance she would have in a society with perfect mobility. Areas with lower mobility tend to have more residential segregation, greater income inequality, worse primary schools, lower social capital, and more family instability.[2]

Equality of opportunity also can't be achieved by simply leaving people alone. Let's assume that Joe and Sam grow up equal in just about every way—wealth, intelligence, hard work. They each get married, have a couple of kids, and get good jobs working as IT managers. Because of a few lucky breaks, Joe's boss leaves and he gets promoted at a young age. Sam is doing just fine, but his company gets bought out and he loses his job after the merger. Now let's compare their kids. Joe's kids can take unpaid internships, enroll in test-prep classes for college admissions, and participate in lots of after-school clubs and activities. Sam's kids, in contrast, need to work to help out with the family's finances. Is it really fair to say that Joe and Sam had equal opportunity? How do we make allowance for luck? And what about their children? Is it fair to suggest that all of them, Joe's kids and Sam's kids, enjoy equal opportunity? In reality, their opportunities are shaped by their context, by a variety of background conditions, and in some measure by simple luck, good and bad.

In an age of rising inequality, public options are a way to ensure that every American has access to some of the basic preconditions that are essential for having a meaningful opportunity to succeed. It's very hard to succeed at school or work if you've got a bad illness. Anyone who has had the flu—let alone something far more serious—knows this. Which is why access to health care is so important. In the modern world, it is hard to interact with the economy unless you have a bank account that allows you to deposit and withdraw money. And yet 7 percent of Americans don't. Technology has transformed society, requiring that people be able to connect to the internet to do virtually anything. But 10 percent of Americans don't have access to high-speed connections.[3] With people living longer than ever, spending your golden years in meaningful, rewarding ways—hobbies, travel, family—requires having retirement savings. But more than half of American households are at risk of running out of money in retirement.[4] Of course, some kind of post-secondary education—whether training or a degree—is increasingly essential for success in the economy. But too many students are too financially strapped to get a good education and, as we've discussed, they often end up at for-profit schools that take their money and leave them worse off. In each of these areas, public options can provide everyone with access to the basic prerequisites for success in modern society. And because public options are universal, they apply to everyone, regardless of race, wealth, or geography.

You might wonder why we need these services to be provided by the public instead of by nonprofit community associations like churches, professional associations, or unions. After all, some policy advocates, like conservative reformer Yuval Levin, suggest that such groups are the best path forward for providing social goods and services.[5] We have no objection to these organizations providing services to their members, but we do not think they can fully meet America's needs. The big difference between community provision and public options is that the latter are public and therefore universal. Community associations work only for members of those communities, just as employer-based benefits only work for employees of those companies. At best, Levin's community organization approach will leave us with a patchwork of opportunity. There will always be some people who aren't members of any community, and they will fall through the cracks.

Public options solve this problem; their universality means there is some measure of equality for everyone.

Public options also help get around some of the more controversial political disputes over providing basic services through private associations. Take women's health care, for example. Some organizations—closely held corporations and churches—have objected on religious grounds to offering birth control as part of their health care coverage for employees. In the *Hobby Lobby* case and follow-on cases, the Supreme Court encouraged the government and these parties to find an accommodation that ensures women can get coverage without imposing on the religious convictions of these organizations.[6] Public options are a way out of this tension, as they are open to anyone and do not infringe upon private associations' religious beliefs.

The Private Sector

Perhaps surprisingly, public options can benefit the private sector. First, public options can help create a more fluid labor market. One of the central problems with an employer-based benefits system is that benefits are sticky. It is harder for people to jump from job to job because with each job transition, the worker has to go through the hassle of switching health insurance and retirement providers—or, worse yet, figure out what to do without them. Some economists call this feature "job lock" because benefits keep you locked into a job you don't really want. Public options take away some of this stickiness, making the labor market more fluid.

Studies suggest that job lock is a real phenomenon, not just a theoretical one. A Government Accountability Office review of thirty-one studies on the link between health care and job lock between 2000 and 2010 concluded from the evidence that "workers who rely on their employer-sponsored health benefits are less likely to change jobs, leave the labor market, become self-employed, or retire when eligible, compared to those who have access to alternative sources of coverage."[7] In addition, job lock keeps married people tied to their work unless they can get health insurance from their spouse's employer.[8] One recent study used the fact that states have different standards for Medicaid eligibility to assess job lock. It turns out that in states with higher thresholds (that is, where you can earn more money and still get health care through Medicaid), there is greater job mobility. Interestingly, the study found that as Tennessee lowered its Medicaid threshold (meaning only poorer people could get its health care services), people actually "down-transitioned," an inelegant phrase for the phenomenon of workers taking lower-paying jobs to preserve their access to health care.[9]

While the magnitude of job lock is hard to calculate, it does have an impact on the economy.[10] Even though some businesses might occasionally be on the losing side (after all, employees are going to leave some businesses to join others), a more fluid labor market is generally better for businesses and the business environment. More fluid labor markets make it more likely that the right workers and employers will find each other, leading to higher productivity. Young people and those who want to work part-time will more easily be able to get jobs in a fluid labor market. And during recessions, the economy will likely bounce back faster because workers can migrate to places where jobs are.

Entrepreneurs and small businesses also benefit from public options. Taking the risk to start a new business is difficult if you have to quit your job and lose your and your family's health care or retirement benefits. In an interesting study, a group of researchers showed that when people turn sixty-five and become eligible for Medicare, there is a major jump in the number who own their own businesses. After ruling out other hypotheses, the researchers conclude that these people don't start their own businesses before they turn sixty-five because they're worried about access to health care. They call this "entrepreneurship lock." Once their health care is guaranteed, these older entrepreneurs decide to start their own businesses.[11]

Smaller businesses and start-ups often also cannot afford to provide benefits to their employees—and certainly not generous benefit plans. Some employers, for example, decline to set up pension funds because they are costly: today, one-third of private-sector workers have no pension plan at work and fully half of workers in smaller firms have no pension plan.[12] Employees without a pension plan at work can, in theory, contribute to an individual retirement account (IRA), but the IRA subsidy is smaller, and the individual herself must do the work of setting up the account and choosing investments. Not surprisingly, few take up that option: less than 10 percent of workers without an employer plan make their own contributions to a retirement plan.[13]

A public option would provide, in effect, a simplified retirement plan for all, ensuring universal access to pensions while reducing firms' labor costs. Businesses benefit when workers arrive at work with a portable pension fund invested in secure, low-cost investments. Some employers might find it worthwhile to offer extra bells and whistles—higher contributions or different investments. But employers could also decide not to provide pensions, without dire consequences. Today, a firm that provides no pension is going to attract workers who can command no better choices, and lose workers, arguably the more talented workers, who can.

In some cases, we might even expect that large businesses will benefit from public options. Today, major corporations spend huge sums of money and resources on benefits administration for their employees. In 2008, to take one example, Starbucks spent more money on health care than on coffee.[14] Whether it is Starbucks, Facebook, or Coca-Cola, the core mission of these companies is not to provide health care or retirement services. If businesses didn't have to provide these benefits, some might instead focus more on investing in the business. They would be free to offer benefits as a recruiting tool if they wanted, but they could instead just compete for workers based on wages and leave benefits provision (and administration) to the public.

Shifting to the public option might be helpful to some large businesses financially too, but we don't know by how much. Providing benefits is expensive. In 2011, employers subsidized more than 70 percent of the costs of employee health care premiums.[15] Retirement plans let workers save money on a tax-favored basis, but only if their employers set up and administer the pension plan and manage employee investments (or pay someone else to do it). These are significant costs for businesses. A public option for health care or pensions might decrease these costs (because the company isn't providing the benefit to its employees), but at the same time, *someone* has to pay for the public option. Depending on how public options are funded, these costs could be partly shifted from businesses. However, even if these public options are fully funded through corporate taxes, it is possible that there would be net savings for companies due to scale and because the public option would not need to make a profit.

Stepping back, we think that a vibrant economy with ample business opportunity is part and parcel of Americans' ideal of a good society. Public options promote that ideal by providing a stable platform for everyone in a dynamic, competitive economy.

Competitive Markets

In traditional economic theory, competitive markets provide consumers with choices they want at the lowest feasible price. In this sense, economic efficiency can form part of an appealing notion of fairness. When society ensures a decent foundation for all, a competitive market can then allocate resources in ways that promote consumer welfare.

But in America today, markets have become increasingly concentrated, dominated by monopolies or oligopolies instead of robust competition. Between 1997 and 2012, two-thirds of America's business sectors—everything from consumer products to pharmaceuticals to banking—became more concentrated.[16] Less competition brings higher prices for consumers, worse service, and fewer choices. For example, in some states, there is only one health insurer participating in the Obamacare health insurance marketplace, and that means less choice and competition for consumers. When it comes to high-speed internet (download speeds of 25 Mbps or greater), only 42 percent of Americans had two or more choices for internet providers as of June 2016.[17]

Markets also perform poorly when consumers can't compare quality and price across different products. It's easy enough to compare Empire apples at $2.49 a pound with Empire apples at $1.99 a pound. But in the higher education market, to take one example, comparisons are much harder. Students can find it difficult to ascertain the quality of the education that an institution offers. College rankings, like those offered by *U.S. News and World Report,* attempt to offer more information. But many critics have pointed out the odd metrics those rankings incorporate (like the number of books in the library). Another confounding feature of the higher education market is that financial aid policies vary from college to college, making it difficult to compare the true price of education at different schools. The posted tuition price is paid by only a fraction of students: the majority obtain some mix of subsidized grants and loans that reduce the total price they pay.

Public options can help introduce more competition into concentrated markets and help consumers in confusing markets. With a public option, consumers have the ability to abandon a private product that isn't working for them and instead choose the public option. In effect, government enters the fray as a baseline provider or a head-to-head competitor. Either way, the presence of the public option puts pressure on private actors to provide better service at lower cost.

Economists call this "yardstick" competition, after a comment made by Franklin Roosevelt in a 1932 speech.[18] In response to concerns that monopolistic private utilities were providing bad service at high costs, Roosevelt declared the "undeniable basic right" of governments to set up their own public utility services—in other words, a public option. This public option would compete with the private option, and it would serve as a "yardstick," Roosevelt said, by which to compare the service of the private company.[19]

To go back to an earlier example, if people have low-speed internet connections, high costs, and bad service, they might want to change internet providers. But in many places, including the town in Connecticut where Anne lives, there is a cable and internet monopoly, and consumers have no option to do so. A public option—like municipal broadband—would give them the opportunity to switch internet providers. At the same time, the threat of their leaving should encourage the internet provider to improve its service and cut its prices.

A public option can even create a competitive product where one doesn't exist. Prior to the 1930s, for instance, American mortgages were largely short-term loans. During the Depression, the federal government restructured the mortgage markets. The thirty-year fixed-rate mortgage, which doesn't exist in other countries and didn't exist before, was the consequence. This mortgage option, created through government action, coexists alongside shorter-term fixed- and adjustable-rate mortgages, giving homebuyers more choice and a particularly stable option.

Racial and Geographic Inequality

One of the biggest challenges of our time is addressing racial and geographic inequality. Even as the United States has become wealthier as a country, the gains have not been shared equally—or even relatively close to equally. The racial wealth gap between African Americans and whites is longstanding, and it likely cannot be fixed without structural reforms to the economy.[20] Geographic inequality is also a serious problem. Studies show widening regional inequality, with many rural areas falling behind.[21]

Public options can be a partial, but by no means a total, way to alleviate these problems. Historically, public options have had a shifting, complex relationship with race. Some public options, like swimming pools and public schools, were segregated during the Jim Crow era, which meant there were separate but hardly equal public options. Southerners in Congress forced the Roosevelt administration to exclude huge groups of workers from Social Security—many in jobs held by African Americans in the South. Other public options, however, have had far more success. The expansion of Medicaid—a public option for health care for the poor—has had a major impact in increasing the number of African Americans with health care coverage.[22]

The relationship between public options and rural areas is also not a simple one. Rural areas have not benefited from every public option. Not all small towns in America have a public library, public golf course, or public swimming pool. The reason is simple: public options delivered at the local level are dependent on communities themselves. At the same time, federally provided public options often have helped reduce geographic inequality. Just before the turn of the twentieth century, Congress and the Post Office began to offer free rural delivery of the mail—instead of requiring people in rural areas to pick up their mail from the nearest post office. More recently, the expansion of Medicaid has been a boon to rural areas, where many poor people do not have health care coverage.[23]

When designed well, public options have the potential to reduce some of the most trenchant inequalities in our society. We are not naive, and we don't think they will fully address racial or geographic inequality. But a public option can provide a basic level of health care, connectivity, education, and other benefits to people who otherwise would not be able to get them—and disproportionately that tends to be racial minorities and people living in rural areas. Especially when provided at the federal level, a public option offers universal access to important social infrastructure—not a patchwork of opportunity, limited only to a few.

Democracy

Public options also can contribute to the social coherence that fuels a political commitment to fairness for all. Today, America is increasingly fragmented, divided by race, wealth, and political ideology. People are more likely to live with people like themselves, marry people like themselves, and even get their news from sources that confirm their preexisting viewpoints. The result is social fraying, and with it an erosion of the sense that we are all part of one national community with duties and obligations to each other.

In prior generations, public schools and the military draft were thought to have helped stitch together our diverse society. But between residential segregation and the move to an all-volunteer military, neither institution serves that function to the same degree now. Public options can't entirely compensate for those deep, socially connected ways of building solidarity. But they might help. Programs like Medicare and Social Security are extremely popular across the political spectrum. They are programs that unite us, rather than divide us. The GI Bill was similar. It wasn't a universal program, but it was so widespread among returning servicemembers that it helped members of the Greatest Generation conceive of themselves as part of a single national project.[24] Public options might help serve this function, rebuilding our sense that we are a national community of equal citizens.

How might public options do this? When people see themselves as consumers (rather than citizens) and get all their goods through the private market, they think largely about themselves: their individual desires, the costs to them, and the benefits they receive. But when citizens engage with government programs, they have to consider more than just themselves. They also have to think about what kind of society they, and by extension we, want to live in—what kind of country we are. And if they want to change public programs, they have to vote, write letters to their congressional representatives, petition, and protest. Of course, the lines here aren't perfectly clear. Many socially conscious consumers purchase goods and services based on the private company's values; many citizens think of government in self-serving terms. But while there is a spectrum, we think there is a meaningful difference between how people see themselves when they are market participants and when they are acting as citizens. Public options encourage an active and committed citizenry, which is the essence of a free republic.

3

The Theory of the Public Option

A public option has two hallmarks: it guarantees access to important services at a fixed price, and it coexists with private provision of the same service. This definition is simple enough, but there's more to it than meets the eye. Each design feature reflects a distinctive ideal of fairness, opportunity, and market competition.

First, the idea of guaranteed access at a reasonable price reflects the idea that every individual should have the basic resources necessary for modern life. The nature of these resources evolves with society, of course. Forty acres and a mule might have expressed the ideal in the nineteenth century, but most of us today wouldn't know what to do with the land—or the mule. Instead, our political system should incorporate a dynamic ideal of what a decent life requires, and make it available to all.

By contrast, in a laissez-faire market, people bid for goods with their wealth, which in turn is earned by selling goods and services to others. Not surprisingly, the result is that people with money and highly valued skills garner most of the good stuff. And they will, predictably, try to limit equal opportunity by passing on their wealth advantage to their kids.

This is why markets are inherently a poor way to guarantee universal access to important social goods. By their nature, markets allocate scarce resources based on price. The more in demand a resource is, the higher the price will go. And the wealthy will always have more capacity to bid up prices and to capture the best for themselves. If we're talking about nonessentials, that market dynamic may be perfectly fair. We are fine with the wealthy having, say, more BMWs and more caviar than everyone else.

But price rationing shouldn't be the sole mode of distributing important goods like education, retirement, and child care (to take just a few examples). Public options enter the picture in order to provide a baseline of services, available to all. And a key part of availability is a fixed price set at a reasonable level. Access isn't meaningful unless the price is one that can be paid by everyone. For that reason, public options should set a low price, often zero, for access.

Another critical feature of public options is that they are public, which is to say that they're provided by the government. Government provision guarantees that the public option can provide universal access at a fair price—and that the price will be set by government rather than by private enterprises.

No less an authority than Adam Smith, arguably the founder of the faith in free market economies, explains why public options need to be public:

> It is not from the benevolence of the butcher, the brewer, or the baker, that we expect our dinner, but from their regard to their own interest. We address ourselves, not to their humanity but to their self-love, and never talk to them of our own necessities but of their advantages.[1]

Smith knew that private firms don't act out of philanthropic motives. They act to make profits, and indeed to maximize profits. Economists who walk in Smith's footsteps predict that prices will adjust until market supply meets market demand. The final price for any good or service will ensure that firms can pay their owners a market rate of profit. But there is no reason to suppose that the market will guarantee all citizens access at a fair price.

Consider the more than 17 million cars sold in 2016.[2] Sellers like Ford, GM, Toyota, and others offer consumers an array of options, from energy-efficient cars to monster trucks. Consumers comparison-shop, bargain with dealers, and eventually settle on what they believe is the best deal. The result is what economists would call a well-functioning marketplace. Sellers make a profit sufficient to keep (most of) them in business, and consumers generally feel satisfied with their purchases.

All well and good, except for one key outcome: because price is set by supply and demand, there is no pretense of universal access. Sure, anyone can buy a car, but only if they have the money to pay the going rate. In 2016, for example, the average new car sold in the United States cost $34,000. That is about 80 percent of the annual salary of the average U.S. worker.[3] Those who can't come up with the cash or borrow have to make do with other options: used cars and public transit.

It isn't a coincidence that one of America's most important public options—public transit—coexists with the car market. As a society, we've chosen to let the car market operate on Smith's principles. But we've also chosen to provide a public option so that people with less money—notably, younger people and poorer people—can get around. To be sure, public transit is unevenly provided. Some cities and states do a better job than others, and rural areas are hardest hit by the lack of a public option. But when you consider a locale like New York City or Washington, D.C., you can see how important it is to offer a public option that is deliberately disconnected from the Smithian profit motive.

It's important to note that our justification for public options isn't the narrow and myopic justification that economists usually rely on for government action. Economists like to say that government action is warranted only in cases of market failures—that is, when the market doesn't do a good job of producing enough of a good or service. This is especially true in cases of what economists call public goods—like national defense or the environment—which the market won't be attentive to because each individual doesn't have enough of a selfish interest to produce that good or service.

While we agree that market failures and the provision of public goods can be justifications for having a public option, we think that public options advance a lot of other public values that are independent of markets. Many programs have huge spillover benefits. Think about public schools. When more people have access to education, it means a more competitive workforce and better citizens. That isn't just good for the individual student; it's good for the entire community—and for the country.

Most fundamentally, many areas we think are ripe for public options provide goods that we think are morally desirable for every American to have. Health care and a secure retirement are great examples. Regardless of wealth, class, race, or geography, everyone should have access to good health care and everyone should be able to have a secure retirement. What matters in these cases isn't market allocation or profit. No, what matters is widespread access at a reasonable price, so that everyone can use the service and so that our whole community benefits. With those justifications as our foundation, the question is how society can best provide these goods to all people.

This brings us to the second critical feature of public options—that they coexist with private (which is to say, for-profit) provision. Markets, when well structured, promote consumer choice, and choice is an important part of freedom in a capitalist society. People make meaningful choices when they choose to save for a prized possession, or to forgo a car and invest in some other activity altogether. But there's no need to go to extremes, to create a false choice between private markets and a Soviet-style state monopoly on car production. The combination of markets plus public options is superior to either of these extremes.

To be sure, sometimes the government should claim a monopoly on important goods and services. National defense and the monetary system are good examples. Everyone in the United States benefits from the military, and there isn't a private option. No matter how rich you are, you aren't permitted to fund your own army and wage war as you choose. The government also operates a monopoly on printing currency, so the dollar is the only unit of exchange in the marketplace. Today bitcoin, a virtual currency, claims to be challenging the government monopoly. It's unlikely to supplant the dollar, but if one day we start thinking of dollars in terms of bitcoins instead of the other way around, the greenback may become a public option.

Where to draw the line—when to have exclusively public or private provision—is a serious and continuing debate. Consider the court system, which is traditionally a government monopoly. Increasingly, the courts are a public option: they exist alongside a huge, private industry of private dispute resolution services, from arbitration to mediation and beyond. Indeed, many of us have agreed to use those services when we hastily click "agree" to those unreadable "terms and conditions" in our bank accounts and credit card agreements. Many banks, for instance, require credit card holders and borrowers to settle disputes through arbitration, and the American Arbitration Association is the principal private arbitrator of choice.[4] Should we allow the arbitration system to take over citizens' traditional right to have their day in court? Questions like these are hard, but our point here is simply that they *are* hard questions. We shouldn't think that the only solutions are exclusively public or exclusively private.

What's a Reasonable Price?

A public option guarantees access at a reasonable price, but people may not agree on what is "reasonable" to pay for a given item. A standard $135 monthly Medicare premium, for instance, may seem cheap to an upper-middle-class retiree but prohibitive for a retired minimum-wage worker. Another issue arises because many public options impose conditions other than price. You can't register your child for public school unless you can provide proof of residency and vaccinations. And you can't claim Social Security unless you're a worker with a substantial, documented work history (or that worker's spouse).

For all these reasons, there can be no magic formula for setting the price of a given public option: social context and public discussion will and should inform public pricing. Take Social Security as an example. We all "buy" Social Security by paying taxes that are deducted from our paychecks. Today, the payroll tax that funds Social Security retirement benefits is 12.4 percent.[5] So a worker who makes $100 per paycheck pays $12.40, while a worker who makes $1,000 per paycheck pays $124.00.[6]

Whether Social Security taxes are reasonable depends, of course, on your views about Social Security. One might expect Americans to have polarized views on the subject, given the polarized politics that dominate Washington these days. But four out of five Americans think the program works well, and they are happy to pay current taxes and even a bit more if need be.[7]

Setting a reasonable price for public options is a classic task for politics, and one that politics often does well, because price is transparent and highly salient. If the State of Connecticut tried to raise the daily parking fee for Hammonasset Beach from $10 to, say, $50, the governor and most members of the General Assembly would hear about it immediately. For nearly anyone, $10 is an affordable price for a day at the beach, especially because that's per car, not per person. But at current income levels, $50 changes the budget equation for many people: that's a dinner out or a couple of bags of groceries.

So even though there is no magic formula, support for programs like Social Security and the adequate transparency and influence of politics help explain why we are not terribly concerned that setting a reasonable price will be a stumbling block for public options. Free is always a happy price, and sometimes it's the reasonable one, as in the case of public schools: the goal in that case is to encourage all parents to send their kids to school. When a non-zero price makes sense, it's usually to prevent waste: the 55-cent price of a stamp is a good example, because it permits anyone to mail a letter but doesn't permit mailers to spam every mailing address for free (the spammers have to go to the internet for that).

At a higher price point, consider Medicare. We tend to think of Medicare as a single program, but technically it has several parts, each priced separately. The premiums for hospital care, doctors' fees, and prescription drugs reflect an effort to ensure universal access while guarding against overconsumption of health care. The result is a complicated pricing system that incorporates a sliding scale based on income (for doctors' fees and prescription drugs). The system isn't perfect: among other defects, the system requires copays that can be very high for people who get sick, and not everyone has the cash to buy a "Medigap" policy to protect themselves.

But, once again, the politics of Medicare pricing work pretty well, because the prices are (fairly) transparent and salient. By contrast, it's much harder for consumers to evaluate the true cost of private insurance policies, which differ by state and by policy terms. (If you really doubt that statement, we invite you to log onto any insurance company's website and click through the many steps needed to price and compare the individual policies for which you're eligible. It took Anne forty-five minutes to figure out how much Aetna would charge for a policy for herself and her kids.)[8]

Let's turn now to the second concern about pricing: non-price conditions. You might reasonably object that access to public options isn't truly universal if people must jump through extra hoops to participate.

Of course, private firms impose non-price conditions as well. Car insurance companies can exclude teenage drivers and people with too many accidents on their record. Banks can deny you an account if you have too little money. Employers can decline to hire you for a wide array of reasons, including your work history, your credit history, and whether they like you. (They can't discriminate based on race or sex, but in many places they can discriminate based on lots of other criteria.)

So the possibility of non-price conditions isn't unique to public options. The real question is whether public options will impose reasonable conditions—or whether politicians will impose unreasonable entry requirements that will defeat our aspiration of providing universal access at a reasonable price.

We agree that, in theory, this kind of thing could be a problem. It would be ridiculous if the government permitted people to use a post office only if they completed a lengthy application at the door and paid for a credit check. That wouldn't be a very good public option at all, because the entry conditions would be onerous compared to the services offered. But we don't see that in the real world. Instead, the Postal Service imposes minimally reasonable conditions: you have to get to a local post office (but geographic coverage is pretty good, and way better than, say, private banks), show up during business hours, and behave appropriately.

Some public options do impose greater burdens. Social Security, for instance, pays retirement benefits only to people who have held on-the-books, paid jobs for roughly ten years during their lifetimes. And Social Security benefits are based on an average of thirty-five years of wages, so people who haven't worked for at least thirty-five years tend to get much lower benefits. Those requirements do exclude some groups (and pay very low benefits to others), including casual workers, like landscapers and domestic workers, who are often paid off the books. Stay-at-home parents and the long-term unemployed can also be disadvantaged.

But there is a vigorous and continuing debate over these conditions, and they have changed over time. For instance, it used to be that a divorced woman could claim benefits based on her husband's work history only if they had been married twenty years. That rule shut out a lot of ex-wives with long marriages: a stay-at-home mother married nineteen years could find herself with zero Social Security benefits. These concerns peaked when the divorce rate spiked in the 1970s. Congress took notice and in 1977 lowered the threshold from twenty years of marriage to ten.[9]

Funding, Federalism, and Framing

Public options are compatible with a variety of funding structures and approaches to implementation. We know those details are critical to any real-world proposal, but our goal is to establish the merits of public options as a general matter. The particulars of how to fund and set up any given public option will necessarily differ based on the policy area. Social Security, for example, is very different from a public library. In later chapters, we look in more detail at specific areas of policy. But it is worth pausing for a moment to look generally at how to fund public options, which level of government should administer them, and how to frame the policy problem for which a public option is the solution.

Start with funding. Some public options would require significant public funding, including our proposals for higher education and public child care. By contrast, other public options we propose wouldn't require much government funding, including our retirement plan and the public option for banking. The reason is that these latter public options are self-funded; that is, they are designed in a way that doesn't require additional government spending.

When a public option requires funding, the money could come from a variety of sources. How that funding model is designed matters, because the funding system could promote—or even reverse—the economic effect of the public option. Take universal child care as an example. Congress could, in theory, fund child care by charging the same fees to all families, rich or poor. That kind of funding would undermine the aspirations of the program, which aims to decrease the price and increase the quality of child care for hard-pressed families. But there are other funding structures that would, overall, be consistent with the public option's mission.[10]

The reason we bracket the issue of how to fund public options is that taxation isn't our comparative advantage in this book. There is a large literature on tax policy, and it lays out a variety of standard funding options, from income taxes to wealth taxes to consumption taxes. The critical point is that any funding source must be compatible with the objective of the public option to offer universal access at a reasonable price.

For similar reasons, we also set aside the problem of federalism—that is, which level of government should fund and implement public options. American federalism is complex and grounded in tradition, and we don't have a particular axe to grind (at least in this book). Sometimes the national government is the obvious choice for a national program: for that reason, we imagine our retirement proposal as a federal initiative. In other cases, though, states or localities would be best placed to implement a public option. Historically, many public options have been provided at the state or local level: public libraries, public swimming pools, public golf courses, public parks. Looking forward, a new generation of public options might also be provided at the local level. Municipal broadband, for instance, is already being offered in some cities. Universal child care provides an interesting example of how funding and federalism can work together. Child care should probably be coordinated with public schools, and so local school districts would be the logical implementers. But given the well-known pathologies of local school finance, the states and the federal government would probably be preferable as funding sources.

Finally, there's the question of how to frame the policy problem to which a public option is a solution. Why is the public option in health care the provision of health insurance? Wouldn't the real public option be public hospitals, with doctors who are government employees? The answer is that it just depends on how you frame the problem. Similarly, a great deal changes if we frame a policy problem as access to a car versus access to transportation. The former might require thinking about a public car rental option—like a public Hertz or Zipcar—while the latter opens up the possibility of buses and trains solving the problem.

As with funding and federalism, there are many ways of framing policy problems, and it is not our goal here to outline a definitive (or even suggested) way for how policy makers should identify or describe the problems they are facing. Our point is simply that a public option is a tool that can be used even if there are multiple ways to frame a problem, as in the example of cars versus transportation. Getting the public option right will depend on identifying the right problem, and that will necessarily turn on the particular issue.

Why Market Subsidies Can't Suffice

An economist might object that, in theory, market subsidies could accomplish all the same objectives, and with less government administration. With minimal direct action by government, the argument goes, strategically placed subsidies could provide universal access to important goods at fixed prices. So why are we so set on the idea that public options can do what market subsidies cannot?

The short answer: because theoretical equivalence isn't plausible in the real world. Take the postal system as an example. The present U.S. Postal Service is a public option: it is government-run and offers universal access to basic mail services at a fixed, low price. The postal system as a whole, however, extends beyond the public program: the Postal Service coexists with private players like FedEx and UPS, which offer additional services at (typically) higher prices. From this starting point, a quick thought experiment will make clear the economist's equivalence point—and its limitations.

Suppose that policy makers wanted to recreate the current postal system using market subsidies alone. FedEx and UPS could continue just as they are. The harder part would be to recreate the offerings of the Postal Service, but in theory at least it could be done. The core business of the Postal Service involves letters, junk mail, and slower packages (for simplicity, we'll ignore Express Mail). Market subsidies would eliminate the U.S. Postal Service as a government agency and would, instead, offer subsidies to private firms to step up and fill the resulting gap in postal services.

What would those subsidies look like? In theory, policy makers could set subsidies for stamps, junk mail, and slower packages with great precision so that private firms would charge exactly the same price to consumers that the Postal Service presently does. To take a simple example: if the true cost of mailing a letter from, say, Massachusetts to Alaska is $1.55, the subsidy would be set at $1 so that a private firm could afford to charge just 55 cents (the current price of a stamp) to the consumer mailing the letter.

The tricky part would be setting the subsidies at exactly the right level. Without perfect knowledge of the cost of providing basic mail service and the rate of return needed (over and above the other costs of doing business) to keep for-profit firms willing to provide basic mail service to all customers, the government would set subsidies too high or too low. Too little subsidy, and private firms would have to charge higher prices, which would restrict access to postal services. Too much subsidy, and private firms could reap a windfall at the government's expense.

Compounding the problem, firms' quest to maximize profits could create wasteful behavior. Firms might provide misleading information to the government and lobby Congress for excessive subsidies. Firms might also profit by cutting corners on service or by shutting down less profitable lines of business.

This thought experiment drives home our point that the case for public options rests on the relative competencies of existing institutions. A science fiction writer could imagine a government with perfect knowledge of private production cost functions, but we don't have that, and we can't see a clear path to get there.

And this discussion isn't entirely hypothetical. All of these problems have surfaced in the health insurance market, because the Affordable Care Act didn't include a full public option. The original legislation did include a partial public option, in the form of a Medicaid expansion, but the Supreme Court gave states the power to avoid expanding Medicaid. As implemented, the central features of Obamacare rely on market subsidies for private insurance companies and voucher subsidies (via the tax code) for individual buyers of health insurance. The problem of pricing has been a difficult one. Despite fairly generous market subsidies, prices for health insurance have risen, and many companies have left the market altogether. The legislation included controversial rules intended to stabilize the cost structure of the system, but pricing and access have been anything but stable.

The critical point, then, is that public options have an institutional advantage when the policy goal is to provide universal access at a fixed and fair price. Market subsidies are best used if the goal is to lower price or change behavior somewhat, but without specific targets for access and final pricing.

Even in such cases, market subsidies don't always work well. Retirement saving provides another real-world cautionary example. There's a wide consensus that Americans save too little for retirement.[11] And Social Security, as we have seen, provides a baseline public option that guarantees (nearly) everyone a decent, if smallish, retirement benefit. At the same time, however, the federal government has subsidized private savings by providing $180 billion per year in tax breaks for firms and workers that sock away money in retirement accounts.[12] The idea behind market subsidies is that they take advantage of the logic of the marketplace. By making it cheaper for firms to offer (and workers to participate in) retirement plans, the hope is that Americans will save more.

One attractive feature of market subsidies is that they require minimal government effort. No need for the government to set up its own retirement savings plans (beyond Social Security): in theory, private firms will compete to offer excellent service to the new savers who will open retirement accounts. So there's no call for the government to expend resources when consumers can choose among Fidelity, Vanguard, TIAA, and more.

The logic of market subsidies also has its appeal. After all, people buy more apples if the price is $2 per apple rather than $5. So retirement saving surely works the same way: make it cheaper and people will do more of it. And this is exactly what tax incentives do. For instance, suppose Matt wants to save $10,000 for retirement every year. Without a subsidy, that costs him $10,000. With a subsidy, it might cost him just $6,000 to put $10,000 into an individual retirement account (or IRA). How does that work? Basically, he can put $10,000 into his IRA and take a $10,000 tax deduction that saves him $4,000 on his taxes if he's in the 40 percent tax bracket. The net cost to Matt is the $10,000 he puts in the account less the $4,000 tax benefit from Uncle Sam. Surely any rational consumer would respond to the subsidy by saving more.

But as appealing as the theory may seem, market subsidies have severe limitations compared with public options. First, market subsidies do not guarantee citizens access to resources at a fair price. This shouldn't be a shock, because they aren't designed to do that. Market subsidies don't aim to set a price for retirement savings. Instead, they just aim to make it somewhat cheaper in order to encourage people to save. Moreover, as the IRA example shows, market subsidies may offer different price reductions to different people. Matt, in the 40 percent tax bracket, gets a subsidy worth $4,000. But Fiona, in the 10 percent bracket, would save just $1,000 on her taxes if she puts $10,000 into her IRA. And on top of all of that, both Matt and Fiona need to know how to take the deduction when tax time comes around—and they need to remember to do it.

Put another way, market subsidies don't guarantee universal access to retirement pensions at a fair price, the way a public option (like Social Security) does. Retirement saving is still too expensive for many Americans, who are struggling to meet today's bills and have no room to think about tomorrow's need. Two statistics tell a grim story: the federal government spends more than $100 billion per year on market subsidies for retirement, but a whopping 66 percent of the subsidies are claimed by taxpayers in the top 20 percent of the income distribution. And 42 percent of Americans have no workplace retirement plan at all.[13]

Adding insult to injury, market subsidies for retirement probably haven't moved the needle on saving rates even among those with retirement accounts. Studies have found that most of the $100-plus billion just subsidizes savings by wealthy people who would have saved the same amount in any event. In other words, our hypothetical Matt is a target saver: he's going to save $10,000 with or without a market subsidy. He'll happily pocket the $4,000 tax benefit, but it won't change his behavior.

We will take a deeper dive into the promise of public options for retirement savings in Chapter 7. For now, though, it's enough to see that market subsidies can't guarantee price, access, or participation.

A Word on Regulation

Readers may wonder whether we've stacked the deck against market subsidies by ignoring the possibility of combining market subsidies with regulation. The government could, after all, just order private firms to offer certain goods at fixed prices. The sting of such an order could then be lightened with subsidies: The same effect as a public option, but without any added government bureaucracy.

There's something to this insight, but in the end, it doesn't undermine the case for public options. Reconsider the U.S. Postal Service example. We concluded that market subsidies would be a poor substitute for the public option (the Postal Service), because market subsidies wouldn't reliably guarantee access or price and might lead firms to cut corners or curtail services. But regulation could fill the gap by setting conditions for the subsidy. To take an example, the government could offer for-profit firms funding to provide traditional mail service, but firms could claim the funding only if they charged 55 cents for a stamp and provided nationwide service. Put another way, it seems that we could combine the carrot of subsidies with the stick of regulation to duplicate the effects of a public option.

Once again, the answer is yes, in theory. But real-world conditions, and in particular the government's lack of information, make the regulatory strategy hard to implement without a significant bureaucracy. To see why, take the problem of the 55-cent stamp. If the government knows that private providers need a subsidy of 29 cents to make that price feasible, then all is well: regulators can mandate the 55-cent stamp price, and firms will happily comply.

But if the government doesn't know the right subsidy price, then it is likely to over- or undersubsidize firms. If the market subsidy is too high, firms will flood into the market and reap excess profits at the government's expense. If the market subsidy is too low, so firms cannot make a market rate of profit on mail service, firms will drop out of the postal market altogether or will even go out of business. Put another way, the government can't force firms to stay in business.

The big picture is that when government has limited information, it can't reliably guarantee access to important goods at fixed (and fair) prices. That's exactly what public options *can* do, of course. In economic terms, public options permit the government to internalize the problems of setting prices and subsidies: the subsidies needed to run the postal system will be quite transparent.

Another form of regulation—one that we think is actually far more promising—is public utility regulation. Public utility regulation is similar to a public option in an important way. Often we want to provide universal access to a good or service at a controlled price, but competition doesn't make sense or isn't possible. In many sectors—for example, electricity—there are natural monopolies. It doesn't make sense to have competition for electricity because different companies would all have to build power lines. One possible solution to this problem is to have nationalized services. But an alternative is public utility regulation. Public utilities are private firms that provide key public services, but government regulators scrutinize the firms' costs and revenues and set prices intended to offer fair access and pricing to consumers while guaranteeing a reasonable measure of profit to investors in the utilities. In essence, a public utility is government outsourcing provision of a service to a private actor. The conditions in the outsourcing contract are regulations.

On the spectrum of policy options from markets to socialism, public utilities are in about the same place as public option, but with the approach inverted. The utilities are formally private. But they are so thoroughly regulated that they don't seek to maximize profits. Instead, they charge prices and earn profits at rates set by the government. A public utility isn't meaningfully under private control. Instead, the structure permits the government to borrow money from private investors to help operate public infrastructure.

To see the point, imagine that an enterprising public utility manager had the bright idea to raise profits by refusing service to rural customers. After all, it costs far more to install and maintain electric lines when people live way out in the country. "Profits would soar," the manager insists. But that kind of profit-maximizing move is precisely what public utilities aren't allowed to do. The government requires them to provide universal access to electricity.

Suppose that the hypothetical public utility manager persists: "If we can't deny service to rural customers, then let's jack up the prices for them, so they pay full freight for the costs we incur." But that initiative, too, would be squelched by government regulators, who would insist on equal pricing for all consumers.

So a public utility is very similar to a public option, even though the utility company is formally a private firm. Setting aside labels and looking to economic substance, we have active government management and monitoring of an enterprise committed to universal access and fair pricing. The big difference is that we often rely on public utility regulation when there isn't much competition in the marketplace among private actors.

As a matter of choosing between public policy options, it is also worth noting that public utilities and public options can be substitutes for achieving similar goals. Consider the problem of corporate monopoly. Monopolies are problematic because without any competition in the marketplace, the monopolist can charge higher prices and simultaneously provide a worse product. Monopolists might also use their market power to pressure other companies they do business with, and they might even use their economic power to try to lobby and pressure government into continuing their privileged status. There are three basic frameworks for addressing monopolies. The most familiar is antitrust, which would suggest breaking up the monopoly. But in cases where we might want concentration or monopoly because of efficiencies in scale or network effects, the public utilities approach suggests regulating the monopoly extensively. And the public options model suggests that the public alternative can compete with the monopoly and serve as a yardstick to measure its performance.[14]

It is also worth noting one more surprising advantage of public options compared with regulation. When a public option exists, it might be possible to have greater deregulation in the private sector. The reason is simple: if the public option provides a robust, high-quality option that is available to everyone, then there might be less reason to regulate private providers as extensively. The old warning "buyer beware" makes more sense in a context when there's a safe, workable version of the same product available. Of course, this would not mean getting rid of all regulations. For example, private utility plants would still have to be prevented from dumping toxic waste into rivers even if there's a public option for energy production. But it is possible that at least some regulations could be rolled back in light of a robust public option—and that conservatives and libertarians, not just progressives and liberals, might therefore be able to get on board with the public option in those cases.

Summing Up

Public options work, both in theory and in practice. Americans have decades or centuries of experience with the U.S. Postal Service, public parks, public colleges, thirty-year mortgages, and Social Security. Politics is never perfect, and yet these public options have succeeded in providing all Americans with access to many of the foundations of a good life.

One of the signal harms of neoliberalism is that it encouraged Americans to believe in an exaggerated distinction between "free markets" and "government intervention." In practice, government and the law are thoroughly—and inevitably—intertwined in the economy, and nearly every institution mixes public and private to some degree.

Public options are suitable both for real-world policy making at the margin—that is, for small changes to existing structures—and for big-think, major reforms for the twenty-first century. As we continue, our approach is to ask what mix of government action and profit motivation can best achieve a given policy aim. We've made the case that public options should be considered whenever policy makers want to make use of the power of government to offer universal access to important goods at a fair price without preempting market competition in the same area. But that doesn't mean that are always the best choice for every policy initiative. Sometimes market subsidies will work better, all in all. Pragmatic policy makers can and should consider all approaches when making policy, including subsidies and regulation, and public options should be in the mix as well.

4

Caveats and Counterarguments

So far we've emphasized the merits of public options, but we don't think they are the best choice in every instance. Later chapters will tackle the details of particular proposals, but here we anticipate some concerns.

Let's start by summarizing where we stand. In Chapter 2, we defended five rationales for the public option: promoting opportunity, assisting business, improving market competition, advancing racial and geographic equity, and supporting democracy. Along the way, we noted that market subsidies have predictable shortcomings: they can't function when markets fail, they can have perverse effects on prices, and they typically can't guarantee quality. It follows that public options are likely to be the best choice when three conditions hold:

- Access is fundamental to liberty or equality.
- Markets don't function well (for example, in the case of limited competition or market failures).
- Government can readily be held to account for price, quality, and access.

Taking the opposite tack, markets (with or without subsidies) will tend to be better options when price and access aren't matters of justice, when markets function well, and when private firms can readily be held to account for quality and access.

These principles can produce powerful insights about how to design public options—and when to use them. For instance, we don't favor a national public option to provide food to the needy; instead, we're fine with the existing SNAP program (sometimes called food stamps), which is a voucher program.

Why? Certainly, food is a primary good—it's hard to be free or equal if you're hungry. But the food market functions well in most places. Competition among stores is robust, and consumers can evaluate their options pretty well. The quality of food is sufficiently transparent: food labeling (a form of regulation) helps, and most adults have decided opinions about quality and taste. And because food purchases are relatively small and repeated, private actors can be held accountable in the marketplace: stores that sell bruised produce or rotten meat will quickly go out of business.

So our criteria suggest that food assistance should probably take the form of market subsidies, like SNAP, rather than a public option. With SNAP, eligible low-income families receive an EBT card (like an ATM card) that can only be used for food purchases. But they shop at private stores, just like everyone else. In theory, we might worry that SNAP, like other voucher programs, could raise food prices: stores might raise prices and capture some of the subsidy, because SNAP dollars increase demand for food. But the theoretical problem isn't a real-world issue: because SNAP customers represent a small fraction of the market, food stamps probably don't raise prices nationally.[1]

Still, the analysis may look different when we get down to the local level. In some high-poverty neighborhoods, market competition can be limited, prices can be high, and SNAP customers can represent a larger fraction of the customer base. In such a neighborhood a public program of some kind could be worth exploring. Nonprofits have begun to take up some of the slack here, and perhaps they'll do the job. In urban New Haven, Connecticut, for instance, some inner-city areas have few grocery options. A nonprofit called CitySeed sponsors farmers' markets around the city, with the goal of ensuring everyone access to fresh, local food.[2] And CitySeed takes SNAP dollars, ensuring that even low-income families can benefit.

As the CitySeed model (and others) develop nationwide, it's worth studying whether a public option should be added to the mix. We wouldn't begin by *assuming* that a public option would be the best way to proceed. Rather, we'll argue throughout the book that the choice of public program (whether public option, market subsidy, or regulation) depends on circumstances.

Another market that works well is the entertainment market. (Is entertainment a primary good, the sort of thing that everyone should have? Luckily, we can sidestep that philosophical question, because the market works so effectively.) Thanks to technology and worldwide competition, Americans can choose from an unprecedented array of entertainment options. Streaming services offer boundless options for a small monthly fee. Video games are available in all price ranges (if you include the market in used systems and games) and increasingly available for free checkout from public libraries. On-demand options on cable bring recent films into our homes for a few dollars.

Still, we do distinguish between entertainment content and broadband service. The market in entertainment content is robust, but the market in broadband can be pretty flawed. For a short period of time under the Obama administration broadband was regulated as a public utility, but under the Trump administration, the Republican chairman of the FCC, Ajit Pai, rescinded the Obama-era "net neutrality" rules, leaving internet service providers free to charge differential prices for content. While there is a strong need to bring back the public utility approach to broadband, a public option for broadband is worth considering as well. Indeed, some U.S. cities have already taken the plunge.

If you're skeptical about public options at this stage, fair enough. We hope that we've begun to demonstrate their promise. But we haven't yet confronted all of the most powerful objections. So let's start there.

Isn't Big Government Bad?

At first glance, public options seem to fit right into the narrative of big, bad government. Government programs, it's often said, are inevitably inefficient and poorly administered, because the discipline of the marketplace is missing. Big government encroaches on individual freedom by levying high taxes and forcing individuals into prescribed ways of life. And many people who worry about big government are concerned that it will lead to socialism or to exclusive and pervasive government provision.

But socialism isn't our agenda—far from it. Our yardsticks for measuring policy success include liberty, equality, and market discipline. Public options expand liberty and equality by promoting real access and meaningful choice. They coexist with private options precisely to impose market discipline on both public and private actors. And our principles suggest that structures for public accountability are critical to the design of sound public options.

Many objections to "big government" rest on an exaggerated dichotomy between public and private. The law serves as the foundation for laissez-faire markets, and yet conservatives don't complain about "big government" when the state takes vigorous action to record, monitor, and enforce property rights, contracts, and other protections for capital. Nor do we hear too many protests about the pro-business subsidies that litter the tax code. In the United States today, pretty much every market mixes subsidies with regulated industries and public options. The question is, what mix best serves the interests of liberty, equality, and good government?

Some people might also worry about public options being a slippery slope to socialism. We don't think so. To believe in the slippery slope argument is to believe that people are incapable of making distinctions between situations that are fundamentally different.[3] A good example is the old story about the frog and boiling water: if you put a frog in boiling water, it'll jump out, but if you put it in cold water and then slowly heat the water to a boil, the frog won't notice and will die. In essence, because of the slow change from cold to boiling water (going down the slippery slope), the frog can't tell the difference between the two situations and gets killed. But here's the thing about this story: it isn't true. Frogs, like people, are completely capable of telling the difference between cold, warm, and boiling water. And when the water gets too hot, frogs jump out.[4]

Public options aren't designed to be socialism, and if they're starting to become socialistic—or if someone proposes socialism under the guise of public options—everyone will be able to tell the difference, and then jump out.

Won't Bureaucrats Screw Up the Implementation?

Maybe. We're not naive about how hard it can be to implement policy in the real world. It is certainly possible that civil servants will make mistakes in rolling out public options and, over time, in keeping them working well. But we don't think that's a good enough reason to forgo the upside that public options can offer.

We can all call to mind examples of government programs that have been badly run. One of the more disturbing recent scandals involved Department of Veterans Affairs (VA) medical facilities, which had long backlogs for veterans seeking treatment. Compounding the problem, some VA administrators manipulated data to try to hide the backlogs. Whistleblowers within the agency revealed the delays, and Congress and the VA have spent years trying to reform the system.[5]

But scandal plagues private industry, too. Martin Shkreli gained infamy when his company, Turing Pharmaceuticals, raised the price of a lifesaving drug from $13.50 to $750 per pill. When Congress convened a hearing to investigate, Shkreli invoked the Fifth Amendment in refusing to testify. Literally moments later, he took to Twitter and called the representatives "imbeciles."[6] In August 2017, Shkreli was convicted for securities fraud.[7]

So the battle of the anecdotes is inconclusive. All organizations—government, churches, colleges, private businesses—are made up of people, and people can be petty, power-hungry, incompetent, lazy, and inefficient wherever they work. There's nothing special about government in that sense. You might respond that government employees often have civil service protections that keep them from getting fired. True, and that is an important difference. But anyone who has worked in a private firm knows that just because people can be fired, it doesn't necessarily mean they will be fired—and it doesn't necessarily mean they will be incentivized to work to the best of their abilities. Office politics, favoritism, and bias can insulate incompetence in any setting.

The reality is that in some regards, the differences between government bureaucracy and other institutions are not as stark as one might think. Indeed, when we look at private firms, we find a lot of the same hassles and irritations that afflict public bureaucracies—and some others, too. Big companies are often loath to innovate (just ask Blockbuster how its business is going). Their top managers often have no idea what bad behavior is going on within the organization, or they condone bad behavior outright (consider Wells Fargo, which was caught creating millions of phony bank and credit card accounts). In small communities, nonprofits can suffer from cronyism and nepotism. This isn't to say that we shouldn't rely on nonprofits or private corporations. It is only to say that if we are going to be serious about designing policies, we can't just look at the deficiencies of government; we have to compare them honestly to the deficiencies of private and nonprofit actors as well.

So let's tackle the serious question: is there reason to think that government is systematically less competent than private actors? It's easy enough to tell a stylized story along those lines. A perfectly competitive market should, in theory, create incentives for private actors to achieve efficiency. Since government officials act outside the market, they may not achieve efficiency—they may have more leeway to waste time or pursue inefficient agendas.

The problem is that the story of perfect competition and efficient markets has several holes. First, there are important mechanisms for making sure government actors do their job well. For one thing, public options *are* subject to market competition:

that's why they're public options and not public monopolies. When baseline public options are not enough or if people don't like competitive public options, they can signal their disapproval through what political scientists call "exit"—leaving the program to rely instead on the private option, and in the process sending a strong signal that the public option isn't serving their needs.[8]

Public options, in effect, prompt markets to function better. If the U.S. Postal Service offers slow service at high prices, let FedEx step in and do better. We are cool with that. Ditto our proposed retirement program (see Chapter 7), which offers workers the chance to sock away money in sound investments for low fees. If JPMorgan Chase can offer a higher return and lower fees, let them! If the public option is inferior, exit is a pretty good mechanism for feedback, and it's exactly the same mechanism that disciplines private firms.

And there is a second source of discipline for public options, one that doesn't exist in the private market: democracy. Presidents and appointed officials are responsible to the public for the success of public options. When public options fail to work, people will raise the alarm with their members of Congress and with the media, putting pressure on the leaders to respond—and reform the deficiencies. Political scientists call this disciplining force "voice" because people use their voices to reform the system rather than abandon it. A good example of this is the Department of Veterans Affairs. In 2014, after reports that veterans were dying because of long delays in receiving care, public outcry led to action. The secretary of the VA resigned, and Congress and the president passed major new legislation that attempted to reduce wait times for veterans. News outlets continue to report on the wait times, keeping lawmakers interested in continued progress.[9]

Finally, the premise of the efficient-market argument is questionable. The Great Recession, sad to say, provided the nation with ample evidence of subpar (in some instances egregiously subpar) governance in private firms. Executives made millions and built a world financial system that collapsed like a sand castle in 2008. The pre-2008 financial industry might have been "efficient" in a very narrow sense, but it permitted elites to capture huge gains at the expense of taxpayers generally and the middle class specifically, and after the collapse, those elites mostly escaped personal responsibility. By our yardsticks of liberty, opportunity, and efficiency, the financial debacle that began in 2008 revealed catastrophic failures in our system.

The broader point is that the theoretical appeal of competitive markets is just that—theoretical. The right comparison for the fantasyland of perfect markets is the fantasyland of perfect government only pursuing the public interest with vigor and honesty. Comparing the fantasy of perfect markets with a craven government doesn't make sense. Nor does it make sense to compare craven markets with perfect government. We should evaluate both government and markets realistically and even-handedly.

Won't Public Options Distort Markets?

We've argued that public options can coexist with private provision, but won't the presence of the public option actually distort the marketplace? This seems like another commonsense objection, but "distortion" is a slippery term. The distortion objection actually incorporates two different points—one that has some merit, and one that we think is off-base.

Economists talk about "distortion" in a very precise sense: they mean that regulation is moving society away from a socially optimal allocation of resources. In the classic model, a perfectly competitive market will allocate resources in a way that maximizes social welfare. A distortion occurs if government action alters the market so that society moves to a less efficient outcome.

To illustrate the economists' point, imagine that there are only two goods, apples and oranges, and that buyers and sellers bargain until they can't make any more productive bargains. The resulting distribution is efficient in the sense that nobody can be made better off without making someone else worse off. A government tax on apples might very well distort this market: in response to the tax, people would buy fewer apples and more oranges. Compared to the efficient distribution just mentioned, this arrangement would mean less happiness in the society overall. (For sticklers: this is true because the tax revenue collected would not completely offset the loss of utility from lower apple consumption, with the result that society suffers a net loss, or "deadweight loss.")

This version of the distortion objection makes a respectable, if limited, point. When markets work well, the government should use caution in altering allocations. But this narrow analysis incorporates two very big assumptions: first, that markets are competitive, and second, that the initial distribution of wealth (that is, inequality) doesn't matter. Here's the problem: *these assumptions do not hold.*

As you'll see when you dive into our policy chapters, public options usually target markets that are imperfect in one or both of these two ways. Over and over again, we find that markets for important goods and services just aren't competitive. Competition in the market for retirement savings, for instance, simply hasn't worked: private firms have found ways to bilk savers by charging high and hidden fees, and the magic of the marketplace has rewarded bad actors instead of punishing them. And, over and over again, we see markets that intensify inequality rather than relieving it. When many Americans can't open a checking account, when young children spend their days in substandard care, and when college costs a fortune, these are outcomes that may be narrowly "efficient," but they aren't fair.

We take the economists' distortion point as a useful cautionary tale. We like markets just fine, but we are also aware of their limits. Put another way: the goal of public options is to improve markets in cases where they aren't competitive or are founded on toxic inequality.

Still, the strict economic version of the distortion point helps flag the limits of public options: public options should be attractive when and to the extent that markets don't work, but they should stop there. To see the point, take the example of the U.S. Postal Service. We kind of love the Postal Service, but we think it has—and should have—a limited mission. It provides mail service to everyone at a reasonable price, and it covers even remote (and urban) areas that private firms shun. But that doesn't mean that it should expand into all possible shipping services and markets.

For instance, we don't think the postal service should compete in the market for high-priced courier service in large cities. In New York, you can have documents messengered from your office to someone else's in just a couple of hours—if you're willing to pay a high fee. This kind of service isn't part of a decent life for most Americans, and so the postal service doesn't have any business doing it.

Now for the second form of the distortion objection, which we see as misguided. Keep in mind that the economists' version of distortion says that it's a bad thing to change the workings of a perfect market. The looser, second take on distortion says that it's a bad thing to change the workings of *any* market.

But this second take on distortion doesn't make any sense. Existing markets should command our allegiance only if they're working correctly (and working toward fair allocations). Bad markets shouldn't command any allegiance at all.

To take an example: The current market for retirement savings is pretty ugly. The market may look okay if you only take a quick look. After all, just about every bank and brokerage firm will happily sell you an individual retirement account. But many of these companies will also happily charge you fees that amount to highway robbery. The fees may sound small—just 2 percent, pennies on the dollar—but over time they can sap your savings. And some of these companies engage in even worse practices, like deliberately dumping bad investments into workers' accounts.

Now imagine that Congress enacted the kind of public option we outline in Chapter 7. The public option would offer every American the chance to save for retirement. Workers could have money withheld directly from their paychecks, and their funds would be invested in a small number of safe, diversified investments with very low fees.

This public option would surely change the market for retirement investments—big-time. And that is exactly what we hope for. To see why, play out the story a little. After a year or so, people have started to become familiar with the public option retirement plan. It's convenient, it doesn't require any investment expertise, and the government is required to disclose all fees every year. With fees at less than one-half of 1 percent per year, the public option is a clear winner compared to Big Bank's price of 2 percent.

Over time, then, workers put more and more money into the public option and less and less into private options—unless the private firms take their game up a notch and offer real value for money. Facing big competition from a public option, firms have to take one of two paths if they want to continue to play in the retirement market. One option is to offer a product with even lower fees. If Big Bank can guarantee that it will provide investments just as sound as those in the public option but at a lower price, then some people will take its offer. Another plan is to charge higher fees but provide better service. If Big Bank can offer services that people really want, then it may be able to charge more and survive.

Yes, Big Bank and other private firms stand to lose a lot of money as workers leave them for the public option, and so they have every incentive to complain about "market distortions." But that complaint should ring hollow, since what's going on here is market improvement: thanks to the public option, American workers would be paying less and getting more. Anyone who wanted something different from the public option could seek it out in the private marketplace.

Stepping back, we can see that this second version of the distortion objection is just a complaint about lost profits. The various types of public options we propose in this book likely would eat into the profits of banks, child care providers, and colleges. But those lost profits aren't "distortions." They're deliberate reforms that improve the markets—and improve options for consumers.

Won't Politics and Lobbying Hijack Public Options?

Another important concern is that politics and lobbying will hijack the public option so that it serves narrow interests instead of the public interest. We readily concede that politics shapes the design and implementation of every policy. Even so, we think public options fare pretty well—and often better than market subsidies and other policy alternatives.

Let's start with one of the most important features of public options: they are simple and salient. That is, everyone knows that government has done something for them, and they know (more or less) what government did. Consider two different kinds of tax cuts. When President George W. Bush and the Republican-controlled Congress passed massive tax cuts in 2001 and 2003, people received a one-time, lump-sum check. The money was given in a simple and highly salient way. As a result, people *felt* like they got a tax cut. Fast-forward almost a decade later. When the Obama administration designed tax cuts as part of the 2009 stimulus package intended to mitigate the effects of the Great Recession, they deliberately did so in a complex and hidden way—they gave people the tax cut by reducing payroll taxes slightly in each paycheck. The problem is that while people did get a tax cut when you added up all the savings, they didn't feel like they got a tax cut. Compared with getting a lump sum, many people don't notice a small change in their paycheck week to week—and even if they notice, they don't necessarily associate the extra cash with Uncle Sam.[10]

Public options are sort of like a lump-sum tax cut—simple and salient. Market subsidies are like the payroll tax cut—complex and hidden. Think about higher education. When people take out federally subsidized student loans (a market subsidy), it's harder to tell that government actually did something. The experience of the program feels like taking out a private loan. In contrast, if college is free (a public option), it's pretty clear that government provided you with an education.

The simplicity and salience of public options have everything to do with why they fare well even in the face of lobbying. When people know about a government program, they can get mobilized around it if lobbyists or special interests try to change, cut, or distort the program. There's a reason Social Security is so resistant to efforts to cut benefits to elderly Americans: people know what the program does, and when elected officials try to cut benefits, voters can get engaged in the political process to block those efforts. In comparison, when government programs are complicated and fly under the radar, it's hard for citizens to know what's going on with the programs, and lobbyists can operate in the shadows with a much lower risk of popular scrutiny. Public options, therefore, might be *less* likely to suffer from the problems of lobbying than complex and hidden policy interventions.

Won't Public Options Excuse State Interference in the Marketplace?

The conservative commentator Yuval Levin has argued that the public options approach is problematic because it "confuses the role of the state in markets, combining the elements of the role of referee and that of a player in market competition in ways that will likely prove unsustainable."[11] Levin doesn't expand further on this criticism, but we don't think it is very persuasive. The role of the state in markets is emphatically and decidedly not limited to "the role of referee," and it never has been. The state creates the marketplace by defining the rules of the game—property law, contract law, antitrust law—and by enforcing those rules through the state-run justice system. But states have almost always also been players in market competition.

We'll go back to a basic example we've used before: public libraries. Public libraries are public entities, a government organization. But they are and have always been a player in market competition. You don't have to borrow books at the public library; you can buy books from booksellers, or even borrow books from private libraries. The public library system is a "player in market competition" alongside those private options.

Or look outside of public options. The federal government purchases pencils and cars and computers. It is a player in those markets. The federal government also contracts with private businesses to build aircraft carriers and fighter planes. There the government *is* the market.

So at a theoretical level, Levin's argument is overly broad. But what about practically? Should we be worried about confusing the role of referee and that of market player? We don't think so. The fact is that our government is a complex organism. It isn't just "the president" or "the government." As scholars like to say, our government is a "they," not an "it."[12] What that means is that we can design public options so that different parts of the government will be market players and referees, and we can create a firewall between them.

There's nothing extraordinary or radical about this. We split up government functions all the time. We have executive branch agencies and independent agencies, for example. The former (like the Environmental Protection Agency) are responsive to the president; the latter (like the Federal Reserve) are insulated from political influence. In fact, our basic constitutional structure is premised on the idea of separating different functions. We separate the legislative, judicial, and executive branches of our government in order to make sure that the same people don't run each of them and have total power. In a similar vein, there's no reason we couldn't separate public option functions from the referee functions of government.

Levin also worries that the government "certainly could not avoid showing preference to the relevant public options over private competitors and supporting them with implicit subsidies and advantages." We agree, but what Levin gets wrong is that this is a feature, not a bug. One of the most important features of public options is that they provide universal access at a fair price. They cost money and are funded by the public through taxes. But the point is that *we want people to have access to those goods.* To take an example: If community college is free, that is definitely going to show a preference for the public option over private nonprofits and for-profits. But that is the goal. We think everyone should be able to get some kind of post-high-school education without having to pay tuition, just like everyone can today get a K–12 education without paying for it.

But to assuage some of Levin's fears, here's a key point: the public options we are describing are rarely going to be Cadillac programs. Baseline public options are just that—baselines. No one living on Social Security alone, for example, is going to be vacationing in the south of France or living large in a Manhattan penthouse. The local community college isn't Harvard, and it shouldn't be. Competitive public options will often be "plain vanilla" options: simple and standardized. A robust market will exist around and above the public options—and some market actors might even want to offer plain-vanilla options that compete with the public option as a loss leader, to familiarize people with their brand for when they want to move to a higher-end product. Here's an example. Imagine a public option for banking services: savings and checking accounts. If everyone had access to those two accounts, it would mean that many people who now are unbanked would be able to access their paychecks without paying fees to check-cashers. But they wouldn't have access to loans of any kind and would only get minimal interest (if any). Would that end the banking business? Of course not. Most people would still prefer to bank with community banks, credit unions, and national banks because they offer many more services.

Levin's third objection is that public options "would not be subject to the kinds of life-or-death pressures" that private companies face. At the level of armchair economic commentary, that is right. Public programs do not depend on profits to stay alive. But in the real world, it isn't clear that the comparison is between apples and apples. First, private companies increasingly face less and less competitive pressure. Monopolization and concentration—not competition—are the defining features of our economy. Depending on the sector, the comparison might be between monopolies or oligopolies, not fiercely competitive little guys, and the public option. In that case, it isn't clear that the monopolies and oligopolies face much by way of life-or-death pressures either. Second, as we've already pointed out, public options do face a different kind of disciplining pressure: democratic voice. The very fact that Levin is skeptical of public options proves our point. He and others like him will be vigilant in making sure that public options are working as they should be. When they aren't working right, we are 100 percent confident that he and others will sound the alarm.

Isn't Personal Responsibility Better?

Let's put a key issue right on the table: aren't public options just another example of softhearted, nanny-state liberalism? Surely people should step up and take personal responsibility for their own education, their own retirement, their own child care.

Once again, two separate objections are smuggled into this one complaint. Let's take them in turn. First, some people who feel this way are committed libertarians, who believe it's always and without exception morally wrong for the state to tax some people for the benefit of others. The poster libertarian along these lines was the late Harvard professor Robert Nozick. In his view, the only defensible government is a minimal one whose sole job is to protect people's property from theft and their bodies from violence. Any more extensive form of government, Nozick believed, would violate individuals' rights to their own labor.[13]

If you're a moral libertarian like Nozick, then we probably can't persuade you to like public options. But then, if you're a Nozickian, you'd be against many, many features of present-day America: you'd want to eliminate Social Security and Medicare, radically downsize the military, abolish public schools, turn all highways into toll roads, and revoke all government contracts and subsidies for business. We can't imagine even a far-right Republican running on that platform. Even Rand Paul and Ron Paul, recent political candidates who pitched themselves as libertarians, didn't go this far.

The second objection based on individual responsibility is pragmatic, and it runs something like this: The government is already big, and taxes are high, so is there really a good case for more of the same? After all, resources are limited, and the state can't, and shouldn't, cushion people against all of life's bumps. Taxes aren't "free money"—they come out of the pockets of real people, and those people have less freedom when the government forces them to fund public programs.

Even worse, this objection continues, some well-meaning government programs can penalize the responsible and subsidize the irresponsible. Partisans of this point of view often use Aesop's fable about the ant and the grasshopper to make the point.[14] In the story, the ant saves diligently while the grasshopper parties away the summer. When winter comes, the ant is cozy and secure, while the grasshopper is destitute. Surely Uncle Sam shouldn't take (much) from the ants to relieve the grasshoppers of the consequences of their own irresponsibility.

But we don't think the pragmatic objection provides good reason to oppose the kinds of public options we propose. Our goal is not to insulate people from their bad decisions. Instead, our goal is to construct a platform that supports people who want to act responsibly. Our worry is that laissez-faire markets and market subsidies have badly served Americans who want to live good lives. Public options aim to ensure access to universally important services when the free market has failed to provide good options for most Americans. Public options won't do much to save the grasshoppers among us: everyone will still have to work to care for their kids and to have money to put in the bank. Indeed, many public options—like higher education, public libraries, child care—strongly benefit the ants who want to work hard.

Why Not Just Use Vouchers?

Another objection is that public options aren't necessary because the government can just give people vouchers to help them pay for private options. Whether called vouchers, tax subsidies, or grants, the basic idea is the same: the role of government is to be, as one critic has memorably said, a "giant coupon machine . . . passing out coupons to discount and subsidize private education, health-care, old-age pensions and a wide variety of other primary goods."[15]

The case for vouchers is that they are supposed to support and increase choice and competition. In theory, vouchers give individuals more choice about what service provider to use; they also increase competition between service providers, and the government can easily fund them at a fixed cost.[16] But vouchers have a number of downsides. The first is that they don't always work as the theory suggests they should. The economist J. W. Mason has explained how basic economics shows the flaws of vouchers. When the supply of a good is highly inelastic (meaning that a decrease in price does not lead to an increase in supply), then a voucher (or tax cut, or whatever other form of market subsidy) will be captured by the producer of the good, and the discount will not be passed on to the consumer in the form of lower prices. Mason uses the example of cutting the gas tax. If oil refineries are running at full capacity and can't produce any more oil, and prices are going up because demand for oil is high, cutting the gas tax won't lower prices. Producers can't produce or refine oil any faster, so the discount won't help. And demand is already outstripping supply because people need the gas (that's why prices are so high in the first place).[17]

With that background, now consider the voucher example in higher education. If the supply of higher education is inelastic, meaning that we can't build more schools or get more spaces opened up at a college or university, then giving every student a $5,000 voucher won't actually decrease prices. Colleges can just increase tuition prices, perhaps even by the entire $5,000, and still have fully enrolled classes. The flip side of this basic economic logic is that spending directly on public schooling will lead to reductions in tuition across the board. If government spends its money on reducing tuition at public colleges, instead of on vouchers for any school, then unsubsidized schools will now need to compete with the public option—and they'll have to keep prices low to get students to attend.

In fact, as Mason argues, this logic will apply in any situation in which there is a monopoly or something close to inelastic supply. In that context, directly providing a public option will actually lower prices, while vouchers will lead to higher prices because most of the subsidy goes to the producer (the university, for example).

Vouchers also have some other downsides. According to Yale political scientist Jacob Hacker, two of the most important problems are distribution and visibility.[18] Vouchers have a distributional problem in that they tend to benefit people who are wealthier. Richer people are more likely to know that vouchers exist and to have the time and ability to figure out how to utilize them. Take tax credits. In order for a tax credit to have any effect, people have to know that the tax credit exists and they have to spend the time when doing their taxes to actually take the credit. If they don't know or if it's too complicated, they won't utilize the credit. And it's only wealthier people who, when they get confused or discouraged, have the resources to hire tax attorneys and accountants to help them navigate the complex tax code.

The problem of visibility is primarily political. Public options make it clear that the *public* is providing the option. People understand that their children attend public schools and that the government and their tax dollars go to support them. That gives citizens a stake in the institution's success—and a reason to monitor the institution. In other words, it gives them a reason to be active citizens. Vouchers, in contrast, are far less visible. As a result, most people don't realize that voucher programs are actually government programs that are helping them. For example, more than 60 percent of people who rely on government discounts to pay for college and more than half of people who take the home mortgage interest deduction in their taxes don't think that they're relying on a government program.[19] The political scientist Suzanne Mettler has called such government policies the "submerged state." The existence of the submerged state is important because it goes back to the issue of accountability for government programs. Public programs emphasize the democratic nature of our government and spur citizens to participate and hold accountable their elected officials. By contrast, hidden government action undermines the ability of citizens to control their government.

Why Not Just Use Regulation?

Another alternative to the public option is regulation. Instead of public provision, the private sector could provide services and the government could establish regulations—rules of the game—that govern provision of those services. We think that regulation is sometimes the right way to go, but as a tool, it suffers from some important drawbacks.

First, regulators can be "captured" by regulated industry. "Capture" is a term that scholars use when government actors pursue policies that are favorable to the regulated industry instead of policies that are in the public interest. Capture can take place when regulators come from private industry and bring with them the views of the industry (or if they plan to leave government service and go right back to the very companies they were just regulating). It can happen when regulators disproportionately hear from industry (informational capture) or when regulators themselves come to believe that what is best for industry is best for the general public, even when it isn't (cultural or intellectual capture).[20]

In our modern government, regulatory capture takes place because we have people from industry doing the regulating and because the regulatory process (appropriately) requires public participation in making new regulations, but industry predominates during that process. While we think the basic process is a sensible one, it does increase the risk of informational capture, because regulated industries have the greatest incentive to lobby hard for what they want. But this is less likely to be a problem for public options. Because public options do not involve regulating industry, government officials will not have to weigh the regulatory costs to industry as part of their analysis. This will make industry views less prominent. Social Security is a good example. When the Social Security Administration deliberates on various policy changes, the views of brokers such as Fidelity or Charles Schwab aren't as relevant. In contrast, when regulations on IRAs or 401(k)s are being debated, Fidelity and Charles Schwab have a lot at stake—and a lot to say. The possibility for capture is heightened.

A second drawback of regulations is that they can be costly and complicated, burdening business in general while at the same time advantaging big business. When regulations become complex (often because of lobbying from industry), they become more difficult and costly to comply with. Businesses and individuals have to hire lawyers, accountants, and compliance teams just to comply with the regulations—all of which take away from resources that could have gone elsewhere. Comparing Obamacare and a public option in health care is a good example. Obamacare is extremely complex, requiring a great deal of effort for both industry and individuals to navigate its provisions. A public option would be simpler.

A third problem with regulations is that they can be evaded. Industry often hires teams of lawyers to help them weasel their way through the rules, finding any possible loopholes. (This of course benefits big businesses; small businesses have a harder time.) The result is that individuals might not actually get the simple, safe, basic services that the regulations were intended to provide. Public options get around this problem. The public option would provide individuals with a service—plain and simple. Because there's no industry trying to game the regulations, the public option would do exactly what it says it does.

Don't Public Options Mean Unequal Services?

Another objection to public options concerns inequality: won't public options relegate poorer Americans to second-tier services, while the well-off opt out and patronize the private sector? There are two ways in which unequal services might arise, and we have to evaluate each one separately. In some cases, we should not be too worried about unequal services. For example, public parks, like Central Park in New York City, serve as a public option for thousands who don't have a private option (that is, a big backyard). But the alternative to the public option isn't yards for everyone in New York City. More likely, it's no yard and no public park. Public libraries are similar. Wealthy people will buy books and build up their personal libraries, but for many people, access to books is enough, even if it is more limited. In these cases, a public option is better than no option at all.

The other and more troubling possibility is that the optional part of a public option can lead to cream-skimming. What we mean here is that the underlying public option might itself be devalued, defunded, or eroded if some people opt for the private option. The classic example of cream-skimming is in health insurance (where it is called adverse selection). The "cream" of people to insure are healthy young people—they are the least costly to insure because they generally don't need much in the way of health care. So insurers have an incentive to try to serve only these people while leaving out others, especially those who are older or very ill. This is part of the reason health care reformers focused a great deal on people with preexisting conditions (who were often excluded from private-market insurance), and it is why some reformers support a single-payer system.

But cream-skimming can be addressed by careful policy design. For instance, a single-payer insurance system enrolls *everyone* in a baseline public health insurance plan. That means there is universal access to health care (no locking out the people with preexisting conditions). But universal coverage also enables cross-subsidies, as the payments from healthy people help fund insurance for less healthy people.

Cream-skimming can affect other public options, too. Public schools stand as a troubling example. K–12 schools vary widely in quality and are segregated by race and class because admission to these schools depends on residence in a town or county, and much of their funding comes from local taxes, including property taxes. What this means is that richer people can move to areas with expensive houses (where poor families can't afford to live) and send their kids to that community's public schools, where their kids are less likely to meet, interact with, or socialize with the poorer kids. If rich parents live in areas with poorer families, they can send their kids to private schools where, again, their kids are self-segregated from poorer families. This is a form of cream-skimming. The public schools in poor areas don't end up with all different types of students—the richer students are skimmed off by private schools. This can have an impact on school and student performance, investment, and more broadly on culture, as children aren't interacting with people different from themselves.

Once again, policy design matters. We agree that public schools need reform, but we reject the suggestion that new public options will necessarily replicate the existing public education experience. Public education in America has been distorted by the shameful legacies of slavery and Jim Crow. Deliberate racial segregation shaped the public schools, and residential segregation (combined with local politics) preserved school segregation long past *Brown v. Board of Education* and into today. Local financing, particularly the link between property taxes and school funding, helps perpetuate economic segregation as well. As Chapter 6 discusses, school reform poses thorny problems, but reform is possible, and there is every reason to think that reforming the public option is a better way forward than turning to voucher systems, which suffer from a variety of problems.

Isn't a Universal Basic Income Better?

Some forward-looking liberals will offer another objection—that a universal basic income could accomplish everything public options can achieve, and perhaps even more. We do have some sympathy for this claim. A basic income could, indeed, promote liberty and equality by improving market access for many lower-income (and younger) people and by setting an income floor for everyone. So we agree that a basic income could do a great deal of good in furthering progressive ends. We agree, too, that a basic income tends to avoid some of the perverse effects of market subsidies (discussed earlier and in Chapter 2) and imposes some market discipline: if prices in one sector rise too high, citizens who have access to a basic income will leave that sector and substitute another good or service. In a sense, a basic income is actually a type of public option—it is a public option for wages.

But we don't think that a basic income is sufficient, because it cannot fully protect freedom and promote opportunity. A basic income operates against a backdrop of institutions, including markets, and it has only a limited capacity to correct matters when markets fail or when prices are so high that they preclude access to primary goods. Take higher education, for instance. A basic income of, say, $10,000 per year could certainly ease the burden of college education by providing living expenses. But the average public university today charges $18,000 for tuition alone. Even a very generous $20,000 basic income would only cover living expenses plus a portion of tuition.

Put another way, basic income can't (and isn't meant to) solve all problems. A basic income can widen the range of life options for many people: everyone will have, say, $10,000 annually to spend as she chooses. But the moral case for basic income assumes that markets set fair prices for scarce resources, based on competing demand among individuals with equal endowments. Implicit is the idea that if one item (say, a college education) is expensive because of high demand, then citizens who don't sufficiently value college will—and should—spend their money elsewhere.

But our society doesn't operate that way. Markets are often incomplete, uncompetitive, or distorted by market subsidies. And individuals do not enter the market on terms of financial or social equality. Higher education provides a telling example. Higher education today is the surest entry to opportunity, and there are extensive market subsidies for college. But the result is not a moral marketplace in which everyone confronts a wide array of options at varying prices and soberly weighs how much they value a particular college option against other uses of their money. Instead, the market charges an exorbitant price and offers a limited array of options, and the subsidies that are available for college are far greater than any provided for competing life options.

Basic income can help by offering equal resources to the college-bound and the non-college-bound. But public options can add value by ensuring baseline access to opportunity and by helping correct some perverse market dynamics. In the end, then, basic income and public options can work together.

Part Two

THE HISTORY OF THE PUBLIC OPTION

5

Public Libraries, Social Security, and Other Successes

The term "public option," in the sense of a benefit provided to the general public at a controlled price, appears to be of relatively recent vintage. The *Oxford English Dictionary* has no entry for the phrase. A Google Books Ngram Viewer search, which tracks mentions of a phrase in printed sources starting in 1500, and a Google Scholar search show that the phrase was used only rarely in the 1980s. It became more common in the early 1990s during the Clinton-era health care reform debates. But while the public option is conventionally associated with health care policy, public options have been all around us for some time.

The U.S. Postal Service, Libraries, and Pools

Take the U.S. Postal Service (by now it should be clear this is one of our favorite examples). In the old days, you could hire a private courier to deliver a message.[1] These days, you can go to private companies like FedEx or UPS. But the Postal Service provides an option that combines universal access at a reasonable price, making it possible for anyone to send postcards, news, contracts, love letters, or holiday presents, regardless of wealth or location.

The Post Office served these functions from the founding of the country. The Constitution empowers Congress to "establish Post offices and post roads," and in the Post Office Act of 1791, Congress did just that. It created a postal system, guaranteed privacy in the mails (by barring officials from searching mail), allowed newspapers to be sent via mail, and established procedures for expanding post roads and postal services westward. The early Post Office was critical to the establishment of democracy in America. With citizens spread across a vast and often wild territory—and with limited transportation making travel difficult—the postal service spread information. With the rate for transporting a newspaper at 1 cent for less than 100 miles and 1.5 cents for more than 100 miles (lower than the cost of a private courier), citizens of the new republic had steady access to events happening all around the country.[2] As one historian has said, "The citizen-farmer had no trouble securing access to a steady flow of information on public affairs, making it possible for him to participate in national politics without leaving the farm."[3]

While the Post Office evolved over time, its core mission remained: to ensure universal access to information. But there were significant ancillary benefits from the start. In the early republic, the creation of post roads helped the country expand westward, and the postal service was critical to subsidizing the stagecoach industry and encouraging road building. The postal service contracted with steamships and delivered mail by rail, even sorting mail on railcars to improve efficiency. In the late nineteenth century it created rural free delivery, linking even the farthest reaches of the country. When the Post Office lowered rates on magazine delivery at the turn of the twentieth century, it contributed to a boom in the magazine industry that helped educate and entertain Americans.[4]

The postal service innovated frequently throughout its history—from stage coach to steam, rail to airmail. When the volume of mail doubled between 1945 and 1970, the Post Office was at the forefront of optical scanning technologies to sort mail more efficiently. In the 1980s and 1990s, leaders of the newly renamed U.S. Postal Service experimented with electronic services, recognizing that they would have to adapt to emerging technologies. The primary reason they failed wasn't a lack of imagination—it was interest group lobbying. Private companies like AT&T, and later internet companies, didn't want the postal system as a competitor, and they lobbied hard to keep it from providing new services. After decades of case-by-case battles, Congress ended the war and declared private companies the victor. The Postal Accountability and Enhancement Act of 2006 banned the postal system from providing any innovative services beyond traditional mail delivery.[5] Today the U.S. Postal Service is sometimes portrayed as a sclerotic institution, slow to adapt to technological change and perhaps even unnecessary in the age of email, FedEx, and now drone delivery. But this reputation isn't deserved. For most of American history, the Post Office was the quintessential public option, and it provided significant spillover benefits to the country in terms of democratic deliberation, infrastructure development, and commercial activity.

Public libraries are another example of a public option that is hidden in plain sight. In a world without public libraries, individuals can buy books and have a personal library. Private organizations (like private universities) can also buy books and let their members use them. But books are expensive, especially if they only get read once. Most people can't afford to purchase a large variety of books. Public libraries therefore provide a public option for books—universal access at a reasonable price (free). And you can still buy all the books you want.

Ben Franklin helped create the library tradition in America in 1731 when he founded the Library Company of Philadelphia, which was the country's first lending library. In the eighteenth century, America had both "social libraries," which lent books for free, and "circulating libraries," which charged a fee (and usually focused on more popular works). In the middle of the 1830s, reformers who believed in civic education established school district libraries. These proved hard to maintain, so by the 1850s libraries became identified with towns. Free public libraries would help schoolkids, house government documents, provide practical information for town citizens, and help the moral development of the community. Midcentury reformers saw part of their goal as ensuring that working-class people had access to information and knowledge so that they could improve their condition. During the Gilded Age, Andrew Carnegie gave millions of dollars to establish more than 1,600 libraries in 1,400 communities around the country.[6]

Public libraries inspired generations of notable Americans. Thomas Edison read about electricity; Hemingway encountered books at the Oak Park, Illinois, library as a kid. A young Martin Luther King Jr. read everything by Gandhi in the Atlanta Public Library. Toni Morrison, Woody Guthrie—the list goes on and on. But the impact of public libraries was much greater than just a few notable names. During the Depression, the National Youth

Administration (one of President Franklin Roosevelt's New Deal agencies) employed 9,000 people at public libraries. The Works Progress Administration built libraries, employed librarians, and funded bookmobiles to reach rural areas. President Lyndon Johnson's Great Society initiative expanded libraries further, from 9,500 public libraries in 1964 to almost 15,000 public libraries in 1980.[7] Today, public libraries not only provide reading material to children and adults who couldn't otherwise afford to amass a private library in their homes but also offer internet and computer access, lectures and readings, art appreciation, puppet shows, and much more. Anyone can take advantage of these opportunities.

Public swimming pools are a third example of a public option, though their history is far more checkered.[8] From the late eighteenth century, working-class people—boys especially—swam in nearby lakes and rivers for enjoyment. By the mid-nineteenth century, Victorian norms of modesty pushed municipalities to ban daytime swimming in lakes and rivers. The result was to block working-class families from both recreation and hygiene, because most were unable to afford baths in their homes or the expense of visiting a private bathhouse. With the emergence of a trend toward physical fitness, the advent of vacations (which made swimming acceptable to those with middle-class sensibilities), and the fear that dirtiness would lead to disease and criminality, municipalities started building public swimming pools.

From the 1890s through the New Deal, public swimming pools went through a series of changes. They were first democratic, bringing together white and black men across class lines and justified for fitness purposes (because the germ theory of disease had become dominant, the "bath" justification was now unnecessary). But the working-class tradition of recreational swimming conflicted with middle-class preference for physical fitness, leading cities to charge fees in order to lock out working people.

Eventually city leaders reopened pools on "free days" in hopes that working-class people wouldn't cause trouble in town during their free time. When pools became integrated by gender, they became segregated by race. Mixing genders meant that pools became sexualized spaces, and fears of black men alongside white women led to segregation, enforced by private violence and intimidation. During the New Deal, the federal government built 750 pools and another almost 1,700 wading pools through the Civil Works Administration, Works Progress Administration, and Public Works Administration.[9] These pools were not just jobs programs; they provided a respite from the economic stress of the Depression and refuge from the heat and drought in the Midwest.

After World War II swimming pools were increasingly desegregated, and in the late 1960s cities started building pools for black neighborhoods that had been excluded during the age of segregated swimming. Whites soon fled public pools, establishing private neighborhood swim clubs and building in-ground backyard swimming pools. In 1950, only 2,500 American families had their own swimming pool; by 1999, 4 million did.[10] With middle-class whites moving to private pools, cities started to ignore the maintenance of the public pools used by the working class and minorities, leaving those facilities increasingly dilapidated. At the same time, Americans lost a central locus for community life—a place where people of different classes could come together.

A Public Retirement Option for the Elderly: Social Security

Thanks to the public options just described, we take it for granted that anyone can mail a letter or package to a loved one, or pay a bill for the cost of a stamp. We can be confident that anyone, rich or poor, can read or use a computer in a safe, clean space with access to plenty of books, movies, and software.

But public options have also accomplished an even more ambitious task: how to provide for old age in a modern society. Today we take Social Security retirement benefits almost for granted, kind of like the Postal Service and public libraries. Shrouded in the mists of history is the program's stunning achievement: it helped protect workers and their families and made possible the development of the United States as a major and thoroughly modern economic power.

Many histories portray Social Security as an effort to address poverty among the elderly during the Great Depression, and that's a reasonable starting point. In the 1930s, many older people faced a life of poverty when they could no longer work. The shortage of jobs in the Depression compounded the situation: older workers were competing with younger workers for scarce jobs. At the time, the only public retirement programs were means-tested, which is to say miserly and limited to the very poor. President Roosevelt's big idea, which would take years to come to fruition, was that the federal government could create, and stand behind, a secure public retirement for all.

Congress passed the Social Security Act in 1935, and for the first time the federal government guaranteed an old-age pension to American workers. The Social Security retirement program has been amended and expanded over time, and today it covers about

85 percent of all workers in the United States and pays an average benefit (to new retirees as of 2016) of $1,400 per month, or $16,800 per year.[11] That may seem like a modest sum. But Social Security is a baseline public option: it provides a decent floor, not abundant riches. (People who want a higher living standard need to save money on their own—an issue we consider at length in Chapter 7.) Still, together with private pensions and private savings, the Social Security program has proved to be one of America's most successful anti-poverty programs. The poverty rate among the elderly as of 2017 was less than 10 percent. If Social Security were suddenly repealed, the poverty rate among those over sixty-five would jump to an astonishing 40 percent.[12]

Social Security remains one of the most popular public programs in the United States. Poll data show that the great majority (about three-quarters) of Americans don't mind paying Social Security taxes, because they believe they'll receive benefits and know that they would have to support their parents if there were no Social Security.[13] Between two-thirds and three-quarters of Americans actually want to *increase* Social Security benefits.[14]

Social Security has endured well beyond the Great Depression because it isn't just an anti-poverty program: it also fills predictable gaps in private retirement provision. Free marketeers like to argue that if Social Security were repealed, workers would save for their own retirement. But the strategy of relying on private markets alone has several problems.

First, workers don't know how long they'll live. The fact that the average life expectancy of a sixty-five-year-old is about twenty more years is a useful statistic, but it doesn't reassure any particular individual that she needs to provide for herself only to age eighty-five.[15] In theory, individuals could buy life annuities from private insurance companies: these annuities pay out a monthly income for as long as one lives, making them very useful hedges against outliving one's savings. There's just one problem, and it's a showstopper: the private annuity market is a failure. Sure, there's a small number of private annuities available, but they are extremely expensive—which makes them very poor investments for the average person.

The reason the private annuity markets fail is the dynamic called "adverse selection." If every sixty-five-year-old adult bought an annuity, there'd be no problem: insurance companies could estimate that the average buyer would live to eighty-five. But in a pure private market, not everyone buys an annuity. And those who do are likely to have information (say, a family history) that leads them to believe they'll live longer than average. We'd all like to be one of those ninety-five-year-old marathon runners, but, realistically, people who are sick or who have a family history of early death won't spend their time shopping for annuities. Instead, it's healthy people with a family history of longevity that will enter the market.

This dynamic might at first seem just fine: shouldn't annuity markets cater to the people who need annuities? The problem is that the skew in the marketplace makes it difficult for insurance companies to estimate average life span. Knowing that mostly longer-lived people will buy their products, the companies price the annuities as if everyone lived to, say, a hundred. But that means some people who expect to live "only" to ninety-five will find it too expensive to buy an annuity, and they'll drop out. The result is a downward spiral, making private annuities scarce and expensive.

Second, workers face additional uncertainty about investment returns. Imagine that you're thirty-five years old and you'd like to accumulate $1 million for retirement at age seventy. If you anticipate interest rates of 8 percent, you can save just $5,800 per year and you'll meet your goal. But if interest rates are much lower (say, 1 percent), you'd have to save way more—a whopping $24,000 per year.[16] Compounding the problem, most workers aren't investment experts, and yet the stakes are high. Workers who fail to diversify or who adopt the latest investment fad (tech stocks in the 1990s, anyone?) could find their retirement savings decimated when booms go bust. And because most people aren't investment experts, it is awfully easy for private firms to sell them low-quality products at high prices.

This isn't just a supposition: this is exactly what has happened in the 401(k) marketplace. You may have heard of the investment management firm Edward Jones, which has storefront locations inviting passersby to "put the power of personal attention to work for you."[17] But the firm's own 401(k) plan reportedly offered its workers subpar investment options at high fees. Edward Jones, employee lawsuits allege, got "partnership fees" from investment providers. Put bluntly, the wealth management firm's own workers believed that the firm cheated their retirement plan in order to receive hidden kickbacks from investment providers.[18]

Third, private markets can't solve a basic dilemma of budget arithmetic: low-income workers find it hard to save. When your earnings are just barely enough to pay for food and rent, saving for retirement just isn't going to happen. Today, for instance, a startling 15 percent of households have a net worth of zero or less than zero. That means one American family in seven has debt that equals or exceeds the value of its assets.[19]

Social Security solves all three problems with a baseline public option. First, the program provides all retirees with a life annuity.

Once workers retire, they receive a Social Security check every month until they die, whether that's ten more years or forty. Social Security can offer a stable annuity in part because the program requires virtually all workers to contribute: because nearly everyone is covered, the program doesn't suffer from the adverse selection that undermines private annuity markets.

Second, Social Security removes investment risk from workers and places it on the community—that is, the government. Every worker receives a defined-benefit pension via Social Security: a guaranteed payment every month, no matter whether interest rates are high or low or whether the stock market has boomed or bottomed out. Defined-benefit pensions have become a rarer and rarer bird in the private employment market, and so this feature of Social Security provides an important financial baseline for everyone.

Third, Social Security helps lower-income workers save for retirement. For one thing, the payroll tax "contribution" is mandatory: all workers pay something toward Social Security with each paycheck. For another, the program offers low-earning workers a far better deal than they could get in the private marketplace: every dollar they pay in taxes "buys" higher benefits than higher earners receive. In other words, retirement benefits through Social Security are better than those through private competitors for the same price. As a result, the Social Security system insures workers against having low earnings by ensuring that even low earners will have a decent retirement income.

Taking the long view, Social Security has not only protected the elderly against poverty but also promoted freedom and equality in myriad ways. In the agricultural era, aging farmers relied on their kids to stay around and work on the farm. Industrial work changed these patterns: no longer would multiple generations live on the same land, and no longer would children take up their parents' way of life. Social Security helped the United States make the transition to this modern, industrial economy, because it allowed Americans to be more mobile. It also permits the elderly to live independently—something that retirees very much want, as do their children. We sometimes like to think that in some bygone era multigeneration families lived happily together. But historian Dora Costa found that older people have always preferred independent living when they could manage it.[20] Having a measure of retirement security means that Americans—and almost all Americans are covered by Social Security—have greater opportunities to live independently.

To be sure, Social Security makes a major claim on federal expenditures. In 2016, for instance, Social Security alone (without Medicare) accounted for 24 percent of federal spending.[21] Budget cutters have made the program a target and have on many occasions predicted that the program will become insolvent. The only solution, some politicians claim, is to privatize the program or cut benefits sharply.[22]

But rumors of Social Security's so-called problems and insolvency have been exaggerated. First of all, the size of the program shouldn't be surprising: it provides retirement security (plus disability and life insurance) for nearly every American worker. Second, we must remember that this isn't an ordinary line item in the budget. Americans have paid into Social Security throughout their lives. Finally, thinking about Social Security only as a matter of the budget misses the point. To address the retirement crisis, many have advocated expanding this highly successful baseline public option. Most Americans want to do so, and with some changes to make its tax provisions more progressive, expanding Social Security is possible.

This is not to say that Social Security is perfect. The program's design merits consideration as social conditions change. For instance, the average sixty-five-year-old has gained seven years of life expectancy since 1900. At the same time, the gap between rich and poor has grown: at age sixty-five, richer men can expect to live more than five years longer than poorer ones. In the near future, then, Social Security will need an update to ensure that its benefit structure remains sustainable and progressive under current conditions.[23]

Still, a note of caution is appropriate when we look beyond Social Security to the broader topic of retirement security. The program continues to succeed at providing a baseline public option. But it was never intended to provide 100 percent of the income individuals need in retirement. Rather, Social Security was designed to coexist with employer pensions and private retirement savings. The real problem is that the latter two have failed most Americans dismally. The demise of the Treaty of Detroit has led more and more employers to cut or eliminate worker pensions. And despite massive tax subsidies, there is a national shortfall in private pension savings, with more than 50 percent of workers having too little retirement savings.[24] Only the well-off find themselves nearing retirement with anything like enough money for a secure old age. In Chapter 7, we'll propose a public option for private retirement savings that would lower costs and improve options for most workers by offering them something like the very successful savings plan that the federal government offers to its own workers.

But even as it is, Social Security works well in three ways: it fosters freedom and equality in ways that private markets cannot, it has a clear and limited mission to provide a baseline of retirement security, and the distribution of monthly checks to retirees is well within the capabilities of public administration. It's a success story all around.

6

Mixed Results in Education and Housing

No policy tool is perfect in every case, and it is essential to take a hard look at some of the less-happy instances, where policy has fallen short of its ambitions. Public schools and public housing are both important public options, but they have both also occasioned bitter controversy. Public housing has been widely criticized, especially (but certainly not exclusively) by politicians on the right. A (Democratic) former mayor of Worcester, Massachusetts, noted, "For many, public housing has become a perverse legacy handed down from one generation to the next."[1] The *New York Times* described Chicago's notorious Robert Taylor Homes, a large public housing project, as "slums" occupied by "drug gangs" and swarming cockroaches.[2]

By contrast, public schools enjoy solid popularity. The overwhelming majority of Americans believe that the government should guarantee a quality public education to all and that the government should spend more, not less, on education.[3] Still, there is a well-known puzzle in people's attitudes toward public schools. Parents give their own children's public schools high marks—77 percent in a recent survey gave their child's own school a grade of A or B. But in the same survey, only 18 percent gave the same rating to the nation's public schools as a whole.[4]

Since the 1980s, right-leaning policy makers have promoted market subsidies as the solution to the problems, actual and perceived, of public housing and public schools, and this approach has accelerated with the Trump administration. Instead of funding public housing, critics say, the government should offer housing vouchers to tenants or subsidies to private developers. And instead of funding public schools, the argument runs, the government should provide vouchers that let families choose any school—public, private, or religious.[5]

As we sorted through the evidence on public schools and public housing, we reached two conclusions. First, the failures of these public options have been exaggerated, usually for political gain. Right-wing think tanks invoke "dilapidated and crime-infested public housing [as] a vivid reminder of the government's failure when it comes to solving social ills."[6] And they dismiss the public schools as failing their students in order to protect lazy, unionized teachers. A memorable 1983 report concluded that "if an unfriendly foreign power had attempted to impose on America the mediocre educational performance that exists today, we might well have viewed it as an act of war."[7]

But these tropes are as dubious as the Reagan-era stereotype of the "welfare queen." They are long on ideology and short on facts, and they play to race and class prejudice. The truth is more mixed. Public housing and public schools have helped many Americans step up to better lives, but they have failed to do enough to advance opportunity for poor and minority Americans. These failures are not, by and large, due to massive incompetence or corruption in government (though we don't ignore the possibility that either might be behind a specific case). Instead, they reflect America's intense residential segregation by race and by class—and the economic and political structures that prevent poor and minority voters from challenging their isolation and gaining access to greater resources. The upshot: although politicians talk about crime-infested "projects" and mediocre public schools, the underlying problems are as much social and political as anything else.

And this brings us to our second key conclusion: vouchers are not a panacea. Without thoroughgoing reform in politics, even ideal market subsidies can't change much. Indeed, robust evidence shows that neither vouchers nor private competition consistently outperforms public options, either in housing or in schools.

The problems plaguing public housing and public education can and should be addressed. Housing and schools are critical prerequisites for equal opportunity, and they merit a public option that works for everyone. The real barriers are both well known and too seldom addressed: residential segregation and political structures that make segregation difficult or impossible to challenge.

Public Schools and the Voucher Debate

Public education is a competitive public option: it provides universal access to free K–12 education, but it isn't mandatory. Parents can choose to pay for private or parochial education, although the vast majority don't. In 2015, 90 percent of children nationwide attended public school.[8]

Public schools have existed since before the American Revolution, but they took a big step toward becoming a public option—

open to all—when states enacted compulsory attendance laws beginning in the nineteenth century. In 1954, the nation took a giant leap toward a true public option with the Supreme Court's decision in *Brown v. Board of Education,* which ended de jure segregation in the schools. Over the centuries, public education has helped create and sustain the American middle class and the transition from an agrarian society to an industrial and technological one.

Public education today faces two major problems. The first is ensuring a quality education for every student. By a number of measures, the United States is behind other major countries in student achievement.[9] Policy wonks and politicians have debated the best fix for the quality problem. Some advocate national standards: this is essentially the approach of the Bush-era No Child Left Behind Act, which has evolved over time to require standardized testing and impose sanctions on low-performing schools. The Common Core, a set of national curricula, was another effort to raise educational quality by promoting national standards.

We think the quality problem is well worth attention, not so much because it reflects a "crisis" but because public reflection on quality and cost are exactly what help public options function well. The merits of testing and metrics remain to be worked out, and there is no easy solution, but—again—all of this is standard operating procedure for a robust public option.

The second problem, which is tied to the first, is segregation by race and by class. While states may no longer formally segregate schoolchildren based on race, residential segregation and local politics have permitted de facto school segregation to flourish. True, lawmakers cannot enact rules that explicitly direct greater resources to rich, white kids. But lawmakers can take notice of a few salient facts that permit them to maintain segregation with plausible deniability.

For one thing, centuries of residential segregation (abetted by Jim Crow and zoning laws, among others) have left poor and minority students largely concentrated in neighborhoods that are geographically distinct from those occupied by richer and whiter kids. For another thing, schools have always been run locally and largely funded by taxes imposed by localities. Putting all this together, school district boundaries effectively segregate poor or minority students into certain school districts. And by funding schools through local taxes, politicians have ensured that poor people will have poorly funded schools.

The funding gap is especially perverse because poorer students need *more* resources if they are to flourish. Poor students enter first grade with lower achievement scores already, and as they advance through the grades, they will predictably face adverse conditions in their neighborhoods and homes that are much less common in richer areas.

Indeed, funding isn't just about schools, nor is education just about funding. Problems like homelessness, untreated medical conditions, family trauma, and drug addiction can—and do—exist everywhere. But they are far more prevalent in poorer communities (both rural and urban). Neighborhoods and communities also have different levels of support networks, economic opportunities, and social capital—all of which are important for fostering an environment where young people can succeed. And there are significant differences in the out-of-school enrichment that kids get, from how much parents read to their children, to whether they make trips to museums, to whether they are involved in outside activities like organized sports or supplementary tutoring.

Take Washington, D.C., as an example. The Washington metropolitan area, taken as a whole, is the richest in the nation, ranking ahead of San Francisco and New York, among others.[10] But that average prosperity masks a high degree of residential segregation. The affluent and the middle class tend to live in places like Bethesda, Maryland, Fairfax, Virginia, and wealthy enclaves in D.C. itself. The very poor tend to live in the District's poorer neighborhoods, like Anacostia.

The District is politically separate from Maryland and Virginia, and it is barred by law from taxing the many suburban commuters who occupy its streets and offices every day. Schools are funded locally, and local district lines are drawn so that poorer people have no chance to vote for higher taxes on their richer neighbors.[11] D.C. does what it can to make up for this unequal distribution; in fact, it has some of the highest per-student spending in the country. But even with these high rates of spending within the District, disparities in resources and in outcomes persist between poorer and wealthier schools.

We believe that de facto segregation and underfunding of poor districts are huge problems and worthy subjects for public debate, as are other topics like raising salaries for teachers and ensuring small class sizes. But we also believe that broader issues—from economic growth and opportunities, to segregation and historic discrimination, to health, family, and social crises—must also all be part of the debate. The key issue, however, isn't whether schools are public. It is that education cannot be divorced from the economic and social context of families and neighborhoods.

The big, splashy reforms in the news are charter schools and, under the rubric of school competition, vouchers, so we will look at both. Before diving into the evidence, though, it's useful to clarify some terminology. You might think that charter schools are a thing, since they've been so widely promoted—and vilified. But, in fact, "charter school" is an umbrella term that covers a wide range of programs. In essence, charter schools are a kind of public-private hybrid, but they range from public schools that test a new educational model to private schools that take state money with very little accountability.[12]

Some of the most successful charter schools have tested educational models that might (in theory) be adapted in public schools. For instance, some Boston charter schools with a "no excuses" philosophy, an approach that sets high behavioral and academic expectations and a strict disciplinary code, have generated some positive results in test scores and four-year college attendance. Still, a shortcoming of the evidence is that the children studied applied for the charter-school lottery and so might not be a representative sample of all students.[13]

But charter schools can also fail spectacularly, especially when they have a weak educational model and limited public oversight. The State of Ohio provides a well-known cautionary tale. The state is one of the top five in the number of charter schools, and has spent millions of dollars on charter schools, including on for-profit firms. But the charter scene turned into an ugly free-for-all because the state engaged in little oversight. Some schools closed midyear. Others "shopped" for friendly monitors who would overlook a little sleight-of-hand on money and school quality.[14]

Take the private firm Electronic Classroom of Tomorrow (ECOT), which sounds kind of futuristic and cool. ECOT's website touts "Education Your Way" and promotes its status as Ohio's largest online charter school.[15] But in practice, the for-profit company bilked the state and offered little to students. Ohio school officials repeatedly gave the chain's schools a grade of F for quality.[16] And in 2015, ECOT billed the state for 9,000 students who didn't actually attend the school.[17]

ECOT is one bad apple in what seems to be a very rotten barrel. Even advocates of charter schools view Ohio as a cautionary tale.[18] The *Akron Beacon-Journal* found that Ohio "charter schools misspen[d] public money nearly four times more often than any other type of taxpayer-funded agency."[19] And Ohio isn't alone: some charter schools nationwide have been caught engaging in very questionable practices.[20] It's no surprise then, that some nationwide studies suggest that charter schools in the aggregate do not raise student achievement.[21]

Overall, we are dubious to agnostic on charter schools, simply because they encompass so many different models. The best charters might permit innovative nonprofits to aid the cause of reform in the public schools—basically, a way of tapping experimental expertise to improve the public option. But as the Ohio scandal suggests, there is no reason to think that the best approach is to give government funds, willy-nilly, to private firms.

Now for school vouchers, which command the allegiance and affection of neoliberals. It's not clear that vouchers have reliably boosted school achievement in the areas where they've been tried. Consider the conclusions of a 2017 study by a Stanford University researcher:

> Studies of voucher programs in several U.S. cities, the states of Florida, Indiana, Louisiana, and in Chile and India, find limited improvements at best in student achievement and school district performance from even large-scale programs. *In the few cases in which test scores increased, other factors, namely increased public accountability, not private school competition, seem to be more likely drivers.*

> And high rates of attrition from private schools among voucher users in several studies raises concerns. The second largest and longest-standing U.S. voucher program, in Milwaukee, offers *no solid evidence of student gains* in either private or public schools.[22]

This is just one study (though a wide-ranging one), and there are conflicting views about school vouchers, including about the data. As a result, it is helpful to think about school vouchers from a broader and more basic perspective. The neoliberal theory of vouchers is that schools will improve as they compete for parents' voucher dollars. On some level, we marvel at the ability of neoliberals to imagine everything as a market. But the reality is that their uncritical faith in markets is very much like the old canard about communism—it sounds great in theory but it doesn't make sense in practice. There are a lot of sociological factors that undermine the simple market analogy. Parents may not understand how vouchers work or may not have time to research schools. It may be inconvenient to send kids to a school that isn't close to their home or to a parent's workplace. And markets might not serve all students well—for example, students with disabilities.

Going beyond parents, the market framework assumes that the problem of performance in schools is that schools and teachers aren't hard-working or innovative enough, and that competition might provide the incentive for them to improve. But it isn't at all clear that this is the problem. The problems with American public schools are far more varied and are often tied up with problems in the community. In addition to funding issues (both for schools and for teacher salaries), less successful schools often have student populations that are poorer, historically have suffered from discrimination and segregation, have fragmented or difficult family situations, don't receive as much out-of-school education and enrichment, and don't get as much social and community support. Even if schools are extremely innovative, it is very hard for schools alone to address such social problems, especially when they are severe.

Adding to all this is the problem of corruption in private markets. A voucher system might lead schools to compete on substance—the quality of instruction. But a private school voucher system, like any private market, can also reward pure marketing and even lies. Schools with an impressive new building may look good but hide an inferior educational "product." And schools may fudge, manipulate, and even falsify their enrollment and performance numbers if they can profit by doing so.

The takeaway, then, is that school reform is important but tricky, and that vouchers are not a magic solution. Background conditions matter, a lot. And public debate over quality is critical. But there is no reason to think (and no sustained experience to show) that turning the schools over to private firms would solve the system's problems.

Public Housing and Housing Vouchers

Public housing is one of the most vilified public options, with critics complaining that housing projects warehouse poor and minority families in substandard conditions in segregated neighborhoods. We'll take a closer look shortly, but before we acknowledge the partial truth in some of these criticisms, it's worth remembering that public housing has helped ease America's housing problems and has promoted equal opportunity for many.

Public housing is just one of several public options that offer universal access to housing at an affordable price. In the Great Depression, the New Deal initiated the federal public housing program, which sought not only to provide decent housing but also, in doing so, to create jobs.[23] Facing a housing shortage and an influx of returning GIs after World War II, the federal government responded with the mortgage subsidies of the GI Bill. In the 1960s, President Johnson's War on Poverty offered subsidies to private developers to build low-income housing. And in the 1970s, Richard Nixon endorsed housing vouchers that subsidized market housing for low-income families.[24]

Housing policy is complex and difficult, not least because programs interact with one another. For instance, mortgage subsidies (through the GI Bill and tax deductions) helped many middle-class families buy suburban homes, so by the 1960s and 1970s public housing had become largely the province of the urban poor.[25] Congressional restrictions on income levels have further transformed the public housing program: in 2015, the average income of public housing families was about $14,000 per year.[26]

So the current debate over public housing is essentially a debate over housing for the very poor. Overall, public housing has provided access to decent and affordable housing to low-income families that otherwise would live in substandard conditions or face unaffordable rents.[27] Today, 1.2 million American households occupy public housing units.[28] The connection to freedom and equality is clear: at its best, decent housing makes it possible for poor parents to provide a safe environment for children and for themselves. At the same time, of course, public housing competes with market housing: no one is required to live there.

Today, the need for affordable housing is particularly great because the cost of housing in many cities has far outstripped wages. More than 21 million households (in 2016) paid rents of more than 30 percent of income (a standard measure of housing affordability), with 11 million of those paying more than 50 percent of their income on rent.[29]

Media images of public housing have highlighted high-poverty, high-crime projects like Cabrini-Green in Chicago (which was demolished in 2011).[30] But in other large cities, including notably New York City, public housing has proved a lasting success. Today, more than 400,000 New Yorkers live in public housing, which—with some missteps—mostly provides decent and affordable housing. Nicholas Dagen Bloom's careful study shows that public administration is key to the success of New York's public housing.[31]

Taking a national view, public housing has had notable successes. In their overview of housing policy research, Robert Collinson and his colleagues found that studies from the 1960s and 1970s showed that public housing appeared to "greatly increase housing affordability."[32] In a 1999 study, economists Janet Currie and Aaron Yelowitz examined data on public housing and concluded that the program has been unfairly vilified. They reported that households in public housing are less crowded and less likely to live in buildings with fifty or more units.[33]

Still, it isn't clear that traditional public housing can cope with the problem of affordability. For one thing, there is a shortage of public housing units relative to need. The U.S. Department of Housing and Urban Development reports that only 60 percent of low-income families with extreme need have access to public housing assistance.[34] In many cities, the waiting list is long: in New York City in 2012, for example, the waiting list stretched to more than 200,000 applicants. With under 6,000 slots opening up each year, most of those families will wait years.[35] Hundreds of thousands of New Yorkers apparently believe that public housing is a good option for them—hence the long waiting list.

For another thing, traditional public housing units are disproportionately located in segregated, poor neighborhoods. Nearly one-third of public housing is located in census tracts with a 40 percent or higher poverty rate, and well over one-third of public housing stands in census tracts with minority populations of 80 percent or more.[36] Indeed, the location and design of public housing locations in the past "helped reinforce patterns of concentrated poverty and racial segregation."[37] These features can make renovating existing public housing an unattractive option.

Over time, the mix of public dollars devoted to housing has also shifted. Over the last two decades, of the number of public housing units has shrunk by 300,000. At the same time, an additional 2.2 million households have gained assistance through housing vouchers and government-subsidized private housing. The result is that today, "privately-owned and operated properties house nearly three-quarters of assisted households."[38]

So public housing as a public option has been on the decline. Given the political roadblocks to increasing funding, even progressive housing advocates have turned to market subsidies instead, in particular to housing vouchers—called Housing Choice Vouchers or Section 8 vouchers. Even the venerable Center for Budget and Policy Priorities, a left-leaning think tank, recognizes housing vouchers for their progressive effects on homelessness, poverty, and opportunity.[39]

Housing vouchers offer families the opportunity to rent private housing and to pay no more than 30 percent of their income each month in rent. Landlords receive a check from the federal government for the balance. So if market rent is, say, $1,000 but the family's contribution is capped at $600, the government pays the landlord the remaining $400.[40] Housing vouchers have proved popular among low-income households, and (relative to no housing subsidy at all) they improve housing affordability and (possibly) housing quality.[41] But vouchers, like public housing, are in short supply, and waiting lists are long.[42]

Housing vouchers also have not markedly changed the location of subsidized housing. "Even though voucher holders have the ability to reside in middle-class neighborhoods that are not racially segregated, most end up in predominantly minority neighborhoods, most of which also struggle with high rates of poverty."[43] And housing vouchers share many of the shortcomings of other market subsidies. Studies have found that landlords charge more to Section 8 tenants than to market tenants, meaning that they reap an extra profit at the government's expense, as we would expect from a voucher-based system.[44]

Government subsidies to private developers have pros and cons as well. The Low-Income Housing Tax Credit, the largest subsidy program, offers tax credits—really, just cash payments—to private developers who built rental units open to low-income families. The program has added millions of affordable housing units to the nation's housing stock. Still, developments tend to be in low-income areas. One recent study found that the program's costs have risen sharply, even as the number of additional units has declined.[45]

When we move the discussion from public housing to private homeownership, most people would be surprised to find out that the market for purchasing a home has also been shaped by a public option. It's sneakier and far more technical, but as the scholars Adam Levitin and Susan Wachter have argued, America once had a public option for housing finance.[46]

After the Great Depression, the government created a variety of "public options" that were integral to the housing finance market. The key features were the Federal Housing Administration (FHA) and the Federal National Mortgage Association (Fannie Mae). The Federal Housing Administration (and also the Veterans Administration) offered insurance on mortgages—but not all mortgages. FHA set standards for mortgages in terms of maximum interest rates, loan to value ratios, and length of mortgages.[47] Fannie Mae created a secondary market for these mortgages, buying up FHA and VA mortgages and expanding liquidity in the mortgage markets. This deep bureaucratic history is the origin of the thirty-year fixed-rate mortgage, which could be offered because long-term loans were insured. In other words, the public option for mortgage insurance actually *created* a wholly new product in the market itself—and in the process helped make America's middle class into a class of homeowners.

Over time, however, Fannie Mae and Freddie Mac were privatized, and adjustable rate mortgages, teaser rate mortgages, and other more complex products expanded. This new world put more and more risk on homeowners, compared to the old world of the public option, which tried to reduce risk for homeowners through a very simple set of products. The result of abandoning the public option in housing finance, Levitin and Wachter conclude, was the great crash of 2008.

The important thing for our purposes, however, is to notice that for housing, the public option wasn't just one thing—government provision of housing. There were really two different approaches to a public option for housing. The housing finance public option was the default for most Americans, for the great middle class who could afford to buy their own homes if the rates were stable and secure. For those who weren't as well off, public housing existed as a baseline safety net.

As the United States has stepped back from public options in housing (much the way it did in education), the larger problem is that policies intended to aid low-income families have operated against a backdrop of political, residential, and economic segregation that has tended to isolate poor families and to cluster them in specific areas.[48]

Looking ahead, a new generation of housing policies can—and should—target racial and economic isolation. For instance, new public housing might be built with greater attention to building mixed-income and mixed-race communities. Low-income housing, whether public or subsidized, might be mixed together with moderate-income housing. And vouchers might be redesigned to help families move out of high-poverty areas.[49]

America's Romance with Private Markets

Today, public options like the U.S. Postal Service, public libraries, Social Security, and public schools continue to serve the vast majority of Americans very well. Ninety percent of Americans consider public libraries important to their communities.[50] More than 80 percent of Americans are willing to pay Social Security taxes because the program provides security and stability to citizens. A majority of Americans give their local public schools high grades for quality.

But even as public options like these continue to define what it means to be American, the idea of direct government services has fallen out of favor. Since the 1970s, U.S. policy makers have been engaged in a romance with the free market. Libertarian ideas were fringe stuff in the 1960s, but by the end of the 1970s, politicians of both parties had succumbed to the allure of the "free market." Economists in the government and the academy spread the gospel, preaching that free markets are best and that government is too bloated and too corrupt to provide reliable services.

But the Great Recession that began in 2008, if it taught us anything, taught us to be skeptical of claims about the honesty, transparency, and efficiency of private firms. This book is a post-romantic effort: we think that analysis rather than faith should guide policy makers. We don't have blind faith in public administration, but neither do we have blind faith in private firms. It's fair and right to ask which is the best form of administration given a particular context, history, and the nature of the task at hand.

Moreover, one of the key contributions of public options is that we need not give an all-or-nothing answer. We see public options as a way of harnessing government's best features and power while also preserving the best features of markets. In the next few chapters, we challenge the status quo and show why public options are worth taking seriously once again.

Part Three

THE PUBLIC OPTION AND PUBLIC POLICY

7

Retirement

The daily news coming out of the Trump White House has pushed other public concerns to the side. And that's a big problem, because policy makers are distracted from dealing with America's retirement crisis, as well as other pressing issues. The typical middle-class household nearing retirement has just $60,000 in pension wealth—not much when retirees can now expect to live twenty years past age sixty-five. Low earners have half that sum.[1] The sobering fact is that more than half of American households are at risk of running out of money in retirement.[2] Social Security will continue to provide a secure floor that staves off the worst destitution, but it was never intended to fully fund anyone's retirement.

From the era of the Treaty of Detroit onward, the plan was that retirement security would be provided in three complementary ways. First, Social Security would provide a baseline public option for a retirement pension.[3] Second, employer-based pensions wouldn't make the ordinary worker rich, but they would add a hefty amount to Social Security's baseline to ensure that retired couples could maintain their middle-class lifestyle.[4] Traditional pensions guaranteed workers a secure monthly benefit, usually calculated as a percentage of their income in a top-earning year. The guaranteed income let middle-class retirees plan ahead—and look forward to a decent living standard in retirement.[5] A generation of middle-class snowbirds flocked to retirement communities in Florida and Arizona, among other places, in part because they had secure, guaranteed pensions on top of Social Security. And third, for those who wanted a little more, private savings would top up retirement income.

Today's workers face a harsher retirement climate. Workers live longer, but they have less financial security. Social Security wasn't meant to bear the whole burden of retirement savings; it simply doesn't cover enough of the cost of living. Many employers dropped pension plans to contain costs. As more workers took service jobs and part-time and temporary work, the percentage of workers with any employer pension plummeted.[6]

Workers with a pension also receive less retirement income than before, largely because defined-benefit pensions have been replaced with defined-contribution pensions.[7] New-style pensions, including 401(k)s, shift risks away from firms and onto workers. Workers' retirement security now depends on their ability to save money out of their paychecks—a tough choice when middle-class families already struggle under the weight of heavy student debt and rising prices for housing and child care. The new pensions also expect workers to decipher the arcane world of finance. The stakes are high: savers who make risky choices or who fail to read the fine print can see their hard-earned money evaporate. Just as bad, a financial crash—like the American market implosions of 2000 and 2008—can decimate pensions for anyone, no matter how frugal and prudent they are.

The looming failure of the U.S. retirement system will affect all of us. Most of us will be old one day. And in the meantime, we care that our parents and coworkers have a secure retirement income. When older people lack retirement security, we all pay the price—because our parents need money or because older colleagues keep working when they can't afford to retire. A secure retirement is part and parcel of freedom and equality for all Americans—and especially for a mobile workforce striving to meet the challenges of the new economy.

The good news is that America can do better. We can't bring back old-style pensions any more than we can bring back the rest of the Treaty of Detroit. But new-style pensions do not need to shift so many risks onto workers' backs. In fact, a better system already exists, and we propose to build on it. Federal employees have a fantastic 401(k)-type savings plan, the Thrift Savings Plan, or TSP, that provides sound investments at a low administrative cost. The TSP is a model for a competitive public option that could be made available to all workers. No one would be required to participate, and market options would compete side by side with it. But a new public option along the lines of the TSP could provide a secure vehicle for retirement savings. Adding to the appeal of the public option is that it would cost the government exactly zero dollars, because savers would pay (modest) fees to defray the system's costs.

Along with the public option, we can—and should—redesign government subsidies for retirement. Today, the federal government subsidizes retirement savings to the tune of $180 billion a year (that's above and beyond the $600 billion Social Security budget). But the subsidies mostly find their way into the pockets of well-off workers who don't need them. In 2013, two-thirds of the government's subsidies for pensions went to the richest 20 percent of taxpayers.[8] Properly redirected, that money could be redeployed to improve retirement security for a wider range of Americans.

Causes of the Retirement Crisis

To see why a public option offers a sensible solution, we need to tease out the multiple problems with today's pension system. At a macro level, the problem is that American retirement policy has never recovered from the implosion of the Treaty of Detroit. The U.S. pension system was engineered on the dual foundation of Social Security and employer pensions. Private savings accounts, like 401(k)s, were meant as a small supplement, a nice-to-have rather than a must-have.[9] So when old-style employer pensions crumbled, Social Security and 401(k)s were left to bear a load beyond their tolerance, as employers shifted four risks of retirement onto workers. Any one of these risks could imperil a worker's retirement. Taken together, the four spell disaster for all but the very wealthiest Americans—those rich enough to fund their own retirement without much help.

Risk #1: No Pension at Work

The first risk that workers face is having no pension at all. The law doesn't require firms to provide pensions, and many employers do not. A recent study showed that only 42 percent of private sector workers have any kind of workplace pension at all.[10] And while policy wonks can debate exactly how to measure pension coverage, by any measure fewer workers have pensions today than in 1979, in large part due to the decline in unionized jobs and the rise in service jobs.[11] Compounding the problem, lower earners and minority workers are least likely to work for firms that offer retirement plans.[12]

Even workers with pensions at work may not be able to save steadily. Today, most workers change jobs pretty often. (Government economists estimate that typical middle-aged workers have held eleven jobs before age fifty.)[13] The result is that many people will have spells of time without pension coverage, either because they take a job with a firm that doesn't offer pensions or because they can't sign up for the pension plan right away. These interruptions in pension savings can be very costly.[14]

Some workers who lack pension coverage at work can save on their own, through individual retirement accounts. But the tax rules are complicated, and it isn't easy to figure out who gets a tax benefit from an IRA. Not everyone does, and the rules span pages and pages of fine print, with variables including whether you choose a regular or Roth IRA, whether you're married, and how much you make.[15] What is certain is that low earners typically receive very little, if any, tax benefit from an IRA.

Compounding the hassle factor, enrollment isn't automatic. To be sure, it's easy enough to find a bank or brokerage willing to take your money—most of them advertise their IRAs. The hard part is figuring out which company offers the best investment options at the lowest cost.

And the whole thing works only if employees can set aside money on a regular basis—something that can be difficult for even middle-class families to do. As student debt balloons and prices rise for basics like housing and child care, it can seem daunting to set aside money for a distant retirement.

Risk #2: Defined Contributions

Even workers with a retirement plan at work are not home free. Once upon a time, a pension meant a monthly income paid by the employer, usually for life. Workers could plan for retirement, because they knew that their company pension would pay a fixed amount, such as 50 percent of the salary they earned in their highest-earning year at the company. Under such a defined-benefit pension plan, a worker who made $50,000 would know that she'd have a retirement pension of $25,000 per year, typically for life.

But as the Treaty of Detroit faded from memory, employers rewrote the pension rules to shift key financial risks off their books and onto workers. Defined-benefit plans have a clear advantage: workers can plan for the future, and any shortfall is the employer's problem. (That's one reason why Social Security is such a stable and successful public option—because it provides a defined benefit.)

Today, though, the vast majority of workers who still have pensions at work have defined-contribution plans, which don't guarantee any level of benefits at all. Instead, workers are guaranteed only whatever money they set aside, plus (or minus) investment gains (or losses). About 70 percent of workers now covered by a pension plan have access to this kind of plan.[16] These are sometimes called 401(k) plans (after the section of the tax code that authorizes them).

The change from defined benefit to defined contribution sounds technical, but it's far from minor. A defined-contribution plan shifts the financial risk of pension saving away from employers and onto workers. Put another way, in this brave new world, retirees are no longer guaranteed an income for life. Instead, they are guaranteed only some unknown amount that's based on a host of contingencies, including their savings rate, their investment choices, and their tax rate at retirement.

Defined-contribution plans shift investment risk onto workers. If workers choose risky investments, they can win big—or lose big. If they choose safe investments, they may not lose much, but they won't make much, either. Economists call this the risk-reward trade-off, and it means workers face a difficult choice.

Part of investment risk lies in choosing the right portfolio of investments, and that simply isn't easy. Even professional money managers, with all the training, talent, and resources that Wall Street can buy, cannot reliably beat the stock market. Warren Buffett, the "Sage of Omaha," is a famous investor who has made money in good times and bad. But he has one simple piece of advice for most investors: Don't try to pick individual stocks. Instead, buy what's called an "index fund," which is a diversified fund that rises and falls with the stock market. And don't pay high fees to do it.

But when ordinary workers have a pot of money, and when their retirement depends on it, it may be tempting to invest in the latest big thing. And there is no shortage of brokerage firms and so-called financial planners that will help you buy and sell individual stocks (for a fee, of course). To take just one example, the home page for the company E*Trade invites investors into the world of trading: "Trade equities and options. ETFs and mutual funds. Bonds and fixed income. Even futures. They're all here, on one platform." How on earth is a real person with a real job, not to mention a family, supposed to wade through all that? But the jargon sounds impressive, and the ad may make people feel that they could make more money if only they traded more.

Even when investors take Warren Buffett's advice and invest in low-cost index funds, they're still hostage to the piece of investment risk that accompanies the boom-and-bust cycle of the stock market. That risk may seem small in good times, like the late 1990s, when tech stocks drove the market to new heights. Some middle-aged, middle-class people became "retirement millionaires" for a few months, as the stock market pushed their retirement accounts to new heights.

But these investors learned, to their horror, that a market crash can decimate retirement accounts. In 2000 the NASDAQ (a stock index heavily weighted toward tech stocks) declined by a whopping 78 percent, and many retirement accounts lost huge portions of their value.[17] Another stock market crash accompanied the Great Recession of 2008. This time, the damage wasn't confined to people heavily invested in tech stocks. The average older participant in a 401(k) lost 25 percent of her money, and many lost more.[18]

How well is the new defined-contribution system working? The news is not good. The typical American with a 401(k) at work has accumulated about $110,000 as he approaches retirement.[19] (That figure excludes the large group of people, around 40 percent at any given time, who do not have a pension plan at all.) That may sound like a substantial nest egg, but it amounts to just $4,400 per year in retirement income.[20]

Risk #3: Being Cheated by Wall Street (or Your Employer)

Most people aren't financial whizzes, and the conventional advice is to seek out an expert to help with money matters. But these experts can take advantage of ordinary workers by overcharging them for subpar financial products. The prospect of being cheated by Wall Street isn't just hypothetical. Law professor Ian Ayres and his coauthor Quinn Curtis studied 401(k) plans and found widespread abuse. Many plans charge exorbitant fees of nearly one percentage point over the cost of basic index funds (like the ones Warren Buffett recommends). A common strategy is to pad investment menus with funds that don't offer any investment advantage over the basic option—yet charge higher fees.[21]

Quibbling over a one-percent difference in investment fees may seem like much ado about not very much. But a little math shows how money management fees can add up. A twenty-five-year-old worker who contributes $5,000 per year to her 401(k) plan will have about $475,000 by age sixty-five if she pays an investment fee of, say, 1 percent per year. She will have just $377,000 if she pays a typical higher fee of 2 percent per year.[22] That extra 1 percent fee translates into nearly $100,000 in lost savings.

In addition, some financial advisors got kickbacks from certain funds as a reward for pushing their customers toward those investments. Funds would send investment advisors on vacations, buy them electronic devices, and even give them cars.[23] This conflict of interest was perfectly legal until 2016, when the Obama administration required that investment advisors act as fiduciaries. (A fiduciary is simply a person who must act in investors' best interests.)[24] You'd think that a regulation holding investment advisors to that standard would be a big yawn. But investment firms have lobbied massively against it, and the Trump administration has signaled that it may repeal the rule.[25]

Risk #4: Outliving Your Savings

The final risk is one that many older people can appreciate. Retirement is always risky because you sacrifice some financial self-sufficiency. No longer can you count on a regular paycheck. And if illness or serious disability strikes, you may not be able to get another job if you need money. So the prospect of running out of money in retirement strikes fear in most of us.

Back in the once-upon-a-time days, workers with pensions didn't have to worry about outliving their savings. Employers typically paid out pensions in the form of an annuity—a monthly sum guaranteed until the worker died. Put another way, the old defined-benefit pension system put longevity risk on employers. Usually it all averaged out: some retirees might live to a hundred, but others might die in their sixties. Prudent employers could also hedge their bets by buying annuities to cover their pension obligations, and the insurance companies that sold those annuities could forecast, with pretty good accuracy, the average longevity of workers in the pension plan.

In the defined-contribution era, though, things don't work nearly so well. Most 401(k) plans pay out benefits as a lump sum, and government regulations do not require plans to offer an annuity option.[26] A lump sum looks attractive, but it has big disadvantages. For one thing, the tax hit can be shockingly high: withdrawals from pension accounts are taxable in full, and workers must pay the tax up-front. Plus, since the withdrawals count as income, the worker looks "rich" in that year and often falls into a much higher tax bracket than usual.

Lump-sum payouts are also problematic because they tempt workers to spend now and worry about later, well, later. Anne's grandmother used to call that "money burning a hole in your pocket," and it's a well-known psychological effect: when people have cash to spend, they tend to spend it, even if they know perfectly well that the money is supposed to last them a long time.[27]

But even the most disciplined and prudent person cannot ensure that her savings will last her lifetime. Investment risk is part of the problem. If Alice lives a long time—say, to age ninety-five—she has to manage her money for thirty years after she retires. With such a long retirement, the markets are sure to bounce up and down, and retirement savings could fall prey to another Great Recession. You might think that a retiree could protect herself by investing only in super-safe investments like bank accounts or Treasury bonds. The problem is that risk-free investments pay very low rates of return. If a worker takes that road, she could find that her savings grow too slowly to preserve her purchasing power, especially over a thirty-year period.

And there's absolutely nothing a worker can do to stretch her money if she lives a lot longer than average. That's the really scary scenario: if she finds herself at age ninety-five with nothing but Social Security to live on, she will either have to cut her expenses to the bone or hope that she'll have family willing to take her in or support her. That's a harsh choice for anyone, and it's one that is especially cruel when it falls on the very old.

You might suppose that a retiree could buy an annuity from an insurance company. As we've noted, some employers used to buy annuities for their workers, and that worked out great, because insurance companies are good at insuring large pools of workers and the long-lived are balanced out by the short-lived. If workers could use their 401(k) payout to buy an annuity, they could rest assured that they would never outlive their money.

The problem is that there is no functional private market for annuities for individuals. Some large employers still buy annuities for their workers, and as long as they have a large pool to insure, the system works just fine. But the individual annuity market suffers from a predictable failure: adverse selection, mentioned in Chapter 5. An example will help explain why this failure occurs.

Imagine a simple society with just two people, Rose and John, both nearing retirement age. Rose's mother, father, and all of her grandparents lived past ninety-five, and she's never been sick a day in her life. She's thinking of running a triathlon next year. John's parents died in their late 60s of heart disease, and he's trying to ignore some recurring chest pain that could signal a heart condition of his own.

Now, imagine that an insurance company offers both Rose and John an annuity on the same terms. The company calculates that the average person lives to about eighty-five. So they offer a guaranteed annuity of $16,000 per year in exchange for a one-time payment (funded out of retirement savings) at age sixty-five of $200,000. Rose jumps at the annuity, because it's a good deal for someone likely to live to a hundred or so. John decides to pass, because he's convinced he'll die by age seventy, and he can come out ahead if he pays his own way.

This is all rational enough, but the dynamic is destructive to the annuity markets. As short-lived people like John leave the market, the people who remain are those likely to live a long time. When the average person in the pool (that is, Rose) is likely to live thirty-five years after age sixty-five instead of just twenty years, the insurance company has to redo its calculations. They can only offer $12,000 per year if they are going to make a profit and stay in business. At that point, Rose may exit the market herself, because what she's being offered is no longer an especially good deal.

Now, you might think that the insurance company could solve the problem by asking Rose and John a few questions and maybe having them agree to a medical exam. If you've ever bought life insurance, you know that's the process: the insurance company is trying to figure out who's likely to die early and who will live a long time. The problem, though, is that the insurance companies can't know as much about you as you do. John's secret chest pain and Rose's triathlon plans aren't observable to the insurance actuaries.

Adverse selection is very real, and it has basically destroyed the individual annuity market in the United States. Technically, an individual can buy a life annuity. The problem is that adverse selection has made annuities a bad financial choice for nearly everyone (except those, like Rose, who just know they'll live to a hundred).[28]

What would it take to offer annuities on reasonable terms that would be attractive to many people? You won't be too surprised by our answer (which happens to be confirmed by both economic theory and real-world evidence): it takes a public option. Let's see why.

A Bold Public Option

Today's retirement system has failed by nearly any reasonable measure, and the result—unless we act—will be to load Social Security with a burden it wasn't meant to bear. We stand at the brink of an unintended experiment, as generations of Americans approach retirement with inadequate savings. If we act now, we can stave off a disruptive future that could create chaos in politics and the economy, as the elderly and their children lobby for aid and orderly retirement becomes a thing of the past.

But the failures of the 401(k) model can serve as a road map to reform. A realistic savings policy should clear a path to retirement security for everyone, not just the rich. A successful program should also meet people where they are: it isn't realistic to expect workers to act like financial experts or to save consistently on their own.

Enter the public option. A public option for retirement savings could:

- Offer coverage to all workers, without gaps when they change jobs
- Enroll workers automatically (unless they opt out)
- Provide simple, sound investment choices with low fees
- Pay out benefits as life annuities

The boldest—and best—idea would be to create a baseline public option that would operate nationwide and enroll everyone automatically. The program could withhold, say, 3 percent or 5 percent from every worker's paycheck. The money would be deposited in a retirement savings account and locked up for retirement. Savers would have limited investment choices, and every item on the short menu would be a low-fee index fund. At retirement, the balance would be converted to a life annuity, paying a guaranteed sum every month for the worker's life.

Automatic enrollment would ensure that all workers can save consistently, even if they work for a firm that doesn't offer a 401(k). Coverage would continue as workers changed jobs. A short menu of low-cost investment options would enable workers to make reasonable decisions without becoming financial experts. And annuitization at retirement would help ensure that workers didn't outlive their savings.

To make all this concrete, let's imagine a hypothetical worker making $50,000 per year. Suppose the public option sets her savings at 5 percent per year. And suppose the fees are 0.5 percent per year. (Actual fees could be lower: the federal government's Thrift Savings Plan averages just 0.33 percent.)[29] If this person worked forty years, she would save $2,500 per year, every year, even if she changed jobs. And thanks to the public option, she would pay investment fees of just 0.5 percent instead of 1 percent. The result? If she retires at age sixty-five, she would have $268,000. But instead of having to manage a lump-sum payout and reinvest the money, she would receive an annuity, calculated on the basis of her balance, of $11,000 per year for life.[30]

The public option wouldn't make this worker rich. But it would help her save more than she could today. And it would guarantee her a steady supplement to her Social Security benefit, no matter how long she lives.

The key feature of the bold public option is that it could, at zero cost to the government, improve retirement security for all Americans. The administrative and investment costs would have to be studied (we give some ranges later in this chapter), but the public option could be entirely self-funded: workers would pay all administrative costs of the program and would fund their accounts entirely through payroll withholding. Firms already withhold Social Security and Medicare taxes, so the new program could be administered using the very same system, which means there would be no learning curve (and no extra costs) for employers.

The bold public option could be a huge boon to business. No longer would firms have to create and administer 401(k)s and track a changing workforce. Pension administration would be centralized in the hands of the government. Small businesses and service firms that don't offer pensions now would benefit from improved morale and productivity in a newly secure workforce—at no extra cost to the firm.

By reforming the U.S. pension system, a public option could motivate policy makers to clean up the existing tangle of tax subsidies for retirement. The federal government spends upward of $180 billion a year on tax subsidies that, in theory, motivate workers to put money into 401(k)s, IRAs, and other retirement savings plans.[31] But these subsidies are doubly flawed. For one thing, they don't actually encourage saving. Economists have concluded that, for the most part, these tax subsidies just pay people who would have saved the same amount even without a subsidy. For another, the beneficiaries of the tax subsidies are overwhelmingly at the high end of the income spectrum.[32]

These subsidies ought to be a national scandal. But without a better program in place, they're hard to repeal, because something seems better than nothing. With a bold public option, however, there would no longer be a defensible rationale for these lopsided subsidies. Policy makers could reform these subsidies so that they benefit all retirement savers equally—or, even better, could redirect the funds to the low earners who need assistance most.

Just to put an idea on the table: Congress could create a universal match, which would add a certain percentage of annual savings to each saver's account (say, 50 percent of the first $2,000 of annual savings). That would mean that an average worker earning $40,000 per year would save $2,000 of her own money (recall the 5 percent rate for the bold public option) and the government would kick in another $1,000, for a total of $3,000.

The public option raises plenty of design issues, and we will highlight some of those in a moment. But the details are less important than the big idea: policy makers could act right now to improve retirement security and benefit business, all at no cost to the public at large. Why on earth wouldn't we do that?

The bold public option may be daring by American standards, but other countries and several U.S. states have enacted similar programs.[33] For instance, the United Kingdom has a competitive public option, the National Employment Savings Trust (NEST).[34] In 2012, the British government required all employers to provide pension coverage for their workers, and it mandated certain standards for investment quality and safety. The NEST program adds a public option to this regulatory approach. Employers can choose to manage their retirement plans on their own, as long as they meet regulatory standards. But employers can also choose to use NEST, which has an easy interface for firms and workers and has a limited set of investment options.[35]

Several states now have automatic IRA-type plans for workers. In California, for instance, the CalSavers program will offer a competitive public option to workers without a workplace pension plan. Firms without pension plans will be required either to offer a private plan or to enroll workers in the CalSavers plan. Those workers will have a portable, defined-contribution pension account.[36]

At a minimum, a public option in retirement should coexist with (not replace) Social Security, should provide universal access at an affordable price, and should exist alongside market options for those who want to save more. The public option should also be designed to mitigate the four risks we highlighted above: the risk of not saving, investment risk, the risk of being cheated, and the risk of outliving one's savings.

Beyond those basics, we can imagine a variety of options. For instance, we propose a baseline public option, but a competitive public option would be a reasonable step too. A competitive public option would permit, but not require, workers to save for retirement via a public plan. Employers could still offer their own 401(k)s, and financial firms could offer IRAs. But all workers would have a secure, basic pension savings option that would be simple and low-cost.

A competitive public option would be a substantial improvement over today's policies. Still, we see three disadvantages. First, a competitive public option would put the burden on workers to sign up for the program and to choose to save. As we've seen, human nature and the high cost of living conspire to make it difficult to save when people have to make an affirmative choice. Many studies have shown that automatic enrollment produces far greater participation.[37]

Second, a competitive public option would impose higher administrative costs, because workers would come into and out of the system, and they could (presumably) elect different savings percentages. Employers would have higher costs, too, because they'd have to track which employees had elected to save via the public option, and firms would have to remit the savings periodically to the public option administrator. That's far more difficult than deducting a straight 5 percent from everyone. And the IRS has not, in the past, had great success in requiring employers to administer optional public programs.[38]

Third and finally, a competitive public option might not surmount the adverse selection barrier to annuitization. As we've seen, annuitization works best with a large, representative pool of retirees. If it turned out that the competitive public option attracted mostly long-lived participants, its annuity program might collapse, just as the pure private market has.

For all these reasons, we think that a baseline public option is the way to go. But even under the umbrella of a baseline public option, there are a number of design issues that require further study. From the government's perspective, the major issues are administrative. For instance, how would the government pick investment managers to invest the fund's money? A public option plan would be a huge customer for any money manager, even with a very small fee. This is a serious issue, because the administrators of the public option should ensure that any private provider acts ethically and efficiently. But interacting with private contractors is a familiar issue throughout government, and there are a variety of bidding and contract structures and other practices already in place.

Still on the administrative side, there is the matter of collecting and coordinating information for 150 million workers so that contributions are tracked accurately. The government also has relevant experience here: the Social Security system tracks those same 150 million workers and monitors their wages, addresses, and work histories. Integrating a new public option retirement fund wouldn't be entirely simple, but it certainly has precedent.

From the citizen perspective, design issues include investment choice. How simple should a simple plan really be? At one end of the spectrum, the plan might offer no choice at all. Everyone of the same age would be invested in the same retirement date fund (these are funds, now offered by firms like Vanguard, that adjust the mix of investments for risk and liquidity based on whether people are near retirement or far away). At the other end of the spectrum, a relatively simple plan could offer three to five investment choices. Still, choice multiplies the opportunity for misunderstanding of risk—and multiplies costs to investors and the cost of customer service.

While some of the details would have to be worked out, the bigger picture is that a public option for retirement savings could go a long way toward addressing the coming retirement crisis in America.

8

Higher Education

Imagine that you've just been hired to head admissions for a for-profit college. Your job is to admit as many students as possible, because your college makes money mostly by tapping student loan programs, Pell Grants, and military aid to pay tuition. You've been told that the job is a numbers game: get them in the door, and don't worry about whether they have what it takes to do college work. And don't ask too many questions about the quality of education your college provides. That's not your department. Anyway, students are adults, and it's up to them to do their due diligence.

Now, maybe you wouldn't take that job to begin with. The red flags are large and numerous. But imagine that somehow you find yourself working under those conditions. You might, logically enough, develop strategies to target people unlikely to have many other college options.

Hollie Harsh and her fiancé, Brian French, certainly fell into the "unlikely to go to college" category. By the spring of 2012, Hollie and Brian had been addicted to methamphetamines, homeless, and living in a tent for about four years. And yet Corinthian Colleges, a for-profit higher education corporation, treated them as promising applicants. The two had decided to clean themselves up and improve their lives, and Brian took the initiative to go online and do some research on grants. The day after filling out an online form, he got a call from a Corinthian recruiter, who offered Brian and Hollie money to tour Heald College. When the two told the recruiter their story, including that they were homeless, he said it wouldn't be a problem and signed them up for classes—as well as $30,000 in student loans.

You can tell that this story isn't going to have a happy ending. Hollie and Brian still didn't have a place to live, so they moved their tent to campus. They cleaned themselves with water from a jug, unless a classmate offered to let them use their bathroom. After three semesters, Hollie and Brian dropped out, with no degree and a mountain of student debt. Brian later said, "What I say I got from Heald was a $16,000 T-shirt."[1]

What's outrageous is that what happened to Hollie and Brian wasn't unique or even particularly surprising. Corinthian and other for-profit schools specifically targeted people like Hollie and Brian: individuals with "low self-esteem," individuals with "few people in their lives who care about them," individuals who were "isolated." In other words, they targeted vulnerable people.[2]

How could Corinthian do this? "Greed," said former California attorney general (and now U.S. senator) Kamala Harris.[3] Greed was certainly part of it. But Corinthian's actions were made possible by the profit motive that drives a segment of higher education in America. Our system of grants, loans, and tax credits has predictable weaknesses, because it operates via private enterprise. To be sure, many nonprofit schools take their educational mission seriously and admit students according to their capacity to do college work. And some for-profit schools do, too. But a system that puts blind faith in the magic of market competition makes Corinthian's business model of recruiting vulnerable people viable.

This system of financing higher education has other adverse consequences as well. Prices at public universities and community colleges are going up far faster than inflation, fueled in part by state disinvestment in higher education and in part by the availability of student loans. As we've pointed out several times, this price effect is one predictable outcome of market subsidies. In the education context, subsidies give students more education dollars to spend, with the result that they tend to bid up the price of tuition. The subsidy dollars may well end up in the pockets of colleges (and student loan brokers). The result is a vicious spiral: as tuition rises, new students must take on larger and larger amounts of debt to pay for college. Given these problems, there's good reason to consider reinvigorating the public option in American higher education.

How American Higher Education Works (and Doesn't Work)

The structure of higher education in America isn't simple or straightforward. There is a dizzying array of options for students—public universities, community colleges, nonprofit schools, and for-profit universities—and a wide range of options within each of these categories. Even within these categories, schools and school systems serve vastly different populations. In New York, for example, community colleges serve many students who are right out of high school—61 percent are twenty-three or younger.

But in other states, older, nontraditional students dominate community colleges; more than half of students in Georgia's system, for example, are over twenty-three years old.[4]

The way our higher education system is funded is also complex, with different programs layered on top of each other. Private nonprofit schools have been around since before America was a country, beginning with the founding of Harvard College in 1636. In 1862, Congress passed the Morrill Land-Grant College Act, which created public universities in states throughout the Union in order to educate Americans in general studies and agriculture. After World War II, the GI Bill sent a generation of veterans to school, and colleges and universities proliferated to meet the new demand.

In the twentieth century, funding programs for higher education expanded with each decade. In 1958, Congress passed the National Defense Education Act, which created student loans for students in areas of critical need, justified on grounds that education was a central part of beating the Soviets in the Cold War. President Lyndon Johnson expanded loan access to education in 1965 through the Higher Education Act. In 1972, Congress established Pell Grants so poor students could get an education without taking out loans.[5] In the 1990s, President Clinton added the Hope Scholarship tax credit and the Lifelong Learning tax credit, allowing deductions of up to $1,500 per student.[6] As a result, American higher education financing today is a combination of state, federal, and personal efforts. States fund a significant portion of public higher education, with assistance from the federal government. Students, in turn, pay tuition with grants, GI Bill funds, federal loans, private loans, tax credits, and their own money.

The American higher education system was a marvel in the post–World War II years, expanding access at affordable rates. But today the system is riddled with flaws. Part of the blame for rising prices certainly lies with universities. Schools compete for the best students and also for the wealthiest students (who can pay full freight), while giving considerable aid to a small number of students. The most egregious build "lazy rivers" and turn education into a leisure activity; more commonly, they spend considerable sums on new dormitories and facilities because students demand them. Many schools expect faculty to both conduct research and teach students, tasks that are very different. Disaggregating the functions of teaching and research could mean better quality in both categories, but it would also mean trading off some of the prestige that comes with having renowned researchers.

But these management problems are far more limited in scope and significance than underlying shifts in public policy. The single most important shift in the past generation has been severe cuts by the states in per-student funding for public institutions of higher education.[7] State governments reduced funding for public universities and community colleges by 26 percent between 1990 and 2009, even as expenses were increasing.[8] The result of these budget cuts has been to shift the financial burden of college squarely onto students. Tuition rose 244 percent between 1980 and 2010 at the average four-year public university.[9] Since the financial crash, these trends have only worsened. In the 2015–2016 school year, forty-six states spent *less* per student than they had before 2009. Nine states slashed per-student spending by more than 30 percent. In that same period, tuition is up 33 percent at the average four-year public school, with rates increasing by more than 60 percent in six states and more than 90 percent in Arizona.[10]

Arizona actually eliminated all state support for two of its major community colleges.[11]

This shift in funding interacts with other parts of our system for financing higher education. Pell Grants, for example, were designed on the assumption that states would continue to provide low-cost, high-quality public education. They weren't designed to accommodate state budget cuts, and as a result, they haven't increased in value even as costs to students went up. In the 1970s, Pell Grants were generous enough to cover about 80 percent of the cost of tuition, fees, room, and board at a four-year public university. But with the explosion in costs, by the 2012–2013 school year Pell Grants would cover only 31 percent.[12] The result is that students are taking on more and more loans. Between 2008 and 2018, total student loan debt in America more than doubled. It now stands at $1.5 trillion.[13]

Some federal government programs may well have contributed to the hike in college prices. The Clinton-era Hope Scholarship and Lifelong Learning tax credits primarily help middle-class students who are already able to afford an education. So instead of increasing access, they make it possible for students to afford more expensive schools than they would have otherwise attended.[14] Harvard professor Bridget Terry Long also points out that schools know that students can get these tax credits, and as a result, they have an incentive to raise prices.[15] This is a classic example of a problem with the market subsidies approach. Providing a coupon for higher education (as these tax credits do) just means that schools can raise prices so that students pay the same amount they would have otherwise. Instead of serving as a discount, the coupon just makes higher prices more palatable.

Most troubling, though, is how the neoliberal approach has rewarded for-profit college corporations that have exploited students, taxpayers, and higher education programs. One caveat before we go further: We're not opposed to all for-profit colleges and universities or to all for-profit education programs. We just don't think taxpayers should be subsidizing corporate profits for low-quality education.

We've already talked a little about how neoliberal ideology turned Pell Grants and student loans into a cash cow for some for-profit college corporations, with taxpayers accounting for 86 percent of their revenues and at least 30 percent of their profits. But let's dig a little deeper. Given our system of taxpayer subsidies, the key for a for-profit college is recruiting. More students means more taxpayer money. As a result, in 2008–2009, for-profits spent 22 percent of their revenues, or about $4.2 billion, on recruiting and marketing.[16] That's more than they spent on instructing students.

But what is astonishing isn't just how much they spent on recruiting; it is also how they recruited students. Hollie and Brian's story is only the tip of the iceberg. An undercover investigation by the nonpartisan Government Accountability Office (GAO) found that for-profits consistently engaged in deception, fraud, and harassment.

For example, recruiters told applicants they had to enroll in the college and pay an application fee before they could even speak with financial aid representatives.[17] One beauty college claimed that barbers can have an annual salary of between $150,000 and $250,000, even though 90 percent earn less than $43,000.[18] Some colleges harassed prospective students who filled out online forms to show interest in attending college; one applicant received twenty-four calls within the first twenty-four hours after filling out the form—and a total of 182 calls in a single month.[19]

The fraud against American taxpayers was even more brazen. The GAO's undercover applicant was told by one financial aid officer to omit $250,000 in personal savings on financial aid forms, and admissions officers at multiple schools advised applicants to add dependents on their applications for federal financial aid so they would become eligible for grants.[20]

In a case of perverse consequences, Congress in 1998 passed the "90–10 rule," which required for-profit colleges to get at least 10 percent of their revenue from a source other than federal higher education dollars.[21] This sounds like a smart reform, but there was a loophole: the GI Bill and military tuition assistance funds are not counted as federal dollars. For-profit colleges quickly learned that they could pass muster by recruiting veterans: for every veteran they recruit, they can claim taxpayer funds for nine other students. As Illinois senator Richard Durbin once remarked, "This is the most heavily subsidized private business sector in America."[22]

The 90–10 rule encouraged the corporate higher education sector to target servicemembers and veterans with the predatory and deceptive practices they had pushed on other students. "The ITT representatives I met with told me that the military would pay for my schooling," one combat veteran said. A few months later, he got bills for both a private loan and a federal student loan. Another veteran was told by for-profit Ashford University that the GI Bill would cover his education. He ended up with an $11,000 charge. "I felt that I have been misled, deceived, or even outright lied to in an effort to gain my contractual agreement," he said.[23]

In perhaps the most offensive case, PBS's *Frontline* investigators discovered that for-profit college recruiters at Camp Lejeune in North Carolina were targeting Marines who had severe brain injuries.[24]

For-profits tend to pad their profits by overcharging for the education they provide. A GAO report, for example, looked at costs for a student working toward a seven-month certificate in computer-aided drafting. The student would have paid $13,945 for the course at the local for-profit, compared to only $520 at the nearby public college.[25] A medical assistant program cost $11,995 at a for-profit college in Illinois, compared to $9,307 at a private nonprofit—and only $3,990 at a public college.[26]

The results are predictable. According to a report from the U.S. Senate Committee on Health, Education, Labor and Pensions, "Ninety-six percent of for-profit students take out student loans. In comparison, 13 percent of students at community colleges, 48 percent at four-year public, and 57 percent at 4-year private non-profit colleges borrow money to pay for school."[27] Students at for-profit institutions carry huge amounts of debt and are more likely to default on that debt (47 percent of all defaults on federal loans are from for-profit students).[28] And what do they have to show for it? Often not even a useful education.

Consider Martha, who signed up for a nursing program through Everest College, part of Corinthian Colleges. She was told she'd make $25 an hour after graduating. But she never once visited a hospital, and when it came time for her "psychiatric rotation," Everest took her on a trip to a museum of Scientology. Her classmates were sent to a day care center to satisfy their "pediatrics rotation." Martha later attended a community college to get her R.N., and told PBS *Frontline* investigators that the experience was completely different. For her psychiatric rotation, she spent a month learning and training in a psychiatric hospital.[29] The cost of her R.N. from community college: $3,000.

Unlike Martha, who stuck it out and earned a degree that couldn't get her a job, many students, like Hollie and Brian, don't finish their degrees and end up deeply in debt. Fifty-four percent of for-profit students who started during the 2008–2009 school year departed within two years—without a degree or certificate. Sixty-three percent of students in two-year associate's degree programs didn't finish. Students at publicly traded for-profits and students in online programs fare the worst.[30] In essence, many for-profits fund themselves with taxpayer dollars, provide a low-quality education to students, and profit handsomely in the process.

With this backdrop, it is easy to see the original sin in the design of our higher education system. When we decided to invest in sending lower-income Americans to college, we used a market subsidy approach instead of directly funding public schools. This meant a huge giveaway to private colleges (both for-profits and nonprofits). The result is that the federal government subsidizes private schools even when they enroll only a tiny proportion of needy students. And it means that the federal government has only indirect influence over those institutions' policies.

The Case for the Public Option in Higher Education

Higher education suffers from serious problems. State funding cuts push costs onto students. Tax credits mean higher prices. And for-profits exploit students in order to get taxpayer subsides. Given these problems, there is a strong case for a more robust public option in higher education. We envision a public option that would guarantee access for any American to some kind of higher education (college or technical training), either for free or at a nominal price.

There are three basic reasons to support a public option in higher education. First, it is increasingly the case that success in the workforce requires some kind of post-high-school education, whether college or technical training. Second, education is important in a republic. For self-government to work, we need citizens who are thoughtful and engaged and who have some knowledge about our constitutional system. Third, given both the economic and civic importance of higher education, access to that education shouldn't depend on the ability to pay for it. Economic opportunity should be open to everyone, regardless of their family wealth—and democratic participation requires that everyone have an education in civics.

These justifications for a public option in education have always lain at the heart of the tradition of public higher education in America. The Civil War–era Morrill Land-Grant College Act set aside 30,000 acres of public land for each representative that a state had; the state could sell the land and use the earnings to establish a public university.[31] Some of the most distinguished state universities were established as land-grant colleges: Iowa State, Penn State, Michigan State, Ohio State, Purdue, and Texas A&M. As historian Allan Nevins once put it, "The central idea behind the land-grant movement was that liberty and equality could not survive unless all men had full opportunity to pursue all occupations at the highest practicable level."[32]

Opponents of a public option might counter that college isn't necessary for everyone in America and shouldn't be forced upon anyone. This objection is unpersuasive for two reasons. Most important, this is a public option. Creating a public option for higher education doesn't force anyone to get more education after high school. It just allows people to do it without worrying about the cost. If you don't want to continue education after high school or if you can find a job without extra schooling, then fine—don't go.

In addition, we don't think the data support the assertion that college isn't increasingly important to success in the workforce. Our argument isn't that college or some kind of post-high-school training is essential for literally everyone. It is that this education is increasingly necessary, or at least strongly desirable. Not only do those who complete college have higher job rates than those who didn't go to college, but the data also show that some college is better than no college.[33] In other words, it is significantly better to have had some kind of post-high-school education.

The second challenge to a public option might be that higher education should not be provided for free. Critics might worry that free provision could produce perverse effects, because students need to have some skin in the game if they are to take maximal advantage of educational opportunities.

We think these arguments are also problematic. First, in other areas where a service or experience is considered necessary or strongly desirable, we have provided it for free. The most apt analogy here is K–12 education. As a country, we decided that primary and secondary schooling were critical for our people—as citizens and as workers—and so we provided as a public option through the public schools. Indeed, in the case of K–12 education, we've gone even further, making school attendance mandatory. For critics of public options who nonetheless acknowledge that some kind of post-high-school education is strongly desirable, it isn't clear why it is any different from K–12 education. In fact, a public option for higher education is actually more compelling because it wouldn't be mandatory.

Second, our current system of student loans, grants, tax credits, and private funding isn't working. For-profit schools engage in widespread deception and fraud. Students take out huge loans and frequently end up drowning in debt. On-time completion rates are abysmal.[34] High levels of debt have negative social and personal consequences for graduates—they are unable to spend money on purchasing a new house or saving for retirement.

Reform is possible, of course. Regulation might increase transparency regarding job outcomes and crack down on fraud by for-profits. We favor these fixes, but they are minor tweaks to a system that is complex and irrationally designed. No one designing a system from the start would advocate layers upon layers of tax credits, grants, loans, scholarships, and private dollars that differ based on school type, veteran status, subject area, future jobs, and a variety of other factors. No one would design a system from the start that forces students and parents to spend huge amounts of time and effort navigating a complex patchwork of financial aid forms, tax documents, scholarship applications, and everything else just to pay for a program that everyone deems necessary or at least strongly desirable.

Third, we are skeptical of the "skin in the game" argument. Our society does not require poor families to pay for their kids to get a K–12 education, because many of them could not manage it, and society views K–12 education as critically important. It is possible that some children would work harder and some parents would be more attentive if they were paying for basic education, but the benefits of free education far outweigh the costs. We believe that the same is now true in higher education.

That said, we are not opposed to a reasonable fee for higher education. Public options don't always have to be free. If you want to send a letter, you have to buy a stamp. Public beaches sometimes charge a small daily parking fee. But the prices are low enough and sufficiently regulated to ensure that access is effectively universal. We would be comfortable with that in the context of higher education, too.

The third argument that opponents might raise is a practical one. Because our existing system is so complicated and has so many stakeholders, it will be hard to transition to a public option. To address that objection, we need to spell out in more detail how a range of public options in American higher education might actually work.

Public Options for American Higher Education

Given the strong case for universal access to debt-free higher education, it isn't surprising that political leaders on both sides of the aisle have tried to expand the public option in higher education. There are a number of options out there, some that have been tried and tested, and some that are more speculative.

Tennessee has one approach. The former Republican governor in that state, Bill Haslam, created Tennessee Promise and Tennessee Reconnect, programs that make community colleges tuition-free for his state's students. Under the Tennessee Promise scholarship, students who maintain a minimum GPA, participate in some community service activity, and attend mentoring meetings are eligible for a "last dollar" scholarship: after taking into account Pell Grants and state scholarship funds, if the student still has tuition and fees to pay, the Tennessee Promise scholarship will cover the remaining amount. The scholarship applies to two-year programs at all of Tennessee's community colleges, technical schools, and schools offering associate's degrees.[35] Tennessee Reconnect operates the same way, but it is a scholarship for adults.[36] Eleven other states have proposed or adopted versions of Promise scholarships.[37] Tennessee's Promise operates as a way to adapt our complicated financing system to what is, in effect, a public option for two-year higher education programs.

Inspired by the success of Tennessee Promise, President Barack Obama proposed a nationwide program for free community college. America's College Promise differs from Tennessee Promise in a few important ways. While it applies to students pursuing two-year degrees, it would also cover the first two years of school for those in four-year degree programs at community colleges. Under the program, the federal government would cover three-fourths of the cost of community college, and states that wanted to participate in the program would cover the rest.

The key difference is that President Obama's plan was a "first dollar" scholarship, not a "last dollar" scholarship like the Tennessee program. Under a "last dollar" scholarship, state funding will go primarily to slightly higher-income students who don't qualify for Pell Grants or other need-based scholarships. (Lower-income students' tuition and fees are largely covered by those other grants, so most of the Promise scholarship money doesn't need to go to them.) Under the "first dollar" approach, the federal and state governments would cover tuition for everyone. That's important because it means that working-class students could still use Pell and other grants to cover room and board, books, and other expenses.[38]

As a result, the "first dollar" approach should expand access to higher education to working-class students who couldn't afford it otherwise.

During the 2016 presidential primaries, Senator Bernie Sanders took another approach to creating a public option for higher education, arguing that all Americans should have the ability to go to college debt-free. Some critics, including then-presidential candidate and former secretary of state Hillary Clinton, attacked Sanders's plan, arguing that taxpayers should not be subsidizing free college for the children of the wealthy. This argument was misguided, because most taxpayers would not be subsidizing the wealthy; the wealthy would end up paying for college through higher tax rates. Indeed, Sanders proposed to fund his plan through a financial transactions tax that would hit upper-income people more than middle- and lower-income people. In fact, K–12 education already works this way: public schools are free for everyone, but the wealthy end up subsidizing the educations of everyone else because they pay higher tax rates.

A more technical problem with Sanders's plan is that it was designed as a matching grant program, in which the federal government would pay two-thirds of costs as long as the states kicked in the other one-third. The virtue of this plan is that it recognizes the reality of our higher education system—it is a patchwork of state and federal programs, with public universities and community colleges operated by the states, not the federal government.[39] The problem is that some states might refuse to expand access, as many Republican states did under the Affordable Care Act's attempt to expand Medicaid. Under Sanders's plan, if states refused to take the matching grants, their citizens wouldn't benefit from a public option.

These are all solid possibilities, despite our caveats. We also want to offer another approach for a public option in higher education to all Americans. We call it Adams University.

Adams University: A National Public Option for Higher Education

On December 6, 1825, President John Quincy Adams declared in his annual message to Congress that "the first . . . instrument for the improvement of the condition of men is knowledge." Adams therefore recommended creating a national university, and imagined it "unfolding its portals to the sons of science and holding up the torch of human improvement to eyes that seek the light."[40]

John Quincy Adams wasn't the first member of the founding generation to believe in the importance of a national university. John Adams, Ben Franklin, Thomas Jefferson, James Madison, Benjamin Rush, George Washington, and Noah Webster all advocated for the creation of a national university. Benjamin Rush said a national university was necessary to "prepare the principles, morals, and manners of our citizens" for republican government.[41] The curriculum needed to ensure that Americans "imbibed federal and republican ideas"—history, law, and commerce, in addition to mathematics, agriculture, biology, botany, and foreign languages.[42] In his Farewell Address, George Washington called for a national university that would educate not just those "who are entrusted with the public administration" but also "the people themselves to know and value their rights."[43] James Madison thought a national university would "enlighten" opinion, reduce "sources of jealousy and prejudice," improve "national character," and increase "social harmony."[44]

Despite the fact that a national university had the backing of some of the most extraordinary people in American history, it's hard to imagine Congress establishing a single national university today, akin to West Point or the Naval Academy. Indeed, with a population of more than 300 million, America would need a lot more than one national university.

But with advances in technology, it is now possible that a national university could scale up and help educate millions of Americans—all for a free or nominal price. We propose calling it Adams University, after John Quincy Adams, the last great champion of a national university in early America.

Here's how it would work. Adams University would be a national public option for basic higher education run entirely online. Many basic courses—Biology 101, Intro to American Government, Introductory Calculus, Fundamentals of Accounting, Econ 101—don't require in-person instruction for lectures. Adams University would offer instruction in all of these areas, and others, to anyone who wants to take them, young or old. Two features of online education make this possible. First, the primary cost is putting together an online platform and producing video or audio alongside course materials. But once that is completed, there is no significant cost per additional student. Whether 1,000 or 10,000 students do the readings and watch the lectures, the cost to the government is the same. Second, basic courses in these areas often don't require small-group instruction, and student performance can be evaluated through standardized tests. Indeed, at many big state schools, introductory courses often have hundreds of students attending large lectures and taking multiple-choice assessments.

To those of us educated in bricks-and-mortar institutions, online education may seem questionable. But, more and more, state schools have already adopted online instruction for large courses, and Adams University represents an extension of that approach. Many state schools offer large catalogs of online courses, and more and more, entire degrees can be earned online.[45]

But a public option would improve on this approach. Right now, many colleges and universities are developing online education—and the federal government is indirectly subsidizing these duplicative efforts through its tuition subsidies. Rather than paying for schools to develop hundreds of these programs, Adams University would develop, offer, and pay for a single online university.

And Adams University could also help transform the rest of the higher education system. Colleges and universities have discretion to accept credits from private online education providers, but the government would require that Adams University credits be transferrable to any public school in the country—four-year, two-year, state, or community colleges. As a result, schools wouldn't need to offer big lecture classes in these areas; students would take basic lecture courses through AU. Public universities and community colleges could rethink their priorities, now allocating dollars to in-person instruction—writing classes, lab courses, and hands-on technical training. To help students who are struggling, schools could offer in-person remedial and supplementary support that operates in conjunction with AU's curriculum. With a more intensive focus on teaching, research universities would not need to hire famous researchers to teach basic introductory courses. They would focus on hiring faculty who will teach full time and establish separate tracks for talented researchers.

Adams University could also provide useful competition for both nonprofits and for-profits. With a national program, a simple fee structure, and quality courses, Adams would offer a compelling alternative to high-pressure, high-cost private options. Low-income students, veterans, and others would quickly learn that AU provides an easily accessed path to a college degree. Middle-class students, too, could begin to see the advantages of earning the first two years of a college education for free.

For those students who wanted to pursue four-year degrees, the system might offer a range of options. Adams University could offer a limited number of degrees in areas in which personalized instruction isn't necessary, just as some public colleges already do. In areas in which personalized instruction is necessary, Adams University credits would work in concert with public schools. We're agnostic as to how funding could work: the Tennessee Promise last-dollar plan, the first-dollar America's Promise program, Sanders's debt-free college plan—all of these programs could work to help students cover the costs of college. The transformative part of Adams University is that it would allow public colleges and universities to save considerable sums on what are now duplicative courses that don't require in-person instruction—and, in turn, lower tuition rates while investing in higher-quality instruction.

Adams University cannot solve every one of myriad problems with American higher education. But we think it should be part of the debate on how to make progress in higher education.

9

Banking

Tens of millions of Americans are "unbanked," a clumsy but descriptive term for people who don't have a checking or savings account. Millions more are underbanked; they have a checking or savings account, but they also use financial services within the fringe banking sector—services like payday loans, money orders, check cashing, pawnshop loans, and the like.[1] According to a report from the Federal Deposit Insurance Corporation (FDIC), 7 percent of American households were unbanked in 2015, and another 20 percent, or nearly 51.1 million adults, were underbanked.[2]

The fringe banking sector wasn't always so significant. In the early and mid-twentieth century, fringe banking was relatively minor. Poor and working-class people gained access to the financial system through a wide variety of cooperatives, community banks, credit unions, and other innovative, small-scale financial institutions.[3] Between the Great Depression and the 1970s, for example, pawnbroking declined steadily, due to the growing economy and the increased availability of credit.[4]

But starting in the mid-1970s fringe banking began to grow, and it expanded massively as a sector in the 1980s.[5] There are a lot of reasons. For one, the advent of the neoliberal era brought banking deregulation. As deregulation increased competitive pressure, banks jettisoned lower-profit services that were mostly used by poor and working-class people.[6] The leading scholar of the rise of fringe banking estimates that between 1977 and 1991 the number of banks offering free accounts plummeted from 35 percent to only 5 percent.[7] Banks also raised fees in order to make more money. The Government Accountability Office estimated that banking fees nearly doubled between 1977 and 1985, from a range of $22–$37 to $41–$55.[8] When combined with increasing economic pressure on working-class Americans and rising economic inequality, more and more Americans migrated into the fringe banking sector.[9] Between 1977 and 1989 the number of American households without a deposit account almost doubled.[10]

Unbanked Americans give a variety of reasons for not having accounts. More than a third say the primary factor is that they simply don't have enough money. About a quarter say that high and unpredictable fees are partially responsible. More than 15 percent say they have a problem with their credit or identification. Another 10 percent find the locations inconvenient. Perceptions of banks are a part of the story as well, with a significant number—almost 30 percent—citing privacy and distrust of traditional banks as a contributing factor.[11] And 55 percent of the unbanked think that banks aren't interested in serving households like theirs.[12]

Many of these concerns are legitimate. Minimum balance requirements, for example, are now high enough to exclude low-earning workers.[13] In addition, banks often screen customers through a service called ChexSystems, which operates like a credit report. In some cases, customers who have previously used fringe banking services, such as overdrafts (that have been repaid), have been denied bank accounts.[14]

So how do the unbanked participate in the economy? While most people (82 percent of the underbanked and almost 88 percent of the banked) receive their income through direct deposit into a bank account, the unbanked instead rely on check cashing and money orders simply to use their hard-earned wages.[15] Some of the unbanked still manage to save money, but they don't save it in banks. Sixty-eight percent save money at home. Another 12.6 percent save through prepaid cards.[16] And while 70 percent of people with bank accounts pay their bills online, only 1.6 percent of the unbanked do. Instead, the unbanked pay their bills with cash, money orders, or prepaid cards.[17]

Lack of access to the banking system is extremely costly, both financially and personally. Take someone who uses a prepaid card to save, pay bills, or just make ordinary purchases. Some prepaid cards have an endless array of fees—activation fees, monthly maintenance fees, ATM fees, reloading fees, transaction (or "swipe") fees. Some prepaid cards have yearly fees as high as $500.[18] Or say you want to cash your paycheck. A check-cashing place might charge up to 5 percent of your paycheck just to give you the cash.[19] Then, if your electric or gas company won't take cash to pay your bills, you'd have to pay between $5 and $20 to get a money order.[20] These fees add up—so much so that a Council of Economic Advisors report estimates that the average unbanked household, with an annual salary of $22,000, will pay more than $1,000 in financial fees in a year.[21]

The unbanked lose time as well as money. Using the fringe banking sector takes more time than banking online because you have to go in person to buy prepaid cards, get checks cashed, or purchase money orders. If you're working two or three jobs and barely making ends meet (or, more likely, falling short), the last thing you need is to spend time waiting in line just to gain access to your income or pay your bills. That's time not spent working and not spent with your family.

From a neoliberal perspective, the system works fine: the fringe banking system is a market-based solution to the financial situation of being poor. Private banks might rationally choose not to provide high-cost, low-profit services, like free or low-fee checking. And people who use fringe banking services have made a rational choice based on the costs—or else they are reaping the consequences of earlier bad behavior.

But this view ignores the social costs of fringe banking. When workers lose money and time to the fringe banking sector, they have less to invest in their children, their jobs, and their future. And it ignores the government's traditional duty to provide means of exchange available to all.

Banking today plays the role that currency played in earlier eras, because the cash economy is becoming obsolete. By the 1950s, checks—not cash—became the norm as a way to pay workers.[22] Today, many workers don't even get checks; it's easier for employers to use direct deposit. Couple that with credit cards, debit cards, and electronic payment systems, and fewer and fewer people and places use cash. These new technologies are largely a positive development. There's no skimming off the top or worries about envelopes of cash getting lost or stolen.

But as the cash economy gives way to the electronic economy, the unbanked don't benefit from these transformations and instead fall further behind.

A Public Option for Basic Banking

We think a public option would be an effective way to connect every American to the financial system. Some of the reasons are ones we've already discussed. There's a real problem: millions of Americans are without access to basic deposit and savings accounts. The market solution isn't working well: the fringe banking sector charges exorbitant fees and results in numerous hours of lost time and productivity, disproportionately hitting those who need it most. But there's another important reason that cuts to the heart of the banking system: banking isn't a purely private activity.

Nothing in the "private" economy is truly private. The private sector works only because of government, which sets up the rules of the game—like contract and property laws—and enforces those rules. But the money side of banking goes further. In every society, across time and geography, money has been the creation of the sovereign state. It's one reason that from ancient Rome to America today, most currencies feature a picture of a revered head of state. Whether the ruler depicted is Julius Caesar, Queen Victoria, or Abraham Lincoln, the message is the same: the sovereign stands behind the currency and will treat it as legitimate for paying debts.

The United States, for example, prohibits the creation of private money and currency without a license (a banking charter). At the same time, most of the money the government issues isn't actually printed and physically distributed (though we highly recommend that you visit the Bureau of Engraving and Printing's presses in Washington, where cash is printed—they have a terrific tour). Instead, the United States, like most governments, "creates money" by increasing and decreasing the credit they give to private banks. In America, it's the Federal Reserve's job to interact with private banks, expanding and contracting the credit available to them. The private banks then lend that money. As the Fed does this and private banks lend more or less, the amount of money in circulation in the economy goes up or down. This function is still a sovereign function—it's just outsourced to private banks. To make sure the outsourced system works well, the United States government provides a variety of backstops to the banks in the form of the full faith and credit of the government, deposit insurance, and subsidies.[23]

The larger point is that the banking system doesn't emerge solely through the efforts of private firms. Banking is based on a social contract: we the people, operating through our government, license bankers to create money, and we give them a variety of privileges in order to operate the financial system. In return, we expect a few things: a safe and sound banking system, consumer protections from fraud and deception, and public access to the banking sector.[24]

Put another way, the financial system is like national defense or public roads. Society can't function without banking (or defense or roads), and it's the job of the government to ensure that everyone has access. In the case of banking, we've just decided to outsource provision of one part of it to banks, instead of having government do it directly. But the presence of private banks in the system doesn't mean that banking is a wholly private concern.

The social contract in banking is so universally understood that most countries—including major developed countries—have adopted some form of a public option in order to guarantee that all of their citizens have free or affordable access to the banking sector. In many countries, these public options operate through the postal system. That made a whole lot of sense when it was implemented. In the era before telephones and electronic devices, it was the postal system that helped stitch together entire countries. Post offices were in virtually every town and city, enabling communication among private citizens and between citizens and their government. In 1861, the United Kingdom created a postal savings system, enabling British citizens to gain access to basic savings accounts—and using the infrastructure of the post office to scale up the service. Canada's postal savings system started in 1868.[25] Japan's postal banking system has 203 trillion yen in assets. China's is the fifth largest bank in that country. France, Italy, and New Zealand have postal banking.[26] Even Switzerland—home to the most famous private banking system in the world—has postal banking.[27]

You might be surprised to learn that the United States also once had a public option for basic banking. From 1911 to 1966, the postal savings system offered Americans a basic savings account via their local post office. Efforts to create a postal banking system started in the wake of the Civil War, and in the early twentieth century, after the financial panic of 1907, the move for postal banking in America gained steam.[28] One of the central motivations at the time was that the distribution of banks around the country was uneven. In the eastern states, excluding New England, there was one bank, on average, for every 57 square miles—compared to one post office for every 14 square miles. In the South, it was one bank per 418 square miles, compared to a post office every 35 square miles. Indeed, because most banks were in cities, the distribution of these banks was skewed even further in rural areas.[29]

Advocates of postal banking argued that the program would address the scarcity of banks and expand access to savings to

Americans across the country. And so the early postal banking system was targeted to serve those who weren't already being served by the banking system. There was a maximum allowable balance—$500 at first, ultimately reaching $2,500 in 1918—and depositors were limited to $100 per month.[30] Postal savers also earned a small amount of interest, 2 percent, which was lower than the market rates at the time. By 1929, the postal savings system had $153 million in deposits from American savers; by 1947, the system had $3.4 billion.[31]

After World War II, the economy boomed. People became wealthier, and banks raised interest rates. Postal savings declined amid the growing economy, dropping to $416 million in 1964.[32] In 1966, the postal savings system was shut down, a casualty of the success of the glorious years of middle-class growth.[33] In the next decade, as we have seen, wages stagnated and economic inequality began to widen, and fringe banking emerged in place of the postal savings system.

So would a public option for basic banking be possible? Legal scholar Mehrsa Baradaran has championed the idea, gaining the attention of many, including Senators Elizabeth Warren and Kirsten Gillibrand. One answer for how to implement it would be to revive and modernize the old postal savings system. For instance, any American could walk into a post office and open a small-scale savings or checking account. The account would be capped at a modest level—say, $5,000. The basic account would pay no interest and have no fees. The account holder could accept direct deposit into the account and use a debit card or ATM card to spend from the account, but without any ATM fees or debit card fees. No overdrafts would be permitted.

Operating this system through the Postal Service would have several benefits. First, as we've seen, around 10 percent of the unbanked report that the absence of a bank near them is an important factor in not having a bank account. Indeed, banks are closing branches all around the country, with lower-income neighborhoods hit hardest.[34] Post offices, in contrast, are a presence everywhere in the country. According to the Postal Service's inspector general, "59 percent of Post Offices are in ZIP Codes with one or no bank branches."[35] Given the tradition of postal savings and the ubiquity of post offices, commentators and politicians have argued in recent years that postal banking is the right path forward.[36]

But a public option in banking doesn't need to be tethered to the postal system. With today's technology, a public option for basic banking could also operate electronically. The basic parameters could be the same—$5,000 cap, no fees, no interest, no overdrafts, direct deposit, and a debit / ATM card—but instead of going to a physical post office, all transactions would take place electronically through a website or smartphone app.[37] The big downside with this approach, however, is that smartphone usage is not universal. Only 77 percent of Americans owned smartphones as of November 2016, and many of the people who would most benefit from a public option for banking—those in rural areas and those with lower incomes—are least likely to own a smartphone.[38] As a result, an electronic public option might not be a substitute for a brick-and-mortar banking option—at least not yet.

A second approach would be for the federal government simply to offer a public option for bank accounts through the Federal Reserve. Right now, banks hold accounts at the Fed that earn a relatively high interest rate, have no minimum balances or fees, are fully non-defaultable (because the Fed is the printer of money), and have immediate clearing. Professors Morgan Ricks, John Crawford, and Lev Menand have argued that citizens and businesses should also have access to what they call "FedAccounts," a bank account directly from the Federal Reserve. This account would have the above-mentioned benefits, in addition to having no interchange fees for using the account at a retailer. FedAccounts would include an online interface, a mobile app, and a brick-and-mortar interface through the post office.[39]

A purely public option isn't the only approach, of course. Some commentators have recognized that another option is to apply a public utility approach to basic banking. Morgan Ricks and Alan White, for example, have each argued persuasively that banks are public utilities and, at a minimum, should have to ensure universal access to basic banking services.[40] Ricks proposes that as a condition of their charter, banks should be required to offer a basic bank account to anyone. Adam Levitin has offered a variation of the public utility approach. Levitin argues for creating a new type of charter for basic banking services. These new basic banks could then operate wherever they like, Levitin suggests, including renting space within post offices.[41] Of course, one could also imagine hybrid versions of these proposals, such as merging Ricks's plan for mandating banks to offer a basic account with the idea of renting space in post offices.

Beyond Basic Banking?

The harder question is whether a public option in banking should extend beyond a basic deposit account to making small loans to individuals. The best argument for offering loans is that the federal government could issue them far more cheaply than fringe bankers, who often charge exorbitant fees. For example, each year 12 million Americans use payday loans.[42] Payday loans are short-term loans, often only for two weeks, that provide the borrower with immediate cash on the theory that they'll pay back the cash on their next payday (these loans require the borrower to have a bank account, which the lender usually has access to in order to get its payment). But the fees and interest rates for these loans are extraordinary. Borrowers pay between $10 to $30 per $100 in fees for these loans, and on average, the interest rate is 339 percent (APR).[43] According to Pew Research, "a person who borrows $400 for a $60 fee for two weeks would have paid approximately $480 in fees after renewing the loan for four months"—and that's before paying off any of the original $400.[44]

A public option might alleviate some of these burdens because the government wouldn't be trying to profit from the loans and because post offices (if the public option worked through the Postal Service) already have their real estate expenses covered. The Postal Service's inspector general estimates that, compared to the average $375 payday loan, which costs the borrower an additional $520, a postal loan would only cost an additional $48.[45] For comparison, most foreign postal banks offer loans, though some do so via private banks.[46]

Some critics oppose a public option because they fear that competition will harm fringe bankers or even mainstream banks. When Walmart, for example, tried to get a banking charter, the banking lobby fiercely opposed it.[47] But it isn't clear that protectionism toward fringe bankers and the credit card industry is a good reason not to move toward a public option for small-dollar lending. The inspector general notes that in 2012 the median income of Americans who filed for bankruptcy was only $26 less than their expenses. Saving money by reducing payday lending fees could prevent thousands of bankruptcies.[48] That's a significant benefit that has to be considered. It's also worth keeping in mind that a public option in small loans might not put fringe bankers out of business. A public option for small-dollar lending would have simple and straightforward terms, and as a result, it wouldn't satisfy the needs of everyone. Many people might still seek out fringe bankers to get riskier products.

The better argument against a public option for small-dollar lending is that it isn't clear that the goal of public institutions should be to spend taxpayer funds to loan money to the poor. If our goal is helping the poorest gain economic security and eventually build wealth, it might be better to spend taxpayer funds on investing in job creation, offering free child care, providing a basic income, or something else entirely. If the problem is that people don't have enough money to make ends meet, it might be better to figure out how to solve that problem rather than just assuming the right way is for them to take out short-term loans.

The case for a public option in basic banking, however, rests on different grounds. People today need to be connected to the financial system. The government creates a uniform system of money, with universal access to everyone. Today, with the changes in banking technology, we need once again to ensure that everyone has access to the financial system.

10

Child Care

Child care is a cornerstone of any society. No matter what else is going on, children have to be cared for. Hunter-gatherers carried their children along as they roamed, and agrarian parents kept their children close by (and, eventually, had them work in the fields). The Industrial Revolution upended these traditional arrangements but eventually created a new one: mothers stayed at home with children while fathers left for the industrial workforce.

Since the 1970s, our society has abandoned that model: the stay-at-home mom went away with the Treaty of Detroit. The expectation that women should be housewives has disappeared along with other relics of the 1950s. Today the vast majority of mothers work, but we have not come up with new social institutions to replace the old ones. Instead, we rely on the neoliberal solution—private markets—to provide child care options. The result is that working parents across the country scramble to find, and to afford, child care.

The stunning fact is that the average cost of child care has nearly doubled since 1985—and that's after taking inflation into account.[1] In two-thirds of states, day care for one infant costs more than public college tuition.[2] One-quarter of American families spend more than 10 percent of their income on child care, and poor families spend nearly 20 percent.[3]

And just finding a slot can be a challenge. In Washington, D.C., some parents put their names on day care waiting lists as soon as they know they are expecting a child, spending hundreds of dollars on nonrefundable deposits just to get a spot on the list.[4] And these parents aren't overreacting. Statistics show a massive shortage of child care slots in the District of Columbia and nearby suburbs, especially for kids under age three.[5] Ditto for Sonoma County, California, and rural counties in Minnesota, just to pick two more examples.[6]

Along with high cost, low quality is a huge problem. Research confirms that children thrive in settings that are healthy, safe, and stimulating—and where adults are warm and encouraging. A low staff-to-child ratio is helpful, and so are small-group settings and educated caregivers. Softer (less measurable) factors matter, too: the best caregivers have a positive attitude and put a priority on sensitive and encouraging interactions with kids.[7] But most American child care settings fall short of these standards. In 2007, a major national study found that most U.S. child care is "fair" or "poor" in quality; only 10 percent of providers ranked as high-quality.[8]

Adding insult to injury, child care—as expensive as it is—often isn't all that reliable. Many day care centers won't take children under three or children who are not yet potty-trained. Day care centers often provide limited hours, even though many parents work nontraditional hours or late shifts. Most day care centers cannot care for sick kids, meaning that parents miss work for every one of childhood's many common colds.

The child care scramble doesn't end when children start school. Public school hours are often inhospitable to working parents—a school day of 9:00 a.m. to 3:00 p.m. is typical. Schools take weeks of vacation during the school year and close all summer. Some schools offer extended care for mornings and late afternoons, but these services are not universally available.

The shortfalls of the U.S. child care system fall disproportionately on women. Although more fathers now take a solid role in raising their children, mothers still take the bulk of the responsibility for child care when a child is sick, or the day care center is closed, or the schools close for the summer.[9]

The subject of child care meshes perfectly with the themes of this book. Our society hasn't yet come to terms with the demise of the Treaty of Detroit: we have not yet replaced the stay-at-home mom with reliable, affordable, and high-quality care for working parents. Instead, we have left child care (outside the public school day) to the private market, which has produced spotty, unaffordable, and low-quality care. We believe that a public option could help rebuild this critical piece of our social foundation by ensuring access and quality at a reasonable price. Let's take a closer look at each of these points in turn.

The Failure of the Private Market

Neoliberals posit that the laissez-faire marketplace should provide ample options for child care. They point out that women's wages have risen over the last few generations, giving them greater purchasing power and creating a vast demand for child care. In theory, then, the free market should respond by offering a range of options—for kids of all ages and parents of all incomes. These very dynamics have produced booming markets in all kinds of convenience goods that cater to busy working families. With no mom at home to make dinner (and wash the dishes), the microwave and dishwasher have become standard in American kitchens, and fast food has, if anything, become too cheap and plentiful. People who want help cleaning their homes need only consult Yelp for a wealth of choices. And cheap, imported fashion is so plentiful that only cultural outliers would consider making their own clothes, as 1950s moms once did.

But, at the risk of stating the obvious, taking care of children is different from making food, cleaning the house, and buying clothes. In fact, the rosy prediction that the laissez-faire market can handle child care founders on three predictable problems.

First, child care is exceptionally labor-intensive. Rising wages for women have created demand for child care, but quality child care is simply expensive. It can't be outsourced to machines or low-wage foreign workers. Children need one-on-one, sustained interactions with adults. The problem isn't that day care workers earn too much. Salaries for day care workers have remained low, and working conditions are poor, since the free market tends to sacrifice quality of care to keep costs down (and profits up).[10]

Even with these compromises on quality, child care remains unaffordable, because the basic math is unavoidable. Imagine an average thirty-five-year-old parent who works full-time and earns $865 per week (the median earnings in the United States in the first part of 2017), or about $43,000 per year for fifty weeks of work.[11] She has two children, and because she is a single parent, her earnings must cover everything—from taxes to rent to food to child care. Now assume that this parent wants to buy child care from a peer who also needs to earn the average wage of $43,000 per year. Even if the child care provider can reliably care for six children, she must charge more than $7,000 per child to make ends meet. That means that our hypothetical parent must pay $14,000 per year, or 32 percent of her pre-tax salary.

The math is cruel because there are limited (if any) economies of scale. Big business may be able to produce cheaper microwaves or T-shirts for consumers who want lower prices. But a day care center cannot reduce staffing levels and other resources per child without severely compromising children's development.

A second problem with the child care marketplace is that quality can be difficult for parents to monitor. In an ideal laissez-faire market, providers might offer an array of options, charging higher prices for higher quality. Perhaps basic day care would cost $7,000 per child (as in the stylized example just given), but enriched care would cost more. (We strongly object to this neoliberal fantasy, because children's care shouldn't depend directly on their parents' budget. Still, let's see why the thought experiment falls apart on its own.)

Studies have shown that parents often can't tell high-quality from low-quality day care.[12] The nice lady down the street may do a great job—or she may park the kids in front of the television and feed them junk food. Child care isn't a standard commodity. If I buy a cheap microwave from Walmart and it conks out after a few weeks, I won't go back for another. But young children can't reliably report what's happening to them, and it's easy enough for canny adults to furnish (misleading) signals of quality. A large room with lots of books and toys is no guarantee that the teachers will warmly engage the children in play. A solid staff-to-child ratio may hide a high turnover rate that creates distress in both the workers and the children.

There is one reasonable proxy for quality in child care: overall, center-based care is of higher quality than informal care. But this is a noisy result, because not all centers are better than all family day care homes. The overall result is explained much more simply: when subsidies permit parents to pay more for care, they often respond by purchasing center care and leaving behind kin care and other informal arrangements. The result is an overall quality improvement. But it isn't evidence that parents can distinguish quality in choosing among centers or well-run family day care homes.[13]

Third, and perhaps most important, child care is too important to be left to the high cost and uncertain quality that the private market provides. Our collective future depends on the children we raise—whether directly, as parents, or indirectly, as members of society. When we force parents to sacrifice quality for the sake of affordability, we damage children's development, with lasting consequences for them and us.

We can express our common stake in children using the economist's idea of externalities. Poor-quality child care has negative externalities, or spillover effects on all of us. Childhood stress can permanently undermine children's ability to learn and to manage adversity. At the same time, high-quality, accessible care has positive spillover effects. Secure, well-educated human beings are more productive and less likely to turn to crime and to drugs.

And there are even deeper values at stake. A society that aspires to freedom and equality must take seriously the task of caring for its youngest members. Children are future citizens who deserve to begin life with a secure foundation that offers them a decent change to shape a good life for themselves.

Why Market Subsidies Fail

Child care also illustrates the shortcomings of market subsidies. In theory, as we discussed in Chapter 3, vouchers can reduce the cost of goods to consumers. And so, in theory, a child care voucher could cut the (after-tax) price of child care paid by families. In Massachusetts, for instance, center-based care for one infant costs $17,000 per year.[14] If the government offered a $5,000 voucher, the net cost to the parents would fall to $12,000. And in theory, the parents would retain valuable choices about the type of care, the location, and so on.

But in the real world, market subsidies cannot provide universal access at a reasonable price, for five reasons. First, a voucher (or refundable tax credit) approach doesn't aim to guarantee affordability to all families. Return to our example of the $5,000 voucher for child care in Massachusetts. The voucher would reduce the price of the child care center from $17,000 to $12,000. But for a worker earning, say, $20,000 per year, that $12,000 price tag is equally out of reach.

A market subsidy could be set to vary by income level using a sliding scale so that a rich family might get no subsidy, while a parent who earns $20,000 a year might get much more, maybe $14,000 per year. This kind of system is appealing in theory but difficult to implement in practice. Measuring income is tricky for a host of technical reasons, and low earners tend to have volatile incomes.[15]

To illustrate, imagine a McDonald's assistant manager who has worked her way up and earns $40,000 in a good year. But she loses her job when the restaurant closes the following year, and bumps back down to minimum wage at a convenience store until she can find a management job or work her way up again.[16] Fairness suggests that she should get a smaller voucher in the first year but a much larger amount in the second year. The problem, in a nutshell, is that it's difficult to design a system that can adjust the market subsidy in a timely way. Tax credits—like the Earned Income Tax Credit—are really bad at this, because they have a built-in one year lag. Our hypothetical McDonald's manager wouldn't qualify for the subsidy she needs until she's earned the minimum wage for a year or more.

Second, market subsidies may not reduce the cost of care at all if the voucher leads providers to raise their prices. Let's go back to our Massachusetts example, where unsubsidized infant care costs $17,000. Suppose that Congress enacts a massive market subsidy of $14,000 per child per year. If the top-line price of child care stays at $17,000, then the net price to parents falls to $3,000. But if child care providers raise their prices in response to the subsidy, the whole scenario looks much less rosy. If day care providers raise prices just as the subsidy hits, they can capture some of the federal largesse. So if over time the unsubsidized price of child care rises to $25,000, then the profits of the day care company will skyrocket—and parents will face a net price of $11,000, less than before the subsidy, but not by much.

This is, of course, an extreme scenario, in which the providers capture the lion's share of the subsidy. Whether prices rise and by how much depends on market conditions and can be hard either to predict or to study. Still, we have some evidence that child care subsidies in California did raise the price of child care.[17]

A third predictable problem of market subsidies is that they can provide wildly uneven assistance to deserving parents. The Trump campaign, for instance, proposed a tax deduction for child care.[18]

At first glance that sounds pretty good, but the well-known pathology of a tax deduction is that it is an upside-down subsidy—it offers a greater dollar subsidy to higher-income families than to lower-income ones.

For instance, suppose that two Massachusetts families each deduct the $17,000 cost of infant care. One family is rich, while one is lower-middle-class. The rich family would get a tax benefit worth $6,200 (37 percent of the price), while the lower-middle-class family would get a tax benefit worth just $1,700 (or 10 percent of the cost). This is backward: if affordability is our goal, then the lower-earning family should get a larger subsidy, not a smaller one.[19]

Fourth, market subsidies often are not tailored to the costs that parents face. The price of child care varies across the country, from $5,000 per child for center-based infant care in Mississippi to $17,000 for similar care in Massachusetts.[20] The result is that a one-size-fits-all subsidy won't work well. A federal voucher for, say, $5,000 per child would pay 100 percent of the cost in Mississippi but just 30 percent in Massachusetts. In theory, market subsidies might be tailored to local costs, but doing this is tricky in practice. For instance, the cost of care in Boston is probably higher than in rural Lenox, Massachusetts, but even a state-by-state approach wouldn't capture that differential.

When market subsidies are set too low, quality tends to suffer. Georgia, for instance, subsidizes day care for young children, but the state sets reimbursement rates so low that poor families have "no choice but to attend the worst day cares."[21] The result is a major quality problem: an independent monitor found that most infants and toddlers go to low-quality programs with few age-appropriate toys, safety hazards, and teachers who lack the language skills needed to foster learning in children.[22]

Fifth is the problem of ensuring quality care for all children. Monitoring is one issue: quality is both critical for child development and hard to monitor, because parents don't have a reliable window on what's going on during the eight- or ten-hour days their child may be in care, and young children aren't reliable reporters. Another issue is that in the hurly-burly of daily life, quality isn't the top priority for all parents. Higher-income parents often put quality at the top of their list, and they tend to choose expensive center-based care. But other parents, pressed for time and money, have to prioritize low cost, a convenient location, and long hours of operation, with the result that they trade off quality of care.[23]

The price-quality trade-off is the dark side of parental choice. Voucher proponents trumpet the value of choice in all settings, but sometimes consumer "choice" opens a back door for opportunists to sell shoddy goods. When parents can't tell high- from low-quality care, they may assume quality or prioritize the lowest price, and so market competition may cause a downward quality spiral, as high-cost and high-quality operations predictably lose out to low-cost, mediocre-quality providers.[24]

In theory, a voucher might condition payment on some measure of quality, so that parents could only use the money for child care providers who have in some way demonstrated the high quality of their product. But there is no national, accepted quality metric for child care. While some "hard" characteristics of quality (like staff-to-child ratios and teacher education) can be measured, some equally important "soft" characteristics (like teachers' positive attitude, the frequency of positive interactions with children, and the frequency of language modeling) cannot.

Failing in Real Time: The Dependent Care Tax Credit

These aren't just academic possibilities. The United States has tried the market subsidy approach, and it has failed parents and children. The federal government devotes $4 billion every year to the dependent care tax credit, a provision of the tax code that offers a tax rebate for child care, and the system founders for most of the reasons we just sketched out.[25]

To begin with, the tax credit doesn't guarantee affordable care. The credit pays a maximum of $1,050 for one child ($2,100 for two), which is just a fraction of the cost of child care anywhere. (To be precise, that's 21 percent of the cost of infant care in Mississippi and 6 percent of the cost of care in Massachusetts.) The credit is not updated for the cost of care (or even for inflation), with the result that it has become less and less useful over time.

The dependent care credit also provides widely varying assistance to families. The credit isn't adjusted for the local cost of care—and so a family in a low-cost area receives a greater percentage of aid than an identical family in a higher-cost area. Perhaps most damning, the tax credit isn't refundable, which means that taxpayers with incomes below about $30,000 get very little or nothing at all, no matter how high their child care costs.[26] The perverse result is that a family earning $100,000 receives more dollars in child care assistance than a family earning just $25,000. And the credit tops out at two children, leaving larger families in the lurch.

The tax credit also has no quality control. Parents can claim $1,050 regardless of the care provider's qualifications, experience, or track record. The regulations do specify that a day care center must meet applicable local licensing and safety regulations, but there's no monitoring mechanism. And only centers must meet the requirements: nannies and smaller home-based day care providers need not meet any quality standards at all.[27]

Some people have proposed reforming the tax credit, and their ideas would certainly improve the program. Making the credit refundable would extend assistance to low- and moderate-income families. Updating the credit amount for the cost of care and for inflation would improve affordability. Expanding the credit for larger families would also address a glaring hole in the program.[28] And the credit might be conditioned on choosing a licensed day care provider.[29]

But even with these well-intentioned reforms, the dependent care tax credit would fall short of the ideal we believe is compelling—a guarantee of high-quality care for every child at a price that is affordable for all parents.

Toward a Public Option for Child Care

A public option could go a long way toward solving the predictable problems of the dependent care tax credit (and of child care vouchers more generally). A public option would offer every child an age-appropriate placement in a local care facility run by the federal (or state) government. The price paid by parents would be affordable, because the government would set the price. Because the centers would be staffed and run locally, the cost to government would adjust for the local cost of living: it would be automatically be cheaper to run a public child care center in a low-cost area. And quality would be built into the model: the public option would set the educational program along with staff qualifications, staff-to-child ratios, and space requirements.

This is all eminently practical. Indeed, we already have a partial public option in child care in the form of the public schools. We understand that public schools aren't perfect. As Chapter 6 acknowledges, public schools provide an uneven education and need reform, including major changes in political boundaries and funding structures. Still, public schools provide much-needed child care for kids age five and up. Parents across the nation don't have to worry about whether the local public school will have a slot for their child, and they don't have to worry about paying the bill every month. They know that their kids will be occupied productively during school hours.

Viewed as part of America's child care system, today's public schools have limitations, which could be addressed. The school day is short, typically just six hours, which fits poorly with parental jobs that last eight hours plus a commute. And starting and ending times are inconvenient for the majority of parents who work full-time: it's the rare worker who can arrive at work at ten o'clock (having dropped off her child at school at nine) and leave at two (to pick up a child at three). Public schools also have numerous holidays and a long summer vacation.

And it's not just the public school day that reflects outdated assumptions about children and families; the yearly school calendar does, too. No longer do children work on the family farm in the summer. And no longer do many families have a stay-at-home parent ready to care for the children during holidays and the summer vacation.

Incremental reform of the public school day and calendar would be a solid first step toward a public option in child care. Today, some schools—but not all—provide before- and after-school care programs, which offer reasonable quality at an affordable price. In

2014, the number of slots demanded for after-care exceeded 50 percent of school-age children. But demand outstrips supply: the parents of nearly 20 million children reported that they would enroll their children in school-based after-care programs but did not have access to one.[30]

Another potential reform is full-year schooling, an idea that has gained some traction. But some of the models still overlook the child care component of public education. Most "full-year" programs still operate only 180 days per year, leaving parents to cobble together care during periodic long vacations. The popular 45–15 plan, for instance, calls for forty-five days of school followed by fifteen days of vacation, repeated for four terms a year. That plan requires parents to gear up child care for four vacations of three weeks each.[31]

We believe America can and should think bigger, moving toward a universal public option for child care. A public option along these lines could incorporate three elements: public infant care (for kids under three), full-day public preschool (integrated with public schools), and public before- and after-care (integrated with public schools).

To see how the public option might work, imagine a hypothetical child, Sophie, born ten years from now, when the public option is securely in place. Both of Sophie's parents work full-time. Her father, Will, is a nurse, and her mother, Jess, is a police officer.

After Sophie is born, and Will and Jess have taken parental leave (ideally, paid leave for three months each—another reform that is well worth considering), Sophie is ready for day care. The local public infant care center received an automatic enrollment from the hospital when Sophie was born, and Will and Jess went online and filled out a registration (much like a public school registration) to confirm the placement. The infant care center is clean and well staffed, with dedicated rooms for newborns, young toddlers, and older toddlers. All the teachers have college degrees in early childhood education, and they tailor activities and schedules to the needs of each age group.

When Sophie nears age three, she graduates from infant care to a guaranteed spot in her local public school's preschool program for three- and four-year-olds. Here, too, the teachers have degrees in early childhood education, but the staff-to-child ratio is higher, because the children are older. The facility is clean and offers stimulating spaces for active play, quiet play, and pre-reading activities. The staff structures the schedule to balance rest and playtime, and they have plenty of outdoor recess and some age-appropriate field trips.

Will and Jess need not worry about how to pay for Sophie's care. Ideally, the public option in child care should be free, just like public schools. But the program's costs could be reduced significantly by charging a fee on a sliding scale. For instance, the program might charge an affordable rate of a few hundred dollars a month, with tuition payments capped as a percentage of family income.

When Sophie reaches age five, she can—just as she can today—attend her local public school kindergarten. The key difference is that Will and Jess can count on affordable, guaranteed before- and after-school care. The care programs include breakfast and dinner as part of the fee, and they provide playtime, homework help, sports, and even music lessons. These programs run until Sophie is fourteen.

All of these programs would run year-round, Monday to Friday, with limited holiday breaks. All of them would guarantee spots to all eligible children. And all of them would have transparent, public standards for staffing, quality, and wages.

Of course, not everyone would take up the public option. Jess's friend Hannah sent her son to public infant care, but she preferred religious schools for her preschool and school-age children. Will's brother, Robert, took the 100 percent private route. Busy lawyers with unpredictable hours, Robert and his wife hired a nanny, then paid for private preschool, and then a private K–12 school. Robert and his wife were able and willing to pay quite a bit for even longer school hours and super-high-end amenities, like fencing lessons and private tutors.

We are not alone in calling for an expanded public role in child care.[32] And a public option already exists for preschools in a few places. For instance, the State of Oklahoma now enrolls 75 percent of children in the public pre-K program, which requires teachers to have college degrees and pays teachers on the public school scale. The program limits class sizes to twenty children per two teachers, and it prescribes a curriculum dedicated to child development as well as academic readiness.[33]

The City of Boston has also implemented a high-quality, universal pre-K program. Boston's pre-K teachers must have the same qualifications as public school teachers and are paid on the same scale. The program operates for a full day, and evaluations have given the program high marks for the educational and emotional quality of teachers' interactions with children.[34]

The evidence on these efforts is in, and it's enormously positive. Both the Oklahoma and Boston programs produce measurable effects on academic achievement for all groups of children, and—in an important step toward social equality—the programs help close gaps in achievement between white and minority children and between children from low-income and higher-income families.[35]

The scenario we've just described might sound like science fiction to American parents. But about 90 percent of this public option scenario exists today in France. The French child care system is famous, and justly so. It encompasses three elements, just as in our hypothetical situation. Public *crèches* provide infant care to children under three. The *écoles maternelles* provide preschool to the three- and four-year-olds.[36] For children age five and up, the French public schools take the reins.

As in America, private options exist alongside the public, but many parents—even well-off ones—prefer the public option. Pamela Druckerman, an American journalist in Paris, was initially skeptical of "government employees changing my baby's diapers." But, having tried the system, she loved it and ultimately sent three children through the system from infancy on.[37]

The French system isn't perfect. In urban areas, the demand for public care, especially infant care, can outstrip demand—parents in Paris are advised to seek a place during pregnancy or adoption planning, and once they have been allocated a spot, they should claim it within ten days.[38]

And, of course, not all of the features of the French system would translate readily to this side of the Atlantic. For instance, French child care—like French public culture more generally—emphasizes a shared culture rather than a heterogeneous one. So French preschoolers sit down to lunch with knives, forks, and cloth napkins. That's kind of cute, but there is (to American eyes) a dark side to the French insistence on cultural homogeneity. For instance, French schools ban religious symbols like crosses, turbans, and head scarfs on the grounds of *laïcité,* the French public commitment to secularism for all.

But none of these cultural features is necessary to the public option. Indeed, the French prohibitions on religious observance would violate our Constitution. The bigger picture is that it is entirely feasible to offer a workable and attractive public option in child care.

Objections

We acknowledge that a public option for child care could be costly, particularly if the cost to parents is zero. But freedom and equality are deeply valuable. Right now, the United States lags the rest of the developed world in its child care spending. In 2013, for instance, we ranked thirty-fifth among thirty-eight developed countries in spending on child care and early education as a percentage of GDP. Put another way, the United States now ranks behind Bulgaria, Slovenia, and Mexico in its public investments in young children.[39]

Even in purely utilitarian terms, the cost of a public option would be recouped as parents experience less stress and children encounter healthier developmental conditions. The universal pre-K program in Tulsa, Oklahoma, for instance, produced benefits (including children's eventual higher earnings, higher tax payments, and lower crime propensity) that outweighed costs by a factor of two to one.[40] A proposed California universal pre-K program was projected to produce similar benefits—not even counting less easily measured benefits like improved worker productivity.[41] And the Chicago economist James Heckman estimates that high-quality preschool produces a 13 percent return on investment for society.[42]

A public option in child care could be a win for American business as well as for parents. Turnover and absenteeism in the workplace are tremendously costly. Secure, high-quality, and affordable child care could transform the workforce. Parents who now must leave work early or worry about a latchkey kid or a shady day care could relax and focus on their work.

Critics might object that a public option would produce low-quality care, with kids warehoused in large, bureaucratic facilities. But public child care need not be impersonal or sterile: just as in the public schools, each teacher would interact with a small group in a small classroom, tailoring the environment to the children and to the curriculum. Studies suggest that public child care can be powerful: when the youngest children (under age three) were enrolled in Early Head Start (rather than informal care), children showed academic readiness and better behavior.[43] Further, school-based preschool programs typically have higher quality and better outcomes than private ones, probably because the school-based programs "are operated under standards set by the education system."[44]

Indeed, the U.S. military has an excellent child care system that answers all these objections. The Department of Defense made child care a priority, because good child care assists military readiness by assuring parents that their children are well cared for. High-quality care is offered in regulated child development centers. And child care teachers are paid on the normal Department of Defense pay scale, which reduces turnover and ensures high-quality staffing.[45]

Only one constituency has a great deal to lose: mediocre private child care providers could find themselves out of business. But that should be counted on the plus side, because it would fix one of the key pathologies of the private market in child care, which is the quality problem. A public option would provide a baseline to all parents. Private providers could compete if they had something additional to offer—whether better amenities, religious education, or something else. The net losers would be the low-quality, low-cost operations that too many parents use today because cost and convenience must take priority over quality. With child care as close as the local public school, no longer would parents scramble for a slot in a cheap, local day care and cross their fingers on matters of safety and quality.

Finally, a common rap on universal preschool comes from conservatives, who say (in effect), "We've already tried it, and it's failed."[46] Many of these critics have in mind the Head Start program, which for several decades has provided government-funded preschool to disadvantaged children. In fact, many studies have found that the Head Start program improves children's health and behavior and can foster lasting academic progress and raise high school graduation rates.[47] The controversial part comes when studies measure Head Start's cognitive impacts (that is, the program's effect on children's IQ scores). Although studies have found that Head Start produces short-run cognitive gains, these effects tend to fade out after the end of the program.[48]

Some critics conclude that cognitive fade-out and modest behavioral and social benefits prove that Head Start—and public preschool more generally—doesn't work. But that's a wild over-reading of the social science evidence. For one thing, many Head Start programs are only short-day and short-term, and they serve a very disadvantaged group of kids. So it's actually kind of amazing that they produce the lasting social and behavioral benefits they do. For another, studies have shown that more intensive, higher-quality preschools can produce major improvements in a range of educational and life outcomes, including educational attainment and adult earnings.[49]

But the Head Start debate is mostly a distraction when it comes to thinking about a universal public option for child care. The intense focus on cognitive fade-out might be critical if preschool were valuable only as an IQ booster. When we take a wider perspective, preschool serves a critical function as quality child care, which benefits parents and kids. Whether or not such programs boost IQ over the long term, they provide safe, stimulating care every day that they're open.

11

Health Care

"I did not come to Washington to hurt people." With statements like that one (from Senator Shelley Moore Capito, a Republican from West Virginia), the effort to completely repeal Obamacare in the summer of 2017 died. For seven years, ever since the passage of the Affordable Care Act in 2010, Republicans fought the nation's new health care law tooth and nail—in Congress, in states across the country, and in the courts. With the election of President Donald Trump in 2016 and majorities in the House of Representatives and the Senate, Republicans were poised to kill the signature achievement of President Barack Obama.

Republicans spent months attempting to draft a bill that could pass, only to find that their reform efforts would result in north of 15 million Americans losing health insurance, massive tax cuts for the wealthiest Americans, and a disaster in the insurance markets. Every time they tried to pivot to a different strategy for repealing Obamacare root and branch, they found themselves trapped between bad and worse options.[1]

A series of close but decisive negative votes in July 2017 left Obamacare in place. Senator John McCain, recovering from brain surgery, cast the vote that "drove a long knife through the cold heart" of efforts to repeal the Affordable Care Act.[2] And just like that, in a matter of weeks, the seven-year effort to repeal the Affordable Care Act was over. Congress was left with only the power to force through a repeal of Obamacare's tax penalty provision, and the vast majority of the Affordable Care Act remained as the law of the land.

Why was it so hard for Republicans to repeal and replace Obamacare? For that matter, why was it so hard for Democrats to pass Obamacare? And now that Obamacare lives on, how can policy makers address the high cost of health care and the millions who remain uninsured? Perhaps predictably, we think public options will play a big part in the unfolding story. But before we get there, we need to start with an understanding of the past, present, and structure of the American health care system.

The Jumble of American Health Care

America's health care system defies logic and common sense. The jumble of providers and insurers, public and private, eligible and ineligible patients reflects generations of layering policy on top of policy, with attempts at progress constrained by the realities of politics. So before we can talk about a public option, we need a brief historical tour of health insurance in the United States.

In the Progressive Era of the early 1900s, what limited health insurance there was operated through associations. Some unions covered their members through health care funds, and Montgomery Ward offered a limited program to its employees starting in 1910. The origins of modern American health insurance are usually pegged to the year 1929, when Baylor University Hospital created a prepaid coverage program for hospital care. The Baylor model spread, and by the end of the 1930s, the American Hospital Association was using a Blue Cross symbol as a way to brand these programs. At the same time, state medical associations started programs for non-hospital care, like office visits and house calls. These became known as Blue Shield plans.[3]

But the critical moment in the creation of America's health care system was World War II. Prior to the war, health insurance was expanding quickly as a benefit of employment. During the war, the government established price and wage controls to prevent the economy from going off the rails. As a result, if companies wanted to recruit workers, they couldn't entice them with higher wages. Companies therefore provided health insurance as a benefit because it was excluded from wage controls.[4] Predictably, the number of Americans with employer-based health insurance continued to increase. After the war, Harry Truman attempted to push for a national health care system, like the ones that countries in reconstructing Western Europe were adopting. But Truman's efforts failed, and America instead doubled down on the employer-based system.

In the decade after the war, there were three moments that turned out to be decisive in entrenching the employer-based system. First, in 1945, the War Labor Board ruled that when the war was over and there was no longer a shortfall in labor, employers couldn't back out of providing health insurance. They had agreed to it by contract and had to keep that commitment. Second, the National Labor Relations Board ruled in 1949 that unions could negotiate for health insurance and other benefits during the collective bargaining process. And finally, in 1954, the IRS determined that money paid for health insurance was excluded from workers' taxable income.[5]

Looking back, this last change was perhaps the most important, although it seemed incremental enough at the time. The IRS decision meant that neither workers nor employers would pay taxes on employee compensation paid in the form of health benefits. The perhaps unintended result was that an extra dollar of (tax-free) health benefits was worth more to workers than an extra dollar in (taxable) wages. That might seem like an innocuous benefit, a smallish giveaway to nudge employers into insuring their workers. But it opened up a Pandora's box. Among other pathologies, the tax benefit encourages more and more expensive health insurance policies. And the federal subsidy is upside-down, shoveling more dollars to high earners than to low earners.[6]

Taken as a whole, the employer-based system America backed into distorts not only the health care system but the economy at large. The system tends to work for well-paid workers at big businesses, which can offer coverage. But it isn't great for small businesses or individuals, who have to buy health insurance on the market without any bulk discount.[7] The system subsidizes expensive "Cadillac" plans. At the same time, it leaves out (or underinsures) the self-employed and low-paid workers. The employer system can also lock workers into their jobs because people don't want to risk losing their health insurance. Would-be entrepreneurs face a double whammy: they not only lose the security of employer-based coverage but must also throw themselves on the mercy of the uncertain market for individual policies.

On the cost side, the employer-based system heaps additional burdens on the economy. The tax subsidy for employer-provided health insurance cost $180 billion in federal revenue in 2017 alone.[8] And the hodgepodge of private coverage has fostered a huge private insurance industry that increasingly regulates health care by setting the terms of payment. These days it might not be your doctor who decides whether you can have surgery:

it could be your insurance company. And the rules differ from provider to provider and state to state. But in the early days of the employer system, no one knew how entrenched it would grow—or how severely it would constrain future health care reform efforts.[9]

In the 1960s, Americans once again came together to expand access to health care. The first effort was Eldercare, a program that covered hospital insurance for poor elderly people. Eldercare was a hybrid state-federal program, with federal grants going to the states and administered by the states.[10] In 1965, Congress passed landmark legislation creating Medicare and Medicaid. The reform established what is known as the "three-layered cake" of public health insurance programs. First was Medicare Part A, a hospital insurance program that was largely supported by President Johnson and the Democrats. Second was Medicare Part B, a program to cover physician visits that was promoted by the American Medical Association (the doctors' industry group) and Republicans. And finally there was Medicaid, an expanded form of Eldercare, which covered a variety of poor Americans—children, the disabled, pregnant women, and mothers of young children.[11]

Fast-forward to the 1990s. By the time President Bill Clinton proposed comprehensive health care reform in 1993, the government's health care efforts had grown more and more complex, with special programs serving special constituencies. Workers whose employers offered health insurance got tax subsidies. The elderly got Medicare; servicemembers got veterans' health and Tricare; and Native Americans had the Indian Health Service. Medicaid itself had grown more and more intricate, with state-by-state rules disbursing federal and state funds to benefit some (but not all) poor children, elderly people, and people with disabilities.

President Clinton's efforts at comprehensive reform failed, but he and his successor managed to enact programs that, once again, both helped some people and added to the jumble of programs. In 1997, the Clinton administration succeeded in enacting the State Children's Health Insurance Program (S-CHIP), which provides federal funding to states to cover uninsured children whose families don't qualify for Medicaid.[12] A few years later, President George W. Bush pushed for (and won) the Medicare Modernization Act, which made two changes to Medicare. One authorized Medicare Advantage, plans under Medicare Part C that provide additional coverage like gym memberships, and the other created Medicare Part D, a prescription drug benefit.

By 2009, when President Obama took office with the hope of accomplishing comprehensive health care reform, the American health care system—and its politics—had grown nearly impenetrable. Each program has its own political constituencies—patients, doctors, hospitals, insurers, employers, unions—for whom "reform" could mean a threat to their health care and their livelihood.

So America's health care jumble means headaches for citizens and politicians alike. Reform, whether incremental or comprehensive, poses a Rubik's Cube–type challenge. As former Obama advisor and noted oncologist Dr. Ezekiel Emanuel observed, "This complexity means there is no 'ideal' system and no final reform."[13]

Obamacare and the Rise and Fall of the Public Option in Health Care

"This is a big f*cking deal." Vice President Joe Biden's private comment to President Obama was picked up by a live microphone at the signing ceremony for the Affordable Care Act in 2010. And he was right, if a bit blunt in his phrasing. The ACA (or Obamacare, as it came to be known) was the most significant reform to American health care since the creation of Medicare and Medicaid in 1965.

In the lead-up to the 2008 presidential election, many progressives had come to believe that the complexity of the American health care system would defy major structural reform. With that caution in mind, they shelved the idea of a single-payer system of national health insurance—even though that system would be the simplest and cleanest approach as a matter of policy design. Instead, they turned to "universal coverage through minimally invasive reform."[14] The conservative approach would build on Medicare and Medicaid, preserve employer-based health care, and rely on markets instead of government. Ironically, the progressive plan closely resembled one that had initially been designed by the conservative Heritage Foundation and implemented by Republican governor Mitt Romney. Health care reformers in 2008 also hoped to placate the major interest groups enough to fend off the hostilities that killed reform in 1993.

As finally enacted, the Affordable Care Act has three major components, all intended to expand access to health care. The first is an individual mandate to purchase health insurance. This was a critical reform because, as any economist could tell you, without a mandate to purchase health insurance, the system would collapse under the weight of adverse selection. The dynamic that worried the economists is pretty intuitive: health care, like any insurance, works only if higher-risk and lower-risk people are all in the risk pool together. If only sick people buy health insurance, while healthy people stay out of the system, the cost of insurance goes up, because sicker people are more expensive to cover. When prices rise, then more people drop coverage, leaving only really, really sick people in the pool. And prices go up again.

The individual mandate aimed to dampen adverse selection by ensuring that healthy people would buy insurance. And that doesn't just benefit sick people. After all, it's a fact of life that today's healthy young people are tomorrow's older, sicker people. If everyone has health insurance, then even healthy people can get the preventive health care that can keep them healthy and reduce the cost to the health care system down the road.

The second component of Obamacare aimed to ensure that all these people could buy health insurance with some minimum standards at a reasonable price. But, instead of a public option, the ACA went for a complex system of market subsidies. Many workers could still get health insurance at work, but everyone else would buy their insurance from private companies in a private market called "the exchange." In a compromise to win over conservatives, the Affordable Care Act didn't create a single national exchange. Instead, it authorized the states to set up their own exchanges. And in an attempt to make insurance affordable to all, the new system offered subsidies to low-income insurance buyers.

The third component was the expansion of Medicaid. Medicaid would now cover anyone who was poor (not just the limited categories of the poor that it covered before), and the ACA expanded coverage to those with incomes at or below 138 percent of the federal poverty level. To sweeten the deal, the federal government set out to pay 90 percent of the costs of this expansion (remember, Medicaid is a hybrid federal-state program). Together, these changes would have massively expanded access to health care for millions of Americans.

So, to recap, Obamacare took a market-based, private-insurance approach to comprehensive reform. But here's the thing: it wasn't the only path forward in 2010. At one stage, there was a real chance that a public option for health insurance—a public health insurance plan available on the exchanges as an alternative to private insurance—could be part of the Affordable Care Act.

A public option in health care first emerged as a serious idea around the time of the Clinton health care reform in the early 1990s, but it wasn't until 2001–2002 that it took root. In California, reformers proposed that the state offer people a public health insurance plan that would compensate health care providers at the same rate as Medicare.[15] Around the same time, Yale professor Jacob Hacker proposed a federal expansion of Medicare to include more people, another version of a public option.[16]

In the run-up to the presidential campaign of 2008, Hacker proposed a comprehensive new solution for American health care that he called Health Care for America (HCFA). In our terms, HCFA was a national, competitive public option for health insurance. Under Hacker's plan, HCFA would offer a public insurance plan modeled on Medicare and available to anyone who lacked insurance via Medicare or an employer plan.[17]

Following on Hacker's move, the public option, in different forms, found traction in national politics. A few weeks later, Senator John Edwards (D-NC), one of the Democratic candidates for president, released a health care plan modeled on the California system. Each state would offer a competitive public option through an exchange that also had private plans available on it.[18] Edwards's plan looked more like what the Affordable Care Act would ultimately be, as it was built around state exchanges, but crucially, it had a public option as part of the solution. Over the next year, liberal activist Roger Hickey and the Campaign for America's Future began trying to persuade the grassroots movement for single-payer health care that a public option would be a more politically palatable way to get to universal coverage.[19]

As 2008 turned into 2009, the public option gained serious momentum. Three committees in the House of Representatives passed a public option. The full House of Representatives passed a public option. The Senate Health, Education, Labor, and Pensions Committee passed a public option.[20] The public option looked like a real possibility. So what happened?

Politics happened. The White House held back on pushing aggressively for a public option. And, at the same time, Senator Joe Lieberman, the former Democratic vice presidential candidate turned independent, threatened to filibuster any bill that had a public option. With razor-thin voting margins in Congress, Lieberman's defection would kill the bill.[21] Adding to the pressure, Republicans and interest groups opposed the public option, knocking it out of the circle of acceptable compromises.

Democrats ultimately abandoned the public option in order to keep their side intact and soften Republican opposition to health care reform. The irony is that these compromises weakened reform without doing much to gain Republican backing. As the most notable historian of American health care reform has observed, "None of the compromises made by Democrats softened Republican opposition in the slightest."[22]

The Ironies of Opposition

Republican opposition to the 2010 Affordable Care Act was swift, unrelenting, and uncompromising. On every possible front, they challenged the health care law. During the Obama administration, Republicans in the House of Representatives voted more than 60 times to repeal the law.[23] Republican governors refused to create state exchanges. Conservative groups challenged the law in court on multiple grounds. The irony is that every effort to weaken, block, or repeal the Affordable Care Act only makes it more likely that health care advocates will push harder for a public option—and that a public option will make even more sense than it did before.

The Supreme Court took one of the first steps toward undermining Obamacare in its 2012 decision in *National Federation of Independent Businesses v. Sebelius*. The NFIB argued that the Affordable Care Act was an unconstitutional exercise of congressional power: Congress couldn't require consumers to buy health insurance, and it couldn't cut funding to states that refused to expand their Medicaid programs.

The challenge to the individual mandate was breathtakingly radical. The core problem in the economics of health insurance is the adverse selection problem we discussed earlier in this chapter. Insurance, whether for health care or car accidents or floods, works only if there is a large and diverse pool of people who are covered and paying into the system. If people can wait to buy health insurance until they're sick, the whole idea of insurance goes down the drain: it's as if people could wait to buy car insurance until after they've had a car accident.

So the NFIB's first argument—that the Court should strike down the individual mandate—would have made the health care market in America work far less well by stripping the mandate from the system. Ultimately, the Court held that the Affordable Care Act's mandate was constitutional because, as a technical matter, it exercised Congress's broad power to tax.

But even as the Supreme Court accepted one of the three pillars of Obamacare, it knocked down another. The Supreme Court agreed with the NFIB's claim that tying federal funds to the Medicaid expansion was unconstitutional. With that decision, the Court emboldened Republican governors to deny Medicaid coverage to tens of millions of poor people. And they did.

Many of these states had large populations of poor and working-class people who would have benefited from the Medicaid expansion. As a by-product, the states would have seen economic benefits from a healthier workforce. But Republicans declined to voluntarily expand Medicaid even when the federal government paid 90 percent of the cost. For progressive health care advocates, the fierce opposition suggested that a national public program—more like Medicare than like Medicaid—would be a better way to guarantee that all Americans have access to health care.

At the same time, many Republican governors across the country refused to create health insurance exchanges. The cynicism and irony of this position cannot be underestimated. The purpose of having state exchanges instead of a single federal exchange was to support a conservative desire for federalism and less national government power in health care. By refusing to set up the exchanges, Republican governors guaranteed instead that the federal government would set up the exchanges in their state. The principle of local control collapsed under ideological opposition to expanding access to health insurance.

When the federal government stepped in to create these exchanges, conservatives challenged that effort in court, too. In *King v. Burwell,* they deployed clever lawyering to claim that the Affordable Care Act didn't allow for the federally created exchanges to offer subsidies to working-class Americans. This challenge, too, would have destroyed the Affordable Care Act because the individual mandate won't work unless there are subsidies for those who can't afford to pay for coverage. This time the Supreme Court rejected this attempt to undermine the ACA.

Not satisfied with attacking the individual mandate and the Medicaid expansion, conservative groups also attacked the scope of health care coverage under the ACA. In *Burwell v. Hobby Lobby Stores* and *Little Sisters of the Poor v. Burwell,* groups challenged the legal requirement that private health insurance plans offer some minimum benefits, one of which was contraceptive health care for women. (To be clear, this wasn't coverage of abortion, which Democrats negotiated away in order to pass the bill; this was coverage for birth control.) *Hobby Lobby* argued that offering its workers a health care plan that paid for birth control was an affront to the corporation's religious beliefs. The Supreme Court agreed, and the federal government offered an accommodation, worked out with health insurers, that enabled women to gain access to birth control separately from their employer-funded plan. In *Little Sisters of the Poor,* the religious order argued that filling out a form telling the federal government that they didn't want to offer birth control coverage to employees (the deal worked out after *Hobby Lobby*) was *itself* an affront to their religion because even filling out a form made them complicit in non-childbearing sexual relationships. The Supreme Court punted on that case, asking the parties to go back and figure out a solution.

Most recently, the Trump administration has weighed in on the Republican side of things. With Congress unable to repeal Obamacare, the president first declared his intention not to enforce the individual mandate and to undermine the ACA's subsidies for insurance companies. Amid the bickering and uncertainty, a number of private companies have either raised health care premiums or exited the exchanges altogether. Finally, in their 2017 tax bill, Republicans pushed through a repeal of the tax penalty for those who don't have health care (the so-called individual mandate).

Conservatives haven't stood alone in their opposition to the Affordable Care Act. In August 2009, some of the nation's largest private insurance companies, including Aetna, Cigna, Humana, UHC, and WellPoint, gave $86.2 million to the Chamber of Commerce, funneled through a group called America's Health Insurance Plans (AHIP), so that the chamber would oppose Obamacare.[24] This political money-laundering allowed them to cover their tracks so that they weren't directly seen as opposing the bill.

All this legal and political wrangling, we think, only strengthens the case for national power in general—and a public option in particular. If the federal government runs exchanges across the country, it only makes sense to consolidate them. That would reduce costs for both the federal government and consumers, because the pool of insured consumers would be larger. If the states won't expand Medicaid despite generous subsidies, then it will take a federal program to cover the poor and near-poor people whom the expansion was intended to benefit. Pushing the point further, if the high cost of subsidies is a stumbling block, perhaps it would be cheaper and easier to have a public option that could enroll anyone who wants it, regardless of income level. A public option would also sidestep the religious objections by parties like Hobby Lobby and Little Sisters of the Poor. If private employers, like corporations and churches, simply can't bear to offer access to essential health care, then the better solution is a public system that offers birth control coverage. Indeed, if we take Hobby Lobby's and the Little Sisters' concerns seriously, then the federal government would have to create a public option for birth control alone. Opposition now *requires* a public option.

Furthermore, a public option would resolve a structural problem that is built into the Affordable Care Act. Because the ACA relies on competition among private companies, it is vulnerable to market forces that erode competition. And, as if on cue, the market in health insurance has become more and more consolidated—which is to say less and less competitive. In 2006, the four biggest health insurance companies covered 74 percent of the national market. In 2014, they covered 83 percent.[25]

The problem of consolidation is compounded by big insurers exiting the ACA marketplace. The best example of this is Aetna. Aetna abandoned eleven of fifteen exchanges, citing the Obama administration's blocking of its merger with Humana as part of the reason.[26] Aetna, of course, wants the greater efficiency and lower costs that come with scale. But with consolidation, there's less competition—and with less competition, fewer choices for those buying health care on the exchanges and higher prices (because monopolies know they can raise prices). As Jacob Hacker has observed: "In a lot of the country, we're getting single-payer health care—it's just a private insurer that's doing the paying."[27]

In these dysfunctional markets, a public option has much to offer. As Hacker has argued, the creation of a public option would give consumers on the exchanges more choice, would ensure there is competition on every exchange with a private option, and would serve as a benchmark to compare costs and prices.[28]

To be fair, public utilities regulation offers an alternative approach. Law professor Nicholas Bagley, for instance, has argued that medicine is a public calling, a service that is akin to many others that have traditionally been understood as something states can regulate to ensure that there is universal access at a controlled price. This kind of regulation, often called common-carrier regulation or public utilities regulation, is particularly useful for essential goods and services and where the market is effectively a monopoly. Electricity is a classic example: it is necessary for modern life, and its provision is a monopoly. As a result, government regulates electric companies to ensure universal access and affordable rates. Bagley suggests the same is true for health care.[29]

In light of massive consolidation, it might be that a public utility model of regulation—in addition to or in lieu of a public options model—is necessary. Indeed, if Hacker is right that we already have a single-payer system, just paid by a private insurer, then public-utility-style regulation will be necessary because monopolies don't face competitive pressures to keep costs down.

The ironies here are abundant. The Republican opposition to the Affordable Care Act was and is opposition to a conservative, market-based approach to health care. The Affordable Care Act isn't a government takeover. There's no single-payer system. There's no public option. In fact, it isn't even implemented as a national program—it operates through *state* exchanges and through *state*-based Medicaid. This is about as conservative a program as one could design (which is why the Heritage Foundation designed it and Mitt Romney adopted it in Massachusetts).

And this is why Republicans had so much trouble repealing and replacing Obamacare under the Trump administration. Even with control of both houses of Congress and the presidency, they couldn't find a health care plan that guarantees expansive coverage without involving the government more heavily. That's because Obamacare was not a radical approach to accomplishing the expansion of health care. By opposing even a conservative, market-based, state-based system of health care, Republicans boxed themselves into a corner.

Some Options for a Public Option

At this stage, the case for a public option in health care is stronger than ever. A public option would guarantee access to health care to everyone at a controlled (and affordable) price; it would serve as a benchmark and competitor to private options without crowding them out; and it would expand people's freedom by decoupling the need for health care from their current employer.

Political battles since Obamacare's passage in 2010 have only strengthened the case for a public option. Republicans have mounted unceasing attacks on the Affordable Care Act, even in the face of compromises that made the program more complicated and less efficient in order to win conservative support. So there is little reason for progressives to embrace those complexities now. If conservatives will oppose *everything* no matter what, then there is no reason not to design a better system. They'll oppose that, too, but at least it'll work better.

And the ACA's dicey experience with market subsidies adds further weight to the case for a public option. The exchanges have been difficult to design, and they haven't fostered robust competition or kept prices down. The cost of subsidies to the federal government is high, and yet many poorer people lack access to affordable coverage, thanks to the Republican states' refusal to expand Medicaid.

A well-designed public option would guarantee access to health insurance to every American. It would ensure that every American has a choice in health care providers, and it would foster competition despite industry consolidation. Indeed, even President Obama, who didn't push hard for a public option during the fight for the Affordable Care Act, has come around to thinking that it would be a good addition now. As he wrote in the *Journal of the American Medical Association* in 2016, "Based on experience with the ACA, I think Congress should revisit a public plan to compete alongside private insurers in areas of the country where competition is limited."[30]

So how might a public option work today? To begin, recall our distinction between baseline public options and competitive public options. Recall that a baseline public option sets a floor—it provides a minimum service for everyone. Further private options exist on top of it. A competitive public option is a program that operates alongside a private option and competes with it. Both kinds of public options are part of the debate, and each has different pros and cons.

The baseline public option is what many people call, misleadingly, "single-payer." (It's misleading because a baseline public option isn't the only game in town. Private companies could offer supplemental coverage, as they now offer Medigap policies to Medicare participants.) A baseline public option (perhaps an expanded form of Medicare) would cover everyone, but with minimum levels of coverage. Private options could exist on top of that for people who wanted to pay for (or for employers who wanted to offer) greater benefits than the baseline public option. This model wouldn't be a "pure" single-payer system, but that's precisely why we like it. Put another way, it wouldn't be a form of socialism with the exclusive government provision of health care.

America already has a baseline public option for people age sixty-five and over: it's called Medicare. Private companies can—and do—compete to offer additional coverage (Medigap policies). This kind of baseline public option is fairly common internationally. The United Kingdom's National Health Service, for instance, allows for private health care provision and insurance on top of the public program.

While the baseline public option is the simplest design for a health care system, it is also demanding administratively and politically, precisely because it would be a big change from the status quo. Today, half of all people who have health care in America get it from a private insurer through their employer.[31] Moving those people from their current insurance to a public system like Medicare would trigger political pushback and practical challenges in implementation. One smaller step forward in the short to medium term would be for advocates of a single-payer system to experiment within the states, in order to see if there is a workable way to make this transition.

The second approach, a competitive public option, is what most people think of when they think about a public option in health care: a public health insurance program that anyone could join if they wanted. The competitive public option could operate within each state, as a public plan that sells insurance through the state exchange. Either the states or the federal government would create and operate this public option. The state version would thus be akin to the California plan that was proposed in 2001–2002 or the Edwards plan from 2007. Alternatively, the competitive public option could be a national plan, created by the federal government and operating in all of the exchanges. The upside to this system is that the national public option would have further benefits of nationwide pooling and a far larger scale.

The most difficult policy challenge in designing a competitive public option lies in the details of managing costs and payments. During the debate over Obamacare, Democrats in the House of Representatives took two different approaches to a public option. Conservative Democrats, who ultimately won the day, argued for a public option in which the government would negotiate prices with providers. In theory, this would help reduce costs (because the government has purchasing power). But the Congressional Budget Office estimated at the time that premiums might actually be higher than premiums from private insurers.[32] Other Democrats advocated for a "robust" public option, in which the public insurer would pay providers at the same rates that Medicare pays. The Congressional Budget Office found that this approach would reduce premiums by 7–8 percent because Medicare simply sets rates for insurers to pay.[33] The problem, however, is that tying payments to Medicare rates (or even Medicare rates plus, say, 5 percent) means that hospitals and providers make less money because of Medicare's lower reimbursement rates.[34] This certainly creates a political problem, and we don't know if it will create a financial problem for hospitals and providers because we don't know whether they will make up lower prices with higher volume. This problem, however, is not insurmountable. One could imagine designing a transition period, in which the public plan pays Medicare rates plus 10 percent for the first year (for instance) and then reduces the payment each year after that. This would enable us to see how the new system works and to help providers adapt to the lower rates incrementally.

As President Trump discovered after his first, quick attempt to repeal the Affordable Care Act, "Nobody knew health care could be so complicated."[35] Health care in America *is* complicated, and reform will be challenging. But a public option would be a big step in the right direction—a way to ensure that every American has access to health care at an affordable price.

12

And More

We hope we've persuaded you that the public option has already contributed a great deal to American society and holds the promise to contribute much more. Looking to the future, we've identified a few more opportunities for public options, some concrete and some more speculative. We consider all of them worth a serious look.

Broadband Access

Today, broadband internet access is critical for communities. It's the equivalent of access to the mail in the nineteenth century or telephones in the twentieth. High-speed internet means communication with the larger world, which is increasingly important for commerce, economic innovation and growth, and connection to others.

And yet millions of Americans don't have access to broadband internet. According to the "2016 Broadband Progress Report" prepared by the Federal Communications Commission (FCC),

10 percent of all Americans—some 34 million people—don't have access to high-speed internet (defined as 25 Mbps download and 3 Mbps upload). The distribution largely hurts rural Americans. While only 4 percent of urban Americans can't access high-speed internet, a whopping 39 percent of rural Americans are stuck with sluggish connections, if they have any connection at all. Twenty percent can't even get 4 Mbps download speeds.[1] In a technologically driven world, this is a serious challenge. As Senator Angus King (an independent from Maine) has said, "Failure to provide broadband to rural areas of America is a death sentence for those communities."[2]

In communities that do have high-speed internet access, there's a different problem. Internet is often a monopoly. People have few if any choices. And because the monopoly knows it has customers captive, it charges higher prices for an inferior product. When the FCC studies internet access, it looks at developed census blocks. These areas are smaller than census tracts, which is how the census normally locates people. As of June 2016, the FCC found that 58 percent of developed census blocks have either no high-speed internet or only one option for it. The numbers are even worse if we move from 25 Mbps to 100 Mbps download speeds: 88 percent of developed census blocks have either no option or only one option.[3] And here's the kicker: these numbers are probably undercounting because the data count a census block as competitive even if only some people have two or more options. With such limited competition, it isn't surprising that surveys show Comcast is one of the most hated companies in the country.[4] And it isn't surprising that average prices are higher in America than in comparable cities in Europe and Asia for all speeds.[5]

These challenges haven't gone unnoticed. In cities throughout America, innovative leaders have tried to offer affordable high-speed internet to their citizens—through a public option.

Take Chattanooga, Tennessee. The southern city's Electric Power Board (EPB) decided in 2007 to build a fiber network within a decade in order to provide the community with 1 Gbps internet. By 2015, the EPB was serving 60,000 homes and 4,500 businesses.[6] The result is that Chattanooga is once again chugging into the future. Chattanoogans can get the fastest internet in the world for less than $70 per month.[7] The result has been a tech boom in the city, with new jobs and businesses.[8] Chattanooga's schools have benefited as well, with students getting access to high-speed connections. The city's public library is now considered a model for others across the country.[9] High-speed internet through the public option has also meant benefits for the city's utility. The EPB used broadband to make the city's electric grid a smart grid. Four times an hour, 170,000 electric meters report to the EPB on the city's power. As a result, EPB has saved customers more than $45 million and slashed the length of any power outages that occur.[10]

Another southern city, Wilson, North Carolina, located near the Raleigh-Durham research triangle, also implemented a public option for high-speed internet. Greenlight, the city's service, offers a package of gigabit internet, phone service, and cable, in addition to free Wi-Fi downtown (which means businesses don't have to pay those costs). As a measure of the program's success, all seven of the biggest employers in town use Greenlight.[11] Wilson's experience with Greenlight has also created beneficial competition. Time Warner, the local internet provider, raised rates from 2007 to 2009, including jacking up prices 52 percent in nearby Cary, North Carolina. But in Wilson—where there was competition from the city's public option—Time Warner didn't raise rates.[12]

Seeing such great success, the leadership in Chattanooga and Wilson thought they might help others get access to their high-speed internet services. Residents of the "digital desert" just beyond those cities have "repeatedly requested" that the cities extend their internet to adjacent underserved communities.[13] The challenge is that both Tennessee and North Carolina have laws banning municipalities from offering internet beyond their borders. In 2015, the FCC found that these laws interfered with the federal law charging the Commission with breaking down barriers to broadband investment, access, and competition.[14] It preempted the state laws, allowing Chattanooga and Wilson to offer their services to needy customers.

The public option in Chattanooga and Wilson offered a high-quality service that has improved economic opportunity, reduced costs for businesses and the municipalities, and introduced necessary competition in a monopolistic sector. But unfortunately, that isn't the end of the story. The FCC's decision was appealed in federal court, and in 2016 the appeals court reversed the FCC, upholding the state laws and banning Chattanooga and Wilson from expanding service.[15] To add insult to injury, Tennessee then got pushed even further away from the public option approach. After heavy lobbying, the state legislature passed a bill in 2017 that claimed to be a boon to rural areas without internet access. But the devil was in the details. Instead of allowing municipalities like Chattanooga's EPB to expand its super-fast and cheap internet to these underserved customers, the bill instead subsidizes Comcast and AT&T to provide rural internet to the tune of $45 million in grants and tax benefits. In a shocking display of disregard for rural Americans, the bill also only requires those companies to provide 10 Mbps internet service—nowhere near the high-speed service that communities must have if they are to succeed today. As one commentator said, "Tennessee will literally be paying AT&T to provide a service 1,000 times slower than what Chattanooga could provide without subsidies."[16]

Credit Reporting

In 2017, America's three private credit bureaus—Equifax, TransUnion, and Experian—came under fire when Equifax revealed that hackers had obtained the private information of 143 million Americans. As if the breach weren't bad enough, Equifax waited weeks before notifying consumers about the hack.[17] And Equifax made a hash of the cleanup as well, putting the burden on consumers to freeze their credit reports (a time-consuming, sometimes costly, and cumbersome process) or buy private identity-theft insurance.[18]

In the wake of the Equifax fiasco, many Americans began to focus on the immense power and limited accountability of the three credit reporting companies. Each company collects a raft of sensitive financial and personal information without our consent, and without any payment to us. And each company then uses the information to generate a credit score, according to a secret algorithm, which it then sells to buyers like banks, insurance companies, and employers. Your credit score will determine whether you can get a mortgage, rent an apartment, or even get a job. And the companies are only weakly accountable to consumers for the accuracy of the information they sell about us.

Put another way, credit reporting has become an important foundation for modern economic life, but the private market has notable problems, including weak accountability and lack of transparency. Regulation offers one solution: the law might, for instance, require greater accountability by requiring the credit bureaus to fix erroneous information. All three companies now offer processes for disputing information in your credit report, but unless you are a VIP, you will not speak with a human being or find that the error is resolved quickly. Instead, you will find yourself "herded into a largely automated system" with minimal review. Horror stories abound. Bobby Allyn, an NPR reporter, hit a roadblock when trying to lease an apartment in Philadelphia. The landlord pulled a credit report that included "a clutch of criminal offenses, including two felony firearms convictions." The problem was someone with the same name. Allyn spent six weeks working to correct the error—even after he identified himself as a journalist, an asset not available to most of us.[19]

But even tighter dispute resolution wouldn't solve the underlying problem, which is that the credit bureaus are so sloppy in their information-collecting that one in four Americans has an error on at least one of her three credit reports.[20] Unless you know about that error, you won't know to enter even the best dispute-resolution system.

Some have proposed nationalizing the three credit bureaus in order to turn over the task of credit reporting to a public agency.[21] But instead of full nationalization, a public option may be worth considering, perhaps in conjunction with regulation. A public option could offer much-needed competition in the market for consumer information and credit reporting. Today, consumers have no choice in the matter: they are involuntarily opted in to all three credit bureaus, with no legal right to opt out. A public option might be combined with an opt-out right that could help discipline both the public and the private credit reporters to collect accurate information and offer quick and reliable dispute resolution.

We haven't worked out the details, and many questions remain to be answered. People might be uncomfortable with the government owning so much data about them. But the government already has much of that data and then some, thanks to the tax filing process. And the big credit bureaus have shown themselves to be untrustworthy custodians of the data. We think that a public option should be part of the conversation as Americans come to terms with the failure of the present model and look to alternatives.

A National Jobs Guarantee

Throughout America, millions of people are unemployed or underemployed. They want to work full-time but can't find a private sector job. In some cases, people just give up. In other cases, they take a temporary, part-time, or seasonal job. Both joblessness and underemployment are serious problems for society. They are economic problems: people without jobs don't have enough money to buy things and expand demand. They are social problems: people without jobs can end up homeless, lonely, susceptible to drugs and crime, or just disaffected from society. And they are fiscal problems: the jobless and unemployed are more likely to use social services like food stamps and unemployment insurance, costing taxpayers money.

A public option for jobs could help solve these problems, putting millions of Americans to work for productive ends while improving the economy. The idea itself, while it might seem radical, isn't new. During the Great Depression, President Roosevelt's New Deal created a variety of jobs programs that employed millions of Americans in productive work throughout the country. The most famous were the Works Progress Administration (WPA), which built schools, buildings, roads, and other infrastructure, and the Civilian Conservation Corps (CCC), which put people to work on environmental and conservation projects all across the country. For a generation after the successes of Roosevelt's experiment, many Americans sought to address the challenges of unemployment through a national jobs guarantee. A robust full employment bill almost passed into law in the 1940s. Martin Luther King Jr., A. Philip Randolph, and Bayard Rustin pushed for a jobs guarantee in the 1960s because they thought it essential to freedom for all Americans. In the 1970s, Congress passed the Humphrey-Hawkins Full Employment Act, which didn't establish a jobs guarantee but did direct the Federal Reserve to consider employment when pursuing monetary policy.

In recent years, however, some policy entrepreneurs have resurrected the idea of a jobs guarantee.[22] The way it would work is simple: the federal government would guarantee that any adult who wants to work could do so, and it would get that person a job. The program would be voluntary (it is a public option, after all), funded either entirely or mostly by the federal government, and administered locally with input and participation from local communities. Workers would get paid a living wage, have health, retirement, and other fringe benefits (perhaps through other public options), and, like all other workers, get vacation time. The work itself would vary considerably but would focus on beneficial projects to communities and the public more broadly. Examples might include repairing and building infrastructure; environmental cleanup and conservation; urban blight removal and revitalization; care and support for the elderly, young, sick, or at-risk; and other projects that local communities deem important.

Advocates for a jobs guarantee have identified a number of benefits. First, it would give millions of Americans a job, both taking them out of despondency and putting money in their pockets. Second, it would help the economy. With millions of people having more money and engaging in productive work, the economy would grow—both because of wages being spent in the marketplace (therefore expanding the market) and because of the investment in growth-creating infrastructure and other services. Because unemployment is countercyclical (more people don't have jobs in a recession), the jobs guarantee would help smooth out the ups and downs from economic cycles. People who lose their private sector job could move into the public option until they can get a new private sector job. A jobs guarantee would also set a wage and benefits floor, improving wages and working conditions throughout the private sector economy. Finally, it would mean reduced spending on a variety of social services that target those who are poor or unemployed. While a jobs guarantee would undoubtedly be expensive, this public option could provide many benefits to the economy.

Public Defense

A storied but sometimes troubled public option grew out of the constitutional right to counsel. Clarence Earl Gideon was arrested, tried, and convicted of felony breaking and entering, all without the assistance of a lawyer despite his request to the Florida judge.

His case made it all the way to the Supreme Court, which held in *Gideon v. Wainwright* in 1963 that every criminal defendant must be provided with counsel, free of charge.[23]

The constitutional right to counsel ensures universal access to an important service, but it doesn't always operate as a public option, because not all public defender services are government-run. Instead, in many places, the work of public defense is hired out to private lawyers.

In our terms, then, public defense spans two models for government provision. One is a true public option: a government agency provides free criminal defense and exists alongside private defense options. In New Jersey, for instance, public defenders work for an agency run and financed by the state.[24] A second model is a privatized system: in this system, the government pays private lawyers to take cases. In New York, for instance, many counties pay private lawyers to act as public defenders; these lawyers may be in private practice or may be employed by nonprofit legal aid organizations.[25] Public defense is notably fragmented in its organization, not only among states but across counties within states.[26]

In popular culture and many television shows, the public defender has a bad reputation: overworked at best, lazy and negligent at worst. Indeed, the heavy caseloads shouldered by public defenders and the underfunding of public defense pose a serious threat to justice, as do poor training and spotty oversight of private lawyers engaged in public defense.[27]

Still, there is evidence that the public option outperforms privatization. A 2017 study focused on San Francisco, where most cases are handled by the state or federal public defender's office, but some cases are handled by private lawyers paid by the government (typically in cases of conflict of interest). Controlling for differences among defendants, the study found that private lawyers paid on a case-by-case basis performed worse than public defenders employed by the government. Even controlling for the better credentials of salaried public defenders (compared to private attorneys paid by the case), public defenders still had greater success.[28] Measuring such differences can be tricky, it's true.[29] But other studies have reached a similar conclusion.[30]

Reforming public defense is a critical item on the nation's agenda, because the promised right to counsel requires diligent, skilled lawyers who have reasonable caseloads and access to the resources they need to investigate cases and defend their clients. Expanding the public option is—and should be—very much on the table.

Notes

1. The Limits of Private Action

1. Nelson Lichtenstein, *The Most Dangerous Man in Detroit* 280 (1995).
2. AARP Public Policy Institute, "The Social Compact in the Twenty-First Century" 1 (2009), http://assets.aarp.org/rgcenter/ppi/econ-sec/d19224-sc.pdf.
3. AARP, "Social Compact," at 22. On the relationship between wartime policies and health care, see Ezekiel J. Emanuel, *Reinventing American Health Care* 30–32 (2014). Most accounts focus on wartime policies, though some scholars argue that the shift happened before those policies took effect. See Timothy Stoltzfus Jost, *Health Care at Risk: A Critique of the Consumer-Driven Movement* 59–61 (2007).
4. This is not to say that this model was the lived reality for Americans. For a discussion of both breadwinner liberalism and its limits, see Robert O. Self, *All in the Family: The Realignment of American Democracy Since the 1960s* (2012).
5. Economic Policy Institute, "The Top Charts of 2014," at chart 2 (Dec. 18, 2014), www.epi.org/publication/the-top-10-charts-of-2014; U.S. Census Bureau, Historical Income Tables, table P-2: "Race and Hispanic Origin by Median Income and Sex," available at www.census.gov/hhes/www/income/data/historical/people;

St. Louis Federal Reserve Bank, "Real Gross Domestic Product," FRED Economic Data, available at https://research.stlouisfed.org/fred2/series/GDPC1.

6. Jacob Hacker, *The Great Risk Shift: The New Economic Insecurity and the Decline of the American Dream* (2006).
7. AARP, "Social Compact," at 12.
8. Gallup, "How Millennials Work and Live," www.gallup.com/reports/189830/millennials-work-live.aspx.
9. See U.S. Department of Labor, Bureau of Labor Statistics, "Number of Jobs, Labor Market Experience, and Earnings Growth at 50: Results From a Longitudinal Survey" (2017), at https://www.bls.gov/news.release/pdf/nlsoy.pdf. For skepticism of multiple career transitions, see Carl Bialik, "Seven Careers in a Lifetime? Think Twice, Researchers Say," *Wall Street Journal* (Sept. 4, 2010); Ben Casselman, "Enough Already about the Job-Hopping Millennials," *FiveThirtyEight* (May 5, 2018).
10. David Weil, *The Fissured Workplace: Why Work Became So Bad for So Many and What Can Be Done to Improve It* (2014).
11. Shayna Strom & Mark Schmitt, "Protecting Workers in a Patchwork Economy," Century Foundation (Apr. 7, 2016), https://tcf.org/content/report/protecting-workers-patchwork-economy.
12. U.S. Bureau of the Census, "Income and Poverty in the United States: 2017," Figure 2; The Hamilton Project, "Median Annual Earnings since 1964," www.hamiltonproject.org/charts/median_annual_earnings_since_1964; David Wessel, "The Typical Male U.S. Worker Earned Less in 2014 than in 1973," Brookings Institution (Sept. 18, 2015), www.brookings.edu/opinions/the-typical-male-u-s-worker-earned-less-in-2014-than-in-1973.
13. On household income stagnation, see Federal Reserve Economic Data (hereinafter FRED), "Real Median Household Income in the United States," https://fred.stlouisfed.org/series/MEHOINUSA672N; Ben Casselman, "The American Middle Class Hasn't Gotten a Raise in 15 Years," *FiveThirtyEight* (Sept. 22, 2014), http://fivethirtyeight.com/features/the-american-middle

-class-hasnt-gotten-a-raise-in-15-years. On the broader phenomenon, see Elizabeth Warren & Amelia Warren Tyagi, *The Two-Income Trap: Why Middle Class Parents Are Going Broke* (2003).

14. FRED, "Civilian Labor Force Participation Rate: Women," https://fred.stlouisfed.org/series/LNS11300002.
15. David Singh Grewal & Jedediah Purdy, "Introduction: Law and Neoliberalism," 77 *Law and Contemporary Problems* 1–3, 6 (2014).
16. Angus Burgin, *The Great Persuasion: Reinventing Free Markets since the Depression* (2012).
17. See David Harvey, *A Brief History of Neoliberalism* (2005).
18. On privatization, see John Donahue, *The Privatization Decision* (1989); E. S. Savas, *Privatization: The Key to Better Government* (1987). On neoliberalism in general, see Manfred B. Steger & Ravi K. Roy, *Neoliberalism: A Very Short Introduction* (2010); Harvey, *A Brief History.*
19. On the failures of privatization, see Jody Freeman & Martha Minow, *Government by Contract* (2009); Jon D. Michaels, *Constitutional Coup: Privatization's Threat to the American Republic* (2017).
20. United States Senate Committee on Health, Education, Labor, and Pensions, *For Profit Higher Education: The Failure to Safeguard the Federal Investment and Ensure Student Success* 3 (July 30, 2012), www.help.senate.gov/imo/media/for_profit_report/PartI.pdf.
21. Senate Committee, *For Profit Higher Education,* at 1–3.
22. Federal Deposit Insurance Corporation, "2015 FDIC National Survey of Unbanked and Underbanked Households" 1 (Oct. 20, 2016), at www.fdic.gov/householdsurvey/2015/2015report.pdf.
23. Naomi R. Lamoreaux, *The Great Merger Movement in American Business, 1895–1904* 2, 5 (1985); Alan Trachtenberg, *The Incorporation of America: Culture and Society in the Gilded Age* 4 (1982).
24. Ganesh Sitaraman, *The Crisis of the Middle-Class Constitution: Why Economic Inequality Threatens Our Republic* 141–160 (2017).
25. "Pushing the Limits," *Economist* (Dec. 12, 2015).
26. "Too Much of a Good Thing," *Economist* (Mar. 26, 2016).

2. Why Public Options?

1. 26 U.S.C. section 1402(g) provides a limited exception for members of religions (e.g., the Old Order Amish) whose beliefs prohibit them from participating in a public retirement scheme. Under the statute, religious objectors must apply for exemption and must waive all Social Security benefits.
2. Raj Chetty et al., "Where Is the Land of Opportunity? The Geography of Intergenerational Mobility in the United States," 129 *Quarterly Journal of Economics* 1553 (2014).
3. FCC, "2016 Broadband Progress Report" (Jan. 29, 2016), www.fcc.gov/reports-research/reports/broadband-progress-reports/2016-broadband-progress-report.
4. Alicia H. Munnell et al., "NRRI Update Shows Half Still Falling Short," Boston College Center for Retirement Research (Dec. 2014), http://crr.bc.edu/briefs/nrri-update-shows-half-still-falling-short.
5. Yuval Levin, *The Fractured Republic: Renewing America's Social Contract in the Age of Individualism* (2016).
6. *Burwell v. Hobby Lobby Stores,* 537 U.S. (2014); *Zubik v. Burwell,* 578 U.S. (2016).
7. GAO, "Health Care Coverage: Job Lock and the Potential Impact of the Patient Protection and Affordable Care Act," 5 (Dec. 15, 2011), www.gao.gov/assets/590/586973.pdf.
8. GAO, "Health Care Coverage," at 6.
9. Ammar Farooq & Adriana Kugler, "Beyond Job Lock: Impacts of Public Health Insurance on Occupational and Industrial Mobility," NBER Working Paper (March 2016), www.nber.org/papers/w22118.
10. GAO, "Health Care Coverage"; Austin Frakt, "Job Lock," *The Incidental Economist* (Mar. 19, 2014), http://theincidentaleconomist.com/wordpress/job-lock-introduction, http://theincidentaleconomist.com/wordpress/job-lock-conclusion; Dean Baker, "Job Lock and Employer-Provided Health Insurance: Evidence from the Literature," AARP Public Policy Institute (March 2015), www.aarp.org/ppi/info-2015/job-lock-and-employer-provided-healthcare.html.

11. Robert W. Fairlie, Kanika Kapur, & Susan M. Gates, "Is Employer-Based Health Insurance a Barrier to Entrepreneurship?," RAND Working Paper (2010), www.rand.org/pubs/working_papers/WR637-1.html.
12. Department of Labor, Bureau of Labor Statistics, "Employee Benefits in the United States" (March 2016), www.bls.gov/news.release/pdf/ebs2.pdf.
13. Tom Perez & Jeffrey Zients, "Helping Workers Save for Retirement in an Ever-Changing Economy," *Obama White House Archives* (Jan. 26, 2016), https://obamawhitehouse.archives.gov/blog/2016/01/26/helping-workers-save-retirement-ever-changing-economy.
14. Beth Kowitt, "Starbucks CEO: 'We Spend More on Health Care than Coffee,'" *Fortune* (June 7, 2010).
15. GAO, "Health Care Coverage."
16. "Too Much of a Good Thing," *Economist* (Mar. 26, 2016).
17. FCC, "Internet Access Services: Status as of June 30, 2016," 6 (Apr. 2017), http://transition.fcc.gov/Daily_Releases/Daily_Business/2017/db0503/DOC-344499A1.pdf. This uses developed census blocks; the actual number might be lower because not all service providers might offer service to every household within a census block.
18. Andrei Schleifer, "A Yardstick Theory of Competition," 16 *RAND Journal of Economics* 319 (1985); Robert Nordhaus, "Yardstick Competition in a Deregulated Electric Utility Industry," 12 *Natural Resources and the Environment* 256 (1998).
19. Franklin D. Roosevelt, campaign address in Portland, Oregon (Sept. 21, 1932).
20. William Darity Jr. et al., "What We Get Wrong About Closing the Racial Wealth Gap," Samuel DuBois Cook Center for Social Equity, Apr. 2018, https://socialequity.duke.edu/sites/socialequity.duke.edu/files/site-images/FINAL%20COMPLETE%20REPORT_.pdf.
21. For a review of some of the recent studies, see Richard Florida, "America's Worsening Geographic Inequality," *The Atlantic*, Oct. 16, 2018.

22. Peggy Bailey et al., "African American Uninsured Rate Dropped by More Than a Third Under Affordable Care Act," Center for Budget and Policy Priorities, June 1, 2017, https://www.cbpp.org/research/health/african-american-uninsured-rate-dropped-by-more-than-a-third-under-affordable-care.
23. Julia Foutz et al., "The Role of Medicaid in Rural America," Kaiser Family Foundation, Apr. 25, 2017, https://www.kff.org/medicaid/issue-brief/the-role-of-medicaid-in-rural-america/.
24. Suzanne Mettler, *Soldiers to Citizens: The G.I. Bill and the Making of the Greatest Generation* (2005).

3. The Theory of the Public Option

1. Adam Smith, *The Wealth of Nations,* book I, chapter II, section I.2.2.
2. Bill Vlasic, "Record 2016 for U.S. Auto Industry; Long Road Back May Be at End," *New York Times* (Jan. 4, 2017).
3. Kelley Blue Book, "New-Car Transaction Prices Jump More than 3 Percent Year-over-Year in May 2016," at http://mediaroom.kbb.com/new-car-transaction-prices-jump-more-than-3-percent-year-over-year-may-2016; Department of Labor, Bureau of Labor Statistics, "Household Data, Annual Averages," Table 37, www.bls.gov/cps/cpsaat37.pdf.
4. Thomas Stipanowich, "Living with 'ADR': Evolving Perceptions and Use of Mediation, Arbitration, and Conflict Management in Fortune 1,000 Corporations," 19 *Harvard Negotiation Law Review* 1 (2013); Thomas Stipanowich, "Arbitration: The 'New Litigation,'" 2010 *University of Illinois Law Review* 1 (2010); Katherine V. W. Stone, "Alternative Dispute Resolution," in *Encyclopedia of Legal History* (Stan Katz ed., 2004); Rory Van Loo, "The Corporation as Courthouse," 33 *Yale Journal on Regulation* 547 (2016); Consumer Financial Protection Bureau, *Arbitration Study* 10 (2015), http://files.consumerfinance.gov/f/201503_cfpb_arbitration-study-report-to-congress-2015.pdf.
5. Workers pay half, or 6.2 percent, while employers pay another 6.2 percent, for a total of 12.4 percent. See Social Security

Administration, "Program Data," www.ssa.gov/OACT/ProgData/taxRates.html.

6. The payroll tax is capped at annual earnings of $127,200 in 2017, so no one pays more than $15,773 in Social Security taxes (taking into account both the worker's and the employer's shares). See Social Security Administration, "Cost of Living Adjustments," www.ssa.gov/OACT/COLA/cbb.html#Series.
7. See Elisa A. Walker, Virginia P. Reno, and Thomas N. Bethell, "Americans Make Hard Choices on Social Security: A Survey with Trade-Off Analysis," 8, 11, National Academy of Social Insurance (2017), www.nasi.org/sites/default/files/research/Americans_Make_Hard_Choices_on_Social_Security.pdf, finding that 81 percent of Americans "don't mind paying Social Security taxes because it provides security and stability to millions of retired Americans" and that 77 percent "would pay more taxes if needed to preserve Social Security." Strikingly, these findings hold true across age groups and political party affiliation.
8. As of June 30, 2017, Aetna offered just one Connecticut health plan, a silver-level plan (see www.aetna.com/plan-info/individual/health-plans/2017/connecticut.html), but the summary sheet included only copays, not monthly premiums. Clicking on the full plan document, at www.aetna.com/plan-info/individual/health-plans/2017/connecticut.html, accessed a long PDF with more detail on coverage but, again, no information on monthly costs. Scrolling down, we finally found monthly rates but had to work through a lengthy document with county-by-county pricing: www.aetna.com/individuals-families/document-library/rates/2017/Rates_2017_CT.pdf. After reading the fine print, Anne was able to figure out that she had to add her premium ($781) to the premiums for each of two kids ($234 each) for a total of over $1,200 per month.
9. Social Security Administration, "Annual Statistical Supplement" (2016), www.ssa.gov/policy/docs/statcomps/supplement/2016/2a20-2a28.html.

10. For a range of progressive tax proposals, see, e.g., Anne Alstott & Bruce Ackerman, *The Stakeholder Society* (1999) (proposing, inter alia, a wealth tax and an inheritance tax); Anne Alstott, *A New Deal for Old Age* (2016) (proposing progressive tax increases in the context of Social Security); see also Michael Lind, "The Liberal Case for Regressive Taxation," *Salon* (Aug. 10, 2010).
11. Joelle Saad-Lessler, Teresa Ghilarducci, & Kate Bahn, "Are U.S. Workers Ready for Retirement?," *New School for Social Research* (2015), www.economicpolicyresearch.org/images/docs/research/retirement_security/Are_US_Workers_Ready_for_Retirement.pdf; Keith Miller, David Madland, & Christian E. Weller, "The Reality of the Retirement Crisis," Center for American Progress (Jan. 26, 2015), www.americanprogress.org/issues/economy/reports/2015/01/26/105394/the-reality-of-the-retirement-crisis.
12. Joint Committee on Taxation, "Estimates of Federal Tax Expenditures for Fiscal Years 2016–2020" 53, JCX-3-17, www.jct.gov/publications.html?func=startdown&id=4971.
13. Congressional Budget Office, *The Distribution of Major Expenditures in the Individual Income Tax System* (2013), www.cbo.gov/publication/43768; Alicia Munnell, Rebecca Cannon Fraenkel, & Josh Hurwitz, "The Pension Coverage Problem in the Private Sector," Boston College Center for Retirement Research (2012), http://crr.bc.edu/briefs/the-pension-coverage-problem-in-the-private-sector.
14. For a comparison of these three forms, see K. Sabeel Rahman, "The New Utilities: Private Power, Social Infrastructure, and the Revival of the Public Utility Concept in a Changing Economy," 39 *Cardozo Law Review* 1621 (2018); K. Sabeel Rahman, "Challenging the New Curse of Bigness," *American Prospect* (Nov. 29, 2016).

4. Caveats and Counterarguments

1. The effect of food stamps on consumer behavior is complex. For instance, in a 2014 study, Hilary Hoynes and her coauthors found

that most SNAP recipients spend more than their benefit allotment on food, so SNAP benefits likely serve as a general consumption supplement; that is, recipients experience them as a cash boost rather than as a restricted food grant. (To see why, imagine that a family spends $500 per month before they receive food stamps. They then receive a SNAP benefit of $400. They can use the food stamps to free up $400 in their budget—the $400 they would've spent on food anyway.) Hilary Hoynes, Leslie McGranahan, & Diane Schanzenbach, "SNAP and Food Consumption," in *SNAP Matters: How Food Stamps Affect Health and Well-Being* (Judith Bartfeld et al. eds., 2015).

2. CitySeed, Who We Are, http://cityseed.org/who-we-are-2.
3. Frederick Schauer, "Slippery Slopes," 99 *Harvard Law Review* 361 (1985); Eugene Volokh, "The Mechanisms of the Slippery Slope," 116 *Harvard Law Review* 1026 (2003).
4. See, for example, James Fallows, "The Boiling Frog Myth: Stop the Lying Now!," *Atlantic* (Sept. 16, 2006).
5. See, for example, Drew Griffin et al., "Veterans Still Facing Major Delays at VA Hospitals," CNN (Oct. 20, 2017).
6. Anjali Athavaley & Melissa Fares, "Shkreli Insults Congress on Twitter after Refusing to Testify," Reuters (Feb. 4, 2016).
7. "'Pharma Bro' Martin Shkreli Defies Attorney's Advice to Lay Low before Trial," Fox News (June 26, 2017).
8. Albert O. Hirschman, *Exit, Voice, and Loyalty* (1970).
9. Dave Phillips, "Did Obama's Bill Fix Veterans' Health Care? Still Waiting," *New York Times,* Aug. 5, 2016; Quil Lawrence et al., "Despite $10 B 'Fix,' Veterans Are Waiting Even Longer to See Doctors," *Morning Edition,* NPR (May 16, 2016).
10. Jack Meserve, "Keep It Simple and Take Credit," *Democracy: A Journal of Ideas* (Feb. 3, 2017).
11. Levin, *Fractured Republic,* at 239–240 n. 29.
12. For the classic statement, see Kenneth A. Shepsle, "Congress Is a 'They,' Not an 'It': Legislative Intent as Oxymoron," 12 *International Review of Law and Economics* 239 (1992); see also Cass R. Sunstein,

"The Office of Information and Regulatory Affairs: Myths and Realities," 126 *Harvard Law Review* (2013) (noting that the White House is also a "they," not an "it").

13. Robert Nozick, *Anarchy, State, and Utopia* (1974).
14. See, for example, Gary Shapiro, "The Election of the Ant and the Grasshopper," *Forbes* (Aug. 15, 2012).
15. Mike Konczal, "No Discount: Comparing the Public Option to the Coupon Welfare State," 2, New America Foundation (Dec. 2012), https://static.newamerica.org/attachments/4165-no-discount-comparing-the-public-option-to-the-coupon-welfare-state/Konczal_Mike_PublicOption_NAF_Dec2012.73ec1576c8a14f248cf792a954387e36.pdf.
16. Konczal, "No Discount," at 2.
17. J. W. Mason, "Public Options: The General Case" (Sept. 5, 2010), http://jwmason.org/slackwire/public-options-general-case.
18. Jacob Hacker, *The Divided Welfare State: The Battle over Public and Private Social Benefits in the United States* 40–41 (2002).
19. Konczal, "No Discount," at 3 (citing Suzanne Mettler, "Reconstituting the Submerged State: The Challenges of Social Policy Reform in the Obama Era," *Perspectives on Politics* [Sept. 2010], 803–824).
20. Ganesh Sitaraman, "Reforming Regulation: Policies to Counteract Capture and Improve the Regulatory Process," Center for American Progress (Nov. 1, 2016), www.americanprogress.org/issues/economy/reports/2016/11/01/291499/reforming-regulation.

5. Public Libraries, Social Security, and Other Successes

1. From the early days, there was a postal monopoly—a mandate that no other actor could operate postal services akin to those of the Post Office. This monopoly was essential to ensure that there wouldn't be cream-skimming: that is, that the most valuable routes wouldn't be taken by private postal carriers, leaving the government with the most expensive routes. But the laws still allowed private couriers. See "United States Postal Service, Universal Service and the Postal

Monopoly: A Brief History" (Oct. 2008), https://about.usps.com/universal-postal-service/universal-service-and-postal-monopoly-history.pdf. For an older take, see George L. Priest, "The History of the Postal Monopoly in the United States," 18 *Journal of Law and Economics* 33 (1975).

2. Richard R. John, *Spreading the News: The American Postal System from Franklin to Morse* 36 (1995)
3. John, *Spreading the News,* at 15.
4. For histories, see generally John, *Spreading the News;* Winifred Gallagher, *How the Post Office Created America* (2016); Devin Leonard, *Neither Snow nor Rain: A History of the United States Postal Service* (2016).
5. See generally John, *Spreading the News;* Gallagher, *How the Post Office Created America;* Leonard, *Neither Snow nor Rain.*
6. Wayne A. Wiegand, *Part of Our Lives: A People's History of the American Public Library* 8, 24–26, 94 (2015)
7. Wiegand, *Part of Our Lives,* at 37, 77, 138–39, 145–46, 193.
8. These paragraphs draw on Jeff Wiltse, *Contested Waters: A Social History of Swimming Pools in America* (2007).
9. Wiltse, *Contested Waters,* at 93–94.
10. Wiltse, *Contested Waters,* at 182.
11. Social Security Administration, "Annual Statistical Supplement" (2017), www.ssa.gov/policy/docs/statcomps/supplement/2016/oasdi.html, and in particular table 5.B4, "Number, Percentage, and Average Monthly Benefit, by Year of Entitlement as Retired Worker and Sex, December 2016," https://www.ssa.gov/policy/docs/statcomps/supplement/2017/5b.html.
12. U.S. Bureau of the Census, Income and Poverty in the United States: 2017, Table 3, https://www.census.gov/content/census/en/library/publications/2018/demo/p60-265.html; Kathleen Romig & Arloc Sherman, "Social Security Keeps 27 Million Americans Out of Poverty," Center on Budget and Policy Priorities, Oct. 25, 2016, www.cbpp.org/research/social-security/social-security-keeps-22-million-americans-out-of-poverty-a-state-by-state.

13. Elisa A. Walker, Virginia P. Reno, & Thomas N. Bethell, "Americans Make Hard Choices on Social Security: A Survey with Trade-Off Analysis," National Institute for Social Insurance (Oct. 2014), www.nasi.org/sites/default/files/research/Americans_Make_Hard_Choices_on_Social_Security.pdf.
14. Social Security Works, "New Polling: Americans Are United in Support of Expanding Social Security" (Oct. 26, 2016), www.socialsecurityworks.org/2016/10/26/new-polling-americans-are-united-in-support-of-expanding-social-security; Social Security Works, "New Polling on Social Security, Medicare, and Prescription Drug Prices" (Mar. 16, 2018), www.socialsecurityworks.org/2018/03/16/new-polling-social-security.
15. Social Security Administration, "Benefits Planner: Life Expectancy," www.ssa.gov/planners/lifeexpectancy.html (last visited June 21, 2018); Michael J. Graetz & Jerry L. Mashaw, *True Security* 95–96 (1999).
16. Authors' calculations based on interest rates of 1 percent and 8 percent over thirty-five years.
17. EdwardJones.com (last visited June 21, 2018).
18. Carmen Castro-Pagan, "Edward Jones Hit with Second ERISA Lawsuit over 401(k) Fees," *Bloomberg News* (Nov. 15, 2016).
19. Olivier Armantier, Luis Armona, Giacomo De Giorgi, & Wilbert van der Klaauw, "Which Households Have Negative Wealth?," *Liberty Street Economics* (Aug. 1, 2016), http://libertystreeteconomics.newyorkfed.org/2016/08/which-households-have-negative-wealth.html.
20. Dora Costa, *The Evolution of Retirement* 128–130 (1998).
21. Budget of the U.S. Government, FY2018, Historical Tables, Table 1.1 (total budget outlays of $3.85 trillion for 2016) and Table 11.3 (expenditures on Social Security and railroad retirement of $919 billion for 2016), www.whitehouse.gov/omb/budget/Historicals.

22. Sahil Kapur, "Inside Paul Ryan's Plan to Privatize Social Security," *Talking Points Memo* (Aug. 14, 2012).
23. Anne L. Alstott, *A New Deal for Old Age* (2016).
24. Alicia H. Munnell, "Falling Short: The Coming Retirement Crisis and What to Do about It," Center for Retirement Research at Boston College, Paper 15-7 (April 2015), http://crr.bc.edu/wp-content/uploads/2015/04/IB_15-7_508.pdf.

6. Mixed Results in Education and Housing

1. Raymond V. Mariano, "The Failure of Public Housing: Temporary Help Has Become a Permanent Way of Life," *Huffington Post* (Nov. 10, 2015).
2. Pam Belluck, "End of a Ghetto: A Special Report; Razing the Slums to Rescue the Residents," *New York Times* (Sept. 6, 1998).
3. Ray Teixeira, "The Public Opinion Paradox: An Anatomy of America's Love-Hate Relationship with Its Government" 3–4, Center for American Progress (June 2010), https://cdn.americanprogress.org/wp-content/uploads/issues/2010/06/pdf/dww_public_opinion.pdf.
4. Shane J. Lopez, "Americans' Views of Public Schools Still Far Worse than Parents'," Gallup (Aug. 25, 2010), www.gallup.com/poll/142658/Americans-Views-Public-Schools-Far-Worse-Parents.aspx.
5. See, e.g., Robert Pear, "Reagan Proposes Vouchers to Give Poor a Choice of Schools," *New York Times* (Nov. 14, 1985); Amit R. Paley, "Bush Proposes Adding Private School Vouchers to 'No Child' Law," *Washington Post* (Jan. 25, 2007); Tad DeHaven, "Five Decades of Failure Is Enough," Cato Institute (Feb. 9, 2010), www.cato.org/publications/commentary/five-decades-failure-are-enough.
6. Dehaven, "Five Decades of Failure Is Enough."
7. National Commission on Excellence in Education, *A Nation at Risk* (1983), www2.ed.gov/pubs/NatAtRisk/risk.html.

8. U.S. Department of Education, National Center for Educational Statistics, "Public and Private School Comparison, Fast Facts," https://nces.ed.gov/fastfacts/display.asp?id=55.
9. See, e.g., Drew Desilver, "U.S. Students' Academic Achievement Still Lags That of Their Peers in Many Other Countries," Pew Research Center (Feb. 15, 2017), www.pewresearch.org/fact-tank/2017/02/15/u-s-students-internationally-math-science.
10. U.S. Bureau of the Census, "Household Income: 2015," table 2, www.census.gov/content/dam/Census/library/publications/2016/acs/acsbr15-02.pdf.
11. For an overview of the sources of residential segregation, see Richard Rothstein, "Why Our Schools Are Segregated," 70 *Education Leadership* 50 (May 2013).
12. For a discussion of the hybrid nature and wide range of charter schools, see James Forman Jr., "Do Charter Schools Threaten Public Education? Emerging Evidence from Fifteen Years of a Quasi-Market for Schooling," 2007 *University of Illinois Law Review* 839 (2007); Jeffrey R. Henig et al., The Influence of Founder Type on Charter School Structures and Operations," 111 *American Journal of Education* 487 (2005); Los Angeles Times, Graphic: Types of Charter Schools, Jan. 10, 2010, http://www.latimes.com/local/la-011010-me-charter_stats-g-graphic.html (describing types of charter schools and their relationship to the LA Unified School District).
13. Joshua Angrist et al., "Stand and Deliver: Effects of Boston's Charter High Schools on College Preparation, Entry, and Choice," 34 *Journal of Labor Economics* 275 (2016).
14. Kimberly Hefling, "Charter School Scandal Haunts John Kasich," *Politico* (Mar. 14, 2016).
15. ECOT, www.ecotohio.org (last visited June 21, 2018).
16. Patrick O'Donnell, "Dealing with E-Schools: Is the Drop from C Grades to F's for Online Schools Accurate?," *Cleveland Plain Dealer* (Sept. 28, 2015).
17. Patrick O'Donnell, "ECOT Attendance Inflated by 9,000 Students, Audit Finds; $60 Million in State Funding in Jeopardy," *Cleveland Plain Dealer* (Sept. 27, 2016).

18. Patrick O'Donnell, "Ohio Is the 'Wild, Wild West' of Charter Schools, Says National Group Promoting Charter Standards," *Cleveland Plain Dealer* (July 28, 2014).
19. Doug Livingston, "Charter Schools Misspend Millions of Ohio Dollars as Efforts to Police Them Are Privatized," *Akron Beacon-Journal* (May 30, 2015).
20. Jeff Bryant, "The Truth about Charter Schools: Padded Cells, Corruption, Lousy Instruction and Worse Results," *Salon* (Jan. 10, 2014).
21. National Center for Education Evaluation and Regional Assistance, "The Evaluation of Charter School Impacts: Final Report" (June 2010), https://ies.ed.gov/ncee/pubs/20104029; National Assessment of Educational Progress, "A Closer Look at Charter Schools Using Hierarchical Linear Modeling" (2006), https://nces.ed.gov/nationsreportcard/pdf/studies/2006460.pdf.
22. Martin Carnoy, "School Vouchers Are Not a Proven Strategy for Improving Student Achievement," Economic Policy Institute (Feb. 28, 2017), www.epi.org/publication/school-vouchers-are-not-a-proven-strategy-for-improving-student-achievement. Emphasis added.
23. Charles L. Edson, "Affordable Housing—An Intimate History," in *The Legal Guide to Affordable Housing Development* (Tim Iglesias & Rochelle E. Lento eds., 2d ed. 2011).
24. Alexander von Hoffman, "History Lessons for Today's Housing Policy: The Political Processes of Making Low-Income Housing Policy," Harvard University Joint Center for Housing Studies (Aug. 2012), www.jchs.harvard.edu/sites/jchs.harvard.edu/files/w12-5_von_hoffman.pdf.
25. Edson, "Affordable Housing," at 5.
26. National Center for Health in Public Housing, "Public Housing Residents," http://nchph.org/about/public-housing-residents (last visited June 21, 2018).
27. Alana Semuels, "The Power of Public Housing," *Atlantic* (Sept. 22, 2015).
28. U.S. Department of Housing and Urban Development, "HUD's Public Housing Program," https://portal.hud.gov/hudportal/HUD?src=/topics/rental_assistance/phprog.

29. "The State of the Nation's Housing 2018," at 30–31, Joint Center for Housing Studies of Harvard University, http://www.jchs.harvard .edu/state-nations-housing-2018.
30. "Demolition Begins on Last Cabrini-Green High Rise," CBS News (Mar. 30, 2011).
31. Nicholas Dagen Bloom, *Public Housing That Worked: New York in the Twentieth Century* (2009).
32. See Robert Collinson, Ingrid Gould Ellen, & Jens Ludwig, "Low-Income Housing Policy" 30, 33–34, NBER Working Paper 21071 (Apr. 2015).
33. See Janet Currie & Aaron Yelowitz, "Are Public Housing Projects Good for Kids?" 27 (July 1999), www.princeton.edu/~jcurrie /publications/Are_Public_Housing_ Projects.pdf.
34. As a rule of thumb, an eligible household is defined as any family making below 50 percent of area median income. See U.S. Department of Housing and Urban Development, "Worst Case Housing Needs: 2017 Report to Congress" (2015), 9–10, https://www.huduser.gov/portal/sites/default/files/pdf/Worst-Case -Housing-Needs.pdf.
35. Mireya Navarro, "227,000 Names on List Vie for Rare Vacancies in City's Public Housing," *New York Times* (July 23, 2013).
36. Collinson et al., "Low-Income Housing Policy," at 36.
37. Susan Popkin, "Public Housing and the Legacy of Segregation," Urban Institute (Aug. 19, 2013), www.urban.org/urban-wire/public -housing-and-legacy-segregation.
38. Collinson et al., "Low-Income Housing Policy," at 13–14.
39. Center on Budget and Policy Priorities, "Policy Basics: The Housing Choice Voucher Program" (May 3, 2017), www.cbpp.org/research /housing/policy-basics-the-housing-choice-voucher-program.
40. U.S. Department of Housing and Urban Development, "FY 2016 Income Limits," www.huduser.gov/portal/datasets/il/il16 /IncomeLimitsBriefingMaterial-FY16.pdf.
41. Collinson et al., "Low-Income Housing Policy," at 29–35, provides a helpful overview of these questions.

42. On the topic of extended wait lists, see Gillian B. White, "America's Invidious Eviction Problem," *Atlantic* (Mar. 1, 2016) (quoting Matthew Desmond as saying, "In cities like Washington D.C., the waiting list is not counted in years but in decades. Young mothers who apply for housing assistance in our nation's capital literally could be grandmothers by the time their application is reviewed").
43. Alex F. Schwartz, *Housing Policy in the United States* 241 (3rd ed. 2015). See also Ingrid Ellen, Michael Suher, & Gerald Torrats-Espinosa, "Neighbors and Networks: The Role of Social Interactions on the Residential Choices of Housing Choice Voucher Holders," *Journal of Housing Economics* (2018); Lisa Sanbonmatsu et al., U.S. Department of Housing and Urban Development, "Moving to Opportunity for Fair Housing Demonstration Program: Final Impacts Evaluation" xvi (2011), www.huduser.gov/publications/pdf/mtofhd_fullreport_v2.pdf (finding that HCV holders moved to less distressed neighborhoods than public housing but to only slightly less minority-centric neighborhoods); Michelle Wood et al., "Housing Affordability and Family Well-Being: Results from the Housing Voucher Evaluation," 19 *Housing Policy Debate* 367, 393–94 (2008) (finding that while voucher families moved to neighborhoods with "slightly lower rates of poverty" than a control group, "the differences in the neighborhoods of voucher users and those without vouchers . . . were not very large").
44. Matthew Desmond & Kristin L. Perkins, "Are Landlords Overcharging Housing Voucher Holders?," 15 *City and Community* 137 (2016); Robert Collinson & Peter Gaining, "How Do Changes in Housing Voucher Design Affect Rent and Neighborhood Quality?" (Feb. 2018), https://papers.ssrn.com/sol3/papers.cfm?abstract_id=2255799; Amy Cutts & Edgar Olsen, "Are Section 8 Housing Subsidies Too High?," 11 *Journal of Housing Economics* 214 (2002).
45. Laura Sullivan & Meg Anderson, "Affordable Housing Program Costs More, Shelters Fewer," National Public Radio (May 9, 2017).
46. Adam J. Levitin & Susan M. Wachter, "The Public Option in Housing Finance," 46 *University of California Davis Law Review* 1111 (2013).

47. Levitin & Wachter, "Public Option," at 1137.
48. See also Richard Rothstein, "Public Housing: Government-Sponsored Segregation," *American Prospect* (Oct. 11, 2012).
49. Raj Chetty, Nathaniel Hendren, & Lawrence Katz, "The Effects of Exposure to Better Neighborhoods on Children: New Evidence from the Moving to Opportunity Project," 106 *American Economics Review* (2016).
50. Kathryn Zickuhr, Lee Rainie, & Kristen Purcell, "Library Services in the Digital Age," Pew Internet (Jan. 22, 2013), http://libraries.pewinternet.org/2013/01/22/library-services.

7. Retirement

1. Benjamin W. Veghte, Elliot Schreur, & Alexandra L. Bradley (eds.), "Report to the New Leadership and the American People on Social Insurance and Inequality," National Academy of Social Insurance (Jan. 2017), Fig. 1, www.nasi.org/sites/default/files/research/Social_Security_and_Gap_in_Retirement_Wealth.pdf.
2. Alicia H. Munnell, "Falling Short: The Coming Retirement Crisis and What to Do about It," Center for Retirement Research at Boston College (Apr. 2015), http://crr.bc.edu/wp-content/uploads/2015/04/IB_15-7_508.pdf.
3. Social Security Administration, "Research Note #1: Origins of the Three-Legged Stool Metaphor for Social Security," www.ssa.gov/history/stool.html.
4. William J. Wiatrowski, "The Last Private Industry Pension Plans: A Visual Essay," *Monthly Labor Review* (Dec. 2012), www.bls.gov/opub/mlr/2012/12/art1full.pdf (data from 1981 to 2011).
5. Employee Benefit Research Institute, *EBRI Databook on Employee Benefits,* chapter 4 (July 2014), www.ebri.org/pdf/publications/books/databook/DB.Chapter%2004.pdf (table 4.4, showing real median income from employer pensions from 1975 to 2011).
6. Center for Retirement Research at Boston College, "Pension Sponsorship and Participation in the Private Sector, 1979–2010" (May 2013), http://crr.bc.edu/wp-content/uploads/1012/01/figure

-14.pdf, and "Workers with Pension Coverage by Type of Plan, 1983, 1992, 2001, and 2013" (Sept. 2014), http://crr.bc.edu/wp-content/uploads/1012/01/figure-15.pdf.

7. Alicia H. Munnell et al., "How Has the Shift to 401(k) Plans Affected Retirement Income?," Center for Retirement Research at Boston College (Mar. 2017), http://crr.bc.edu/briefs/how-has-the-shift-to-401k-plans-affected-retirement-income; Alicia H. Munnell, Dan Muldoon, & Francesca N. Golub-Sass, "An Update on 401(k) Plans: Insights from the 2007 SCF," Center for Retirement Research at Boston College (Mar. 2009), http://crr.bc.edu/briefs/an-update-on-401k-plans-insights-from-the-2007-scf; Edward N. Wolff, "Pensions: The Lost Decade?," NBER Working Paper No. 16991 (Apr. 2011), www.nber.org/papers/w16991.
8. Congressional Budget Office, "The Distribution of Major Tax Expenditures in the Individual Income Tax System" (May 2013), www.cbo.gov/publication/43768 ($92 billion of $140 billion tax savings).
9. *Frontline,* "Can You Afford to Retire?," interview with Alicia Munnell (Feb. 2006), www.pbs.org/wgbh/pages/frontline/retirement/interviews/munnell.html.
10. Alicia H. Munnell, Rebecca Cannon Fraenkel, & Josh Hurwitz, "The Pension Coverage Problem in the Private Sector," Center for Retirement Research at Boston College (Sept. 2012), http://crr.bc.edu/briefs/the-pension-coverage-problem-in-the-private-sector.
11. Munnell et al., "The Pension Coverage Problem."
12. Craig Copeland, "Employment-Based Retirement Plan Participation: Geographic Differences and Trends," EBRI Brief No. 405 (2013), 9–11, figures 1 and 2; Veghte et al., "Report to the New Leadership," figure 2 (showing that a typical white household has more than $100,000 in pension wealth, while a typical black household has only a tenth that much).
13. Bureau of Labor Statistics, "National Longitudinal Surveys, Frequently Asked Questions," www.bls.gov/nls/nlsfaqs.htm#anch41.

14. Example: the pension cost of changing jobs. Suppose that Alice earns a steady income of $50,000 per year. She works from age twenty-five to age sixty-five, and she saves a steady 5 percent of her income for retirement. Assuming an interest rate of 5 percent and investment fees of 1 percent, Alice would accumulate about $238,000 in her retirement account. Now suppose that Alice spends ten years of her career (between ages thirty-five and forty-five) working for small firms that don't offer pensions (changing jobs a few times over the course of a number of years is a typical pattern). The cost to her is pretty high: she loses ten years' worth of pension contributions. The result is that she will have just $172,000 or so at retirement—about 25 percent less than what steady contributions would produce.
15. Internal Revenue Service, Publication 590-A (2016), "Contributions to Individual Retirement Arrangements (IRAs)," www.irs.gov/publications/p590a/ch01.html#en_US_2016_publink1000230352.
16. Center for Retirement Research at Boston College, "Workers with Pension Coverage by Type of Plan, 1983, 1992, 2001, and 2013" (Sept. 2014), http://crr.bc.edu/wp-content/uploads/1012/01/figure-15.pdf.
17. Andrew Beattie, "Market Crashes: The Dotcom Crash (2000–2002)," Investopedia, www.investopedia.com/features/crashes/crashes8.asp; Christian Weller, "What the Market Crash Means for Your Retirement," EPI Report (May 2001), www.epi.org/publication/issuebriefs_ib156.
18. Employee Benefit Research Institute, "The Impact of the Recent Financial Crisis on 401(k) balances," EBRI Issue Brief #326 (Feb. 2009), www.ebri.org/publications/ib/?fa=ibDisp&content_id=4192.
19. Center for Retirement Research at Boston College, "401(k)/IRA Balances for Median Working Household with a 401(k), Age 55–64, by Income Quintile, 2013" (Sept. 2014), http://crr.bc.edu/wp-content/uploads/1012/01/Table-161.pdf.

20. The standard rule (which may now be too generous, overstating potential retirement income), is that a retiree can safely withdraw 4 percent of her lump sum per year. Tara S. Bernard, "Some New Math for the Four Percent Rule," *New York Times* (May 9, 2015).
21. Ian Ayres and Quinn Curtis, "Beyond Diversification: The Pervasive Problem of Excessive Fees and 'Dominated Funds' in 401(k) Plans," 124 *Yale Law Journal* 1346 (2015).
22. Authors' calculations, assuming a 5 percent rate of return before fees.
23. Stan Haithcock, "You Just Gave Your Annuity Agent a Great Vacation," *MarketWatch* (Aug. 12, 2014); Office of Senator Elizabeth Warren, "Villas, Castles, and Vacations: How Perks and Giveaways Create Conflicts of Interest in the Annuities Industry" (Oct. 2015).
24. U.S. Department of Labor, Employee Benefits Security Administration, "Definition of the Term "Fiduciary"; Conflict of Interest Rule—Retirement Investment Advice," Final Rule (Apr. 8, 2016), www.federalregister.gov/documents/2016/04/08/2016-07924/definition-of-the-term-fiduciary-conflict-of-interest-rule-retirement-investment-advice.
25. Presidential Memorandum on Fiduciary Duty Rule (Feb. 3, 2017), www.whitehouse.gov/the-press-office/2017/02/03/presidential-memorandum-fiduciary-duty-rule.
26. Steven A. Sass, "How Can We Realize the Value That Annuities Offer in a 401(k) World?," Center for Retirement Research at Boston College (July 2016), http://crr.bc.edu/wp-content/uploads/2016/07/IB_16-12.pdf.
27. For example, see David Laibson, "Golden Eggs and Hyperbolic Discounting," 112 *Quarterly Journal of Economics* 443 (1997).
28. See Nathan Zahm & John Ameriks, "Estimating Internal Rates of Return on Income Annuities," Vanguard (Mar. 2012), https://personal.vanguard.com/pdf/s284.pdf (finding that rates of return on Vanguard annuities are, for the average purchaser age seventy or older, lower than the rates of return on risk-free Treasury securities).

29. Thrift Savings Plan, "Administrative Expenses," www.tsp.gov /PlanParticipation/BeneficiaryParticipants/administrativeExpenses.html.
30. A standard annuity rule of thumb is 4 percent. Bernard, "Some New Math for the Four Percent Rule."
31. Joint Committee on Taxation, "Estimates of Federal Tax Expenditures for Fiscal Years 2016–2020," JCX-3-17, www.jct.gov/publications .html?func=startdown&id=4971.
32. C. Eugene Steuerle et al., "Who Benefits from Asset-Building Tax Subsidies?," Urban Institute (Sept. 2014), www.urban.org/sites /default/files/alfresco/publication-pdfs/413241-Who-Benefits-from -Asset-Building-Tax-Subsidies-.PDF.
33. See, e.g., Theresa Ghilarducci & Tony James, "A Comprehensive Plan to Confront the Retirement Savings Crisis" 2, Schwartz Center for Economic Research (2016), www.economicpolicyresearch.org /images/Retirement_Project/Retirement_Security_Guarant eed _digital.pdf; see generally Theresa Ghilarducci & Tony James; *Rescuing Retirement: A Plan to Guarantee Retirement Security for All Americans* (2016); Rowland Davis, Nayla Kazzi, & David Madland, "The Promise and Peril of a Model 401(k) Plan," Center for American Progress (Apr. 2010), www.americanprogressaction.org /wp-content/uploads/issues/2010/04/pdf/401k.pdf.
34. National Employment Savings Trust, www.nestpensions.org.uk /schemeweb/nest.html.
35. National Employment Savings Trust, www.nestpensions.org.uk /schemeweb/nest.html.
36. CalSavers Retirement Savings Program, "CalSavers Is Coming Soon," www.treasurer.ca.gov/scib.
37. Richard Thaler & Cass Sunstein, *Nudge* 111–115 (2008).
38. For instance, some employers resisted advance payment of the EITC, which was in theory mandatory but in practice optional. Steve Holt, "Periodic Payment of the Earned Income Tax Credit Revisited," Brookings Institution (Sept. 2015), app. 4–5, www.brookings.edu /wp-content/uploads/2016/07/HoltPeriodicPaymentEITC121515 .pdf.

8. Higher Education

1. PBS *Frontline,* "A Subprime Education" (Sept. 13, 2016), www.pbs.org/wgbh/frontline/film/a-subprime-education (at 1:00 and 17:05); Annie Waldman, "How Corinthian Colleges Targeted the Homeless and Kids with Low Self-Esteem," ProPublica (Mar. 18, 2016), www.valuewalk.com/2016/03/corinthian-colleges-explotation#document/p3/a283694 (original documents).
2. Waldman, "How Corinthian Colleges Targeted."
3. PBS *Frontline,* "A Subprime Education."
4. David Baime & Sandy Baum, "Community Colleges: Multiple Missions, Diverse Student Bodies, and a Range of Policy Solutions," Urban Institute (Aug. 17, 2016), www.urban.org/research/publication/community-colleges-multiple-missions-diverse-student-bodies-and-range-policy-solutions/view/full_report.
5. Suzanne Mettler, *Degrees of Inequality: How the Politics of Higher Education Sabotaged the American Dream* 6 (2014).
6. Mettler, *Degrees of Inequality,* at 81.
7. For a full discussion of state funding cuts and tuition increases, see Michael Mitchell et al., "Funding Down, Tuition Up," Center for Budget and Policy Priorities (Aug. 15, 2016), www.cbpp.org/research/state-budget-and-tax/funding-down-tuition-up.
8. Mettler, *Degrees of Inequality,* at 11.
9. Mettler, *Degrees of Inequality,* at 11.
10. Mitchell et al., "Funding Down, Tuition Up."
11. Ashley A. Smith, "Zeroed Out in Arizona," *Inside Higher Ed* (Mar. 12, 2015).
12. Mettler, *Degrees of Inequality,* at 10.
13. Jillian Berman, "Student Debt Just Hit $1.5 Trillion," *MarketWatch* (May 12, 2018), https://www.marketwatch.com/story/student-debt-just-hit-15-trillion-2018-05-08.
14. Mettler, *Degrees of Inequality,* at 81.
15. Bridget Terry Long, "The Impact of Federal Tax Credits for Higher Education Expenses," in *College Choices: The Economics of Where to Go, When to Go, and How to Pay for It* (Caroline L. Hoxby ed., 2004).

16. United States Senate Committee on Health, Education, Labor, and Pensions, "For Profit Higher Education: The Failure to Safeguard the Federal Investment and Ensure Student Success" 2 (July 30, 2012), www.help.senate.gov/imo/media/for_profit_report/PartI.pdf (hereinafter Senate Committee).
17. Gregory D. Kutz, "GAO Testimony, For-Profit College: Undercover Testing Finds Colleges Encouraged Fraud and Engaged in Deceptive and Questionable Marketing Practices" 11 (Aug. 4, 2010), www.gao.gov/new.items/d10948t.pdf (hereinafter GAO).
18. GAO, at 10 ("A small beauty college told our applicant that barbers can earn $150,000 to $250,000 a year. While this may be true in exceptional circumstances, the Bureau of Labor Statistics (BLS) reports that 90 percent of barbers make less than $43,000 a year").
19. GAO, at 15–16.
20. GAO, at 7.
21. Mettler, *Degrees of Inequality,* at 164.
22. PBS *Frontline,* "A Subprime Education" (at 8:30–8:45).
23. Mettler, *Degrees of Inequality,* at 164.
24. Hollister K. Petraeus, "For-Profit Colleges, Vulnerable G.I.'s," *New York Times* (Sept. 21, 2011).
25. GAO, at 17.
26. GAO, at 17.
27. Senate Committee, at 7.
28. Senate Committee, at 8; Adam Looney & Constantine Yannelis, "A Crisis in Student Loans? How Changes in Characteristics of Borrowers and in the Institutions They Attended Contributed to Rising Loan Defaults," Brookings Papers on Economic Activity (Sept. 10–11, 2015), www.brookings.edu/wp-content/uploads/2016/07/ConferenceDraft_LooneyYannelis_StudentLoanDefaults.pdf.
29. PBS *Frontline,* "A Subprime Education" (starting at 8:47; also 15:15).
30. Senate Committee, at 2, 5.
31. Coy F. Cross II, *Justin Smith Morrill: Father of the Land-Grant Colleges* 84 (1999).
32. Allan Nevins, *The State Universities and Democracy* 16–17 (1962).

33. Pew Research, "The Rising Cost of Not Going to College" (Feb. 11, 2014).
34. National Center for Education Statistics, "Fast Facts: Graduation Rates," https://nces.ed.gov/fastfacts/display.asp?id=40 (last visited Oct. 21, 2018). According to the U.S. Department of Education, for full-time students starting a four-year undergraduate bachelor's program in 2010, the six-year graduation rate was 59 percent at public universities, 66 percent at private nonprofits, and only 26 percent at private for-profits.
35. Tennessee Promise, http://tnpromise.gov/about.shtml.
36. Tennessee Reconnect, www.tn.gov/thec/bureaus/academic-affairs-and-student-success/adult-learner-initiatives/tn-reconnect.html.
37. Executive Office of the President, "America's College Promise: A Progress Report on Free Community College" 5 (Sept. 2015), www.acct.org/files/Advocacy/Progress%2BReport%2Bon%2BCommunity%2BCollege.pdf.
38. White House, "Factsheet: White House Unveils America's College Promise Proposal: Tuition-Free Community College for Responsible Students" (Jan. 9, 2015), https://obamawhitehouse.archives.gov/the-press-office/2015/01/09/fact-sheet-white-house-unveils-america-s-college-promise-proposal-tuitio; Baime & Baum, "Community Colleges."
39. College for All Act, S. 1373, 114th Congress (2015–2016), www.congress.gov/bill/114th-congress/senate-bill/1373/text; Fact Sheet, The College for All Act, https://www.sanders.senate.gov/download/the-college-for-all-act-fact-sheet?id=A2524A5A-CA3F-41F8-8D93-DD10813DC384&download=1&inline=file.
40. John Quincy Adams, Message to Congress (Dec. 6, 1825), www.presidency.ucsb.edu/ws/index.php?pid=29467.
41. George Thomas, *The Founders and the Idea of a National University: Constituting the American Mind* 21 (2014).
42. Albert Castel, "The Founding Fathers and the Vision of a National University," 4 *History of Education Quarterly* 280, 280, 282–83 (1964).
43. Thomas, *Founders and the Idea of a National University,* at 3.

44. Thomas, *Founders and the Idea of a National University,* at 73.
45. See, for instance, University of Connecticut, eCampus, http://ecampus.uconn.edu/courses.html.

9. Banking

1. The classic on fringe banking is John P. Caskey, *Fringe Banking: Check-Cashing Outlets, Pawnshops, and the Poor* (1994). For a more recent account on the unbanked and underbanked, see Lisa Servon, *The Unbanking of America* (2017).
2. Federal Deposit Insurance Corporation, "2015 FDIC National Survey of Unbanked and Underbanked Households" 1 (Oct. 20, 2016), www.fdic.gov/householdsurvey/2015/2015report.pdf (hereinafter FDIC 2015).
3. For a discussion of these avenues, see Mehrsa Baradaran, *How the Other Half Banks: Exclusion, Exploitation, and the Threat to Democracy* 64–101 (2015).
4. Caskey, *Fringe Banking,* at 27–30.
5. Caskey, *Fringe Banking,* at 36.
6. Caskey, *Fringe Banking,* at 87–88.
7. Caskey, *Fringe Banking,* at 89.
8. Caskey, *Fringe Banking,* at 88–89.
9. Caskey, *Fringe Banking,* at 97–100.
10. Caskey, *Fringe Banking,* at 86–87 (noting the increase in households without bank accounts rising from 6.5 million in 1977 to 11.5 million in 1989).
11. FDIC 2015, at 3.
12. FDIC 2015, at 4.
13. Baradaran, *Other Half,* at 142–43.
14. Baradaran, *Other Half,* at 143.
15. FDIC 2015, at 9, 34.
16. FDIC 2015, at 7.
17. FDIC 2015, at 52.
18. Baradaran, *Other Half,* at 174–75.

19. Council of Economic Advisers, "Issue Brief: Financial Inclusion in the United States" 2 (June 2016), https://obamawhitehouse.archives.gov/sites/default/files/docs/20160610_financial_inclusion_cea_issue_brief.pdf. Baradaran, *Other Half,* at 138 (suggesting it might be as much as 10 percent).
20. Baradaran, *Other Half,* at 138.
21. Council of Economic Advisers, "Issue Brief," at 2.
22. Caskey, *Fringe Banking,* at 32.
23. Alan M. White, "Banks as Utilities," 90 *Tulsa Law Review* 1241, 1268–1269 (2016).
24. Mehrsa Baradaran, "Banking and the Social Contract," 89 *Notre Dame Law Review* 1283, 1286 (2014). For a public utility framing that stresses a similar point, see White, "Banks as Utilities," at 1270. ("If we regard banks as public utilities providing essential services, then the present model of banking regulation, with a primary focus on safety and soundness and a secondary focus on consumer protection and community reinvestment, is built on an incomplete set of public goals.")
25. John Anderson, "Why Canada Needs Postal Banking" 28–29, Canadian Centre for Policy Alternatives (Oct. 2013), policyalternatives.ca/sites/default/files/uploads/publications/National%20Office/2013/10/Why_Canada_Needs_PostalBanking.pdf. Canada's system ended in 1968.
26. Anderson, "Why Canada Needs Postal Banking," at 43–44.
27. Anderson, "Why Canada Needs Postal Banking," at 53–55.
28. Maureen O'Hara & David Easley, "The Postal Savings System in the Depression," 39 *Journal of Economic History,* 741, 742 (1979); Edwin W. Kemmerer, *Postal Savings* 2 (1917).
29. Kemmerer, *Postal Savings,* at 10–11.
30. United States Postal Service (USPS), "Postal Savings System" 1, https://about.usps.com/who-we-are/postal-history/postal-savings-system.pdf (hereinafter USPS).
31. USPS, at 1.
32. USPS, at 2.

33. Mehrsa Baradaran, "A Short History of Postal Banking," *Slate* (Aug. 18, 2014).
34. Office of Inspector General, U.S. Postal Service, "Providing Non-Bank Financial Services for the Underserved" 5 (Jan. 27, 2014), www.uspsoig.gov/sites/default/files/document-library-files/2015/rarc-wp-14-007_0.pdf (citing Nelson D. Schwartz, "Bank Closings Tilt Toward Poor Areas," *New York Times* (Feb. 22, 2011), and David Hayes et al., "Banks Follow the Money and Exit Lower-Income Areas," SNL Financial (Apr. 27, 2012), http://www.snl.com/InteractiveX/ArticleAbstract.aspx?id=14485078).
35. Office of Inspector General, "Providing Non-Bank Financial Services," at 6.
36. Baradaran, *Other Half,* at 210–227; Elizabeth Warren, "Coming to a Post Office near You: Loans You Can Trust?," *Huffington Post* (Feb. 1, 2014).
37. Matthew Yglesias, "A Public Option for Banking," *ThinkProgress* (Jan. 16, 2011); Catherine Martin Christopher, "Mobile Banking: The Answer for the Unbanked in America?," 65 *Catholic University Law Review* 221 (2015).
38. Pew Research Center, "Mobile Fact Sheet" (Jan. 12, 2017), www.pewinternet.org/fact-sheet/mobile.
39. Morgan Ricks, John Crawford, & Lev Menand, "Central Banking for All: A Public Option for Bank Accounts," Great Democracy Initiative (June 2018).
40. Morgan Ricks, "Money as Infrastructure" (draft of May 30, 2018), https://papers.ssrn.com/sol3/papers.cfm?abstract_id=3070270); White, "Banks as Utilities."
41. Adam Levitin, "The Public Option in Banking," CreditSlips (Feb. 4, 2014), www.creditslips.org/creditslips/2014/02/the-public-option-in-banking.html.
42. Pew, "Payday Lending in America: Who Borrows, Where they Borrow, and Why" 4 (July 2012), www.pewtrusts.org/~/media/legacy/uploadedfiles/pcs_assets/2012/pewpaydaylendingreportpdf.pdf.
43. Council of Economic Advisers, "Issue Brief," at 5.

44. Pew, "Who Borrows," at 7.
45. Office of Inspector General, "Providing Non-Bank Financial Services," at 13.
46. Anderson, "Why Canada Needs Postal Banking."
47. Mehrsa Baradaran, "It's Time for Postal Banking," 127 *Harvard Law Review Forum* 165, 165 n. 6 (2014) (citing Michael Barbaro, "Bankers Oppose Wal-Mart as Rival," *New York Times* [Oct. 15, 2005]).
48. Office of Inspector General, "Providing Non-Bank Financial Services," at 14–15.

10. Child Care

1. U.S. Bureau of the Census, "Child Care: An Important Part of American Life" (2013), www.census.gov/library/visualizations/2013/comm/child_care.html.
2. Elise Gold & Tanyell Cooke, "High-Quality Child Care Is Out of Reach for Working Families," Economic Policy Institute (2015), www.epi.org/publication/child-care-affordability.
3. Beth Mattingly & Andrew Shaefer, "Child Care Costs Exceed Ten Percent of Family Income for One in Four Families," University of New Hampshire Carsey School of Public Policy, Nov. 10, 2016, https://carsey.unh.edu/publication/child-care-costs.
4. Rachel Nania, "Child Care Shortage: Baby Boom, Operating Costs Lead to Waiting Lists," WTOP (Feb. 13, 2017), http://wtop.com/parenting/2017/02/child-care-shortage-baby-boom-operating-costs-lead-to-waiting-lists.
5. Nania, "Child Care Shortage."
6. Jamie Hansen, "Families Face Shortage of Child Care Options in Sonoma County," *Press Democrat* (July 21, 2015), www.pressdemocrat.com/news/4230795-181/familes-face-shortage-of-child?artslide=0; Marnie Werner, "A Quiet Crisis: Minnesota's Child Care Shortage," RuralMN.org (2016), www.ruralmn.org/a-quiet-crisis-minnesotas-child-care-shortage.
7. See NICHD, *The NICHD Study of Early Child Care and Youth Development, Results for Children up to Age 4 ½ Years* (2006), www

.nichd.nih.gov/publications/pubs/documents/seccyd_06.pdf; Deborah Lowe Vandell & Barbara Wolfe, "Child Care Quality: Does It Matter and Does It Need to Be Improved?," report to the U.S. Department of Health and Human Services (2000), https://aspe.hhs.gov/report/child-care-quality-does-it-matter-and-does-it-need-be-improved-full-report; Margaret R. Burchinai & Debby Cryer, "Diversity, Child Care Quality, and Developmental Outcomes," 18 *Early Childhood Research Quarterly* 401 (2003); Tran D. Keys et al., "Preschool Center Quality and School Readiness: Quality Effects and Variation by Demographic and Child Characteristics," 84 *Child Development* 1171 (2013).

8. NICHD, *The NICHD Study of Early Child Care and Youth Development,* at 11.
9. See, for example, Kim Parker & Wendy Wang, "Modern Parenthood: Roles of Moms and Dads Converge as They Balance Work and Family," Pew Research Center (2013), www.pewsocialtrends.org/2013/03/14/modern-parenthood-roles-of-moms-and-dads-converge-as-they-balance-work-and-family; Lyn Craig, "Does Father Care Mean Fathers Share? A Comparison of How Mothers and Fathers in Intact Families Spend Time with Children," 20 *Gender and Society* 259 (2006).
10. Deborah Phillips et al., "The Early Care and Education Workforce," 26 *The Future of Children* 139 (2016).
11. U.S. Department of Labor, Bureau of Labor Statistics, "Usual Weekly Earnings Summary" (Apr. 18, 2017), www.bls.gov/news.release/wkyeng.nr0.htm.
12. Roberta Weber, "Understanding Parents' Child Care Decision-Making: A Foundation for Policy Making," OPRE Research-to-Policy, Research-to-Practice Brief, Office of Planning, Research and Evaluation, Administration for Children and Families, U.S. Department of Health and Human Services (2011–2012); Suzanne W. Helburn & Carollee Howes, "Child Care Cost and Quality," 6 *Future of Children* 62 (1996); Joe Neel, "NPR Poll: Are Parents Overrating the Quality of Child Care?," National Public Radio

(Oct. 17, 2016); Jennifer Cleveland, Amy Susman-Stillman, & Tamara Halle, "Parental Perceptions of Quality in Early Childhood Education," Child Trends (Nov. 2013), www.childtrends.org/wp-content/uploads/2013/12/2013-44ParentalPerceptionsofQuality.pdf; Naci H. Mocan, "Can Consumers Detect Lemons? Information Asymmetry in the Market for Child Care," NBER Working Paper No. w8291 (May 2001), https://ssrn.com/abstract=269541.

13. Rebecca M. Ryan et al., "The Impact of Child Care Subsidy Use on Child Care Quality," 26 *Early Childhood Research Quarterly* 320 (2011).
14. Child Care Aware of America, "Parents and the High Cost of Child Care" 21 (2016), www.bls.gov/news.release/wkyeng.nr0.htm.
15. Lily L. Batchelder, "Taxing the Poor: Income Averaging Reconsidered," 40 *Harvard Journal on Legislation* 395 (2003).
16. On the difficulty of measuring income in a timely fashion, see Anne L. Alstott, "The Earned Income Tax Credit and the Limitations of Tax-Based Welfare Reform," 108 *Harvard Law Review* 533 (1995); on the volatility of earnings for low earners and the resulting difficulties in designing income-tested programs, see Batchelder, "Taxing the Poor."
17. Grecia Marrufo, Margaret O'Brien-Strain, & Helen Oliver, "Child Care Price Dynamics in California," Public Policy Institute of California (2003), www.ppic.org/content/pubs/report/R_1203GMR.pdf.
18. "Fact Sheet: Donald J. Trump's New Child Care Plan," https://assets.donaldjtrump.com/CHILD_CARE_FACT_SHEET.pdf.
19. For an analysis of the Trump plan, see Lily L. Batchelder et al., "Who Benefits from President Trump's Child Care Proposals?," Tax Policy Center (2017), www.taxpolicycenter.org/publications/who-benefits-president-trumps-child-care-proposals/full.
20. Child Care Aware of America, "Parents and the High Cost of Child Care," at 36.
21. S. Heather Duncan, "Operators: State Subsidy Drives Families into Low-Quality Day Care," Macon, GA, *Telegraph* (Aug. 23, 2010).

22. Ann Hardie, "Study: Many Child Care Centers Low-Quality," *Atlanta Journal-Constitution* (July 4, 2010).
23. See, for example, Vicki Peyton et al., "Reasons for Choosing Child Care: Associations with Family Factors, Quality, and Satisfaction," 16 *Early Childhood Research Quarterly* 191 (2001).
24. For a discussion of this dynamic in the context of child care vouchers, see Chris Herbst, "Obama's Early Education Proposals Leave Federal Efforts Fragmented and Incoherent," Brookings Institution (2013), www.brookings.edu/research/obamas-early-education-proposals-leave-federal-efforts-fragmented-and-incoherent.
25. Joint Committee on Taxation, "Estimates of Federal Tax Expenditures for Fiscal Years 2016–2020" 37 (2017), www.jct.gov/publications.html?func=startdown&id=4971. In addition to the dependent care tax credit, the federal government and the states spend about $8 billion per year to subsidize child care for low-income families, including welfare recipients. U.S. Department of Health and Human Services, Office of Child Care, "FY2015 CCDF Expenditures by State," www.acf.hhs.gov/occ/resource/fy-2015-ccdf-table-4a. The program, called the Child Care Development Fund, offers a block grant to the states, which have wide latitude to spend the money as they choose. But the CCDF doesn't provide guaranteed access to care, and state eligibility standards vary widely.
26. Joint Committee on Taxation, "Estimates of Federal Tax Expenditures," at 46.
27. Treas. Reg. Section 1.21–1(e)(2).
28. Tax Policy Center, "Reforming the Child and Dependent Care Tax Credit" (2007), www.taxpolicycenter.org/publications/reforming-child-and-dependent-care-tax-credit; Katie Hamm & Carmel Martin, "A New Vision for Child Care in the United States," Center for American Progress (2015), www.americanprogress.org/issues/early-childhood/reports/2015/09/02/119944/a-new-vision-for-child-care-in-the-united-states-3.

29. James P. Ziliak, "Supporting Low-Income Workers Through Refundable Child-Care Credits," Brookings Institution (2014), www.brookings.edu/research/supporting-low-income-workers-through-refundable-child-care-credits.
30. Afterschool Alliance, "America after 3 pm: Afterschool Programs in Demand" (2014), www.afterschoolalliance.org/documents/AA3PM-2014/AA3PM_Key_Findings.pdf.
31. National Education Association, "Research Spotlight on Year-Round Education," www.nea.org/tools/17057.htm.
32. For example, see Cynthia G. Brown et al., "Investing in Our Children, A Plan to Expand Access to Preschool and Child Care," Center for American Progress (2013), www.americanprogress.org/issues/education/reports/2013/02/07/52071/investing-in-our-children.
33. See Allison Friedman-Krauss, Steven Barnett, & Milagros Nores, "How Much Can High-Quality Pre-K Reduce Achievement Gaps?," Center for American Progress (2016), appendix B, https://cdn.americanprogress.org/wp-content/uploads/2016/04/01115656/NIEER-AchievementGaps-report.pdf.
34. Friedman-Krauss et al., "How Much Can High Quality Pre-K," appendix B.
35. Friedman-Krauss et al., "How Much Can High Quality Pre-K."
36. Ministère de l'Éducation Nationale, "L'école maternelle," www.education.gouv.fr/cid166/l-ecole-maternelle-organisation-programme-et-fonctionnement.html.
37. Pamela Druckerman, "Catching Up with France on Day Care," *New York Times* (Aug. 13, 2013).
38. Mairie de Paris, "Crèches Municipales," www.paris.fr/creches.
39. OECD, "Public Spending on Childcare and Early Education," http://www.oecd.org/els/soc/PF3_1_Public_spending_on_childcare_and_early_education.pdf.
40. Timothy Bartik et al., "A Benefit-Cost Analysis of the Tulsa Universal Pre-K Program," Georgetown University Center for

Research on Children in the United States (2016), https://papers.ssrn.com/sol3/papers.cfm?abstract_id=2830528.

41. RAND Corporation Research Briefs, "The Costs and Benefits of Universal Preschool in California" (2005), www.rand.org/pubs/research_briefs/RB9118/index1.html.
42. James J. Heckman, "Schools, Skills, and Synapses" (2008), https://heckmanequation.org/assets/2017/01/Schools_Skills_Synapsis.pdf.
43. John M. Love et al., "The Effectiveness of Early Head Start for 3-Year-Old Children and Their Parents: Lessons for Policy and Programs," 41 *Developmental Psychology* 6 (2005).
44. Gosta Esping-Andersen et al., "Child Care and School Performance in Denmark and the United States," 34 *Child and Youth Services Review* 576 (2012).
45. Latosha Floyd & Deborah A. Phillips, "Child Care and Other Support Programs," 23 *Future of Children* 79 (2013).
46. Darcy Ann Olsen, "Universal Preschool Is No Golden Ticket," Cato Policy Analysis (1999), https://object.cato.org/sites/cato.org/files/pubs/pdf/pa333.pdf.
47. Pedro Carneiro & Rita Ginja, "Long-Term Impacts of Compensatory Preschool on Health and Behavior: Evidence from Head Start," 6 *American Economic Journal: Economic Policy* 4 (2014).
48. David Blau, "Child Care Subsidy Programs," in *Means-Tested Transfer Programs* (Robert A. Moffitt ed., 2003); Marianne P. Bitler, Hilary W. Hoynes, & Thurston Domina, "Experimental Evidence on Distributional Effects of Head Start," NBER Working Paper No. 20434 (2014), www.nber.org/papers/w20434.pdf.
49. Jorge Luis Garcia, James J. Heckman, Duncan Ermini Leif, & Maria Jose Prados, "Quantifying the Life-Cycle Benefits of a Prototypical Early Childhood Program" (2017), https://heckmanequation.org/assets/2017/12/abc_comprehensivecba_JPE-SUBMISSION_2017-05-26a_sjs_sjs.pdf; Christopher Ruhm and Jane Waldfogel, "Long-Term Effects of Early Childhood Care and Education," IZA Discussion Paper No. 6149 (2011), https://papers.ssrn.com/sol3/papers.cfm?abstract_id=1968100.

11. Health Care

1. Robert Pear, Thomas Kaplan, & Emily Cochrane, "Health Care Debate: Obamacare Repeal Fails as McCain Casts Decisive No Vote," *New York Times* (July 27, 2017) (noting the 15 million that would lose insurance from the "skinny" repeal).
2. Mark Singer, "John McCain's Health Care Vote Was an Act of Defiance," *New Yorker* (July 28, 2017).
3. Ezekiel J. Emanuel, *Reinventing American Health Care* 27–30 (2014).
4. Emanuel, *Reinventing,* at 30–31.
5. Emanuel, *Reinventing,* at 31.
6. Paul Starr, *Remedy and Reaction: The Peculiar American Struggle over Health Reform* 42 (rev. ed. 2013).
7. Starr, *Remedy and Reaction,* at 19.
8. Joint Committee on Taxation, "Federal Tax Expenditures for Fiscal Years 2016–2020," JCX-3-17, at 37 (January 30, 2017), www.jct.gov/publications.html?func=download&id=4971&chk=4971&no_html=1.
9. Starr, *Remedy and Reaction,* at 19, 42.
10. Starr, *Remedy and Reaction,* at 44–45.
11. Starr, *Remedy and Reaction,* at 46; Emanuel, *Reinventing,* at 47, 207.
12. Starr, *Remedy and Reaction,* at 18–19.
13. Emanuel, *Reinventing,* at 35. On the Rubik's Cube, see James C. Robinson, "The Health Care Rubik's Cube," 27 *Health Affairs* 619 (2008).
14. Starr, *Remedy and Reaction,* at 177.
15. Helen A. Halpin & Peter Harbage, "The Origins and Demise of the Public Option," 29 *Health Affairs* 1117, 1118 (June 2010).
16. Jacob S. Hacker, "Medicare Plus: Increasing Health Coverage by Expanding Medicare," in *Covering America: Real Remedies for the Uninsured* (2001).
17. Jacob S. Hacker, "Health Care for America," EPI Briefing Paper #180 (Jan. 11, 2007), www.sharedprosperity.org/bp180.html.
18. Halpin & Harbage, "Origins and Demise," at 1118.

19. Mark Schmitt, "The History of the Public Option," *American Prospect* (Aug. 18, 2009).
20. Halpin & Harbage, "Origins and Demise," at 1119.
21. Halpin & Harbage, "Origins and Demise," at 1119.
22. Starr, *Remedy and Reaction,* at 23.
23. Jennifer Steinhauer, "House Votes to Send Law to Repeal Health Law to Obama's Desk," *New York Times* (Jan. 6, 2016).
24. Starr, *Remedy and Reaction,* at 218.
25. Jacob S. Hacker, "There's a Simple Fix for Obamacare's Current Woes: The Public Option," *Vox* (Aug. 18, 2016).
26. Scott Lemieux, "Public Option Would Fix Health Insurance Marketplace," *American Prospect* (Aug. 24, 2016); Jonathan Cohn, "Aetna CEO Threatened Obamacare Pullout if Feds Opposed Humana Merger," *Huffington Post* (Aug. 17, 2016).
27. Hacker, "Simple Fix."
28. Hacker, "Simple Fix."
29. Nicholas Bagley, "Medicine as a Public Calling," 114 *Michigan Law Review* 57 (2015).
30. Barack Obama, "United States Health Care Reform: Progress to Date and Next Steps," *Journal of the American Medical Association* (Aug. 2, 2016).
31. Emanuel, *Reinventing,* at 44
32. Nancy LeTourneau, "Democratic Ideas on How to Improve Health Care Are Complicated Too," *Washington Monthly* (Mar. 27, 2017).
33. LeTourneau, "Democratic Ideas."
34. Starr, *Remedy and Reaction,* at 226.
35. Madeline Conway, "Trump: 'Nobody Knew That Health Care Could Be So Complicated,'" *Politico* (Feb. 27, 2017).

12. And More

1. Federal Communications Commission, "2016 Broadband Progress Report" (Jan. 29, 2016), www.fcc.gov/reports-research/reports/broadband-progress-reports/2016-broadband-progress-report.

2. Mariam Baksh, "Municipalities Dream Big on Broadband," *American Prospect* (Aug. 19, 2016).
3. Federal Communications Commission, "Internet Access Services: Status as of June 30, 2016" (Apr. 2017), http://transition.fcc.gov/Daily_Releases/Daily_Business/2017/db0503/DOC-344499A1.pdf.
4. Michael B. Sauter & Samuel Stebbins, "America's Most Hated Companies," *24 / 7 Wall St.* (Jan. 10, 2017), http://247wallst.com/special-report/2017/01/10/americas-most-hated-companies-4; Alexander E. M. Hess & Douglas A. McIntyre, "America's Most Hated Companies," *24 / 7 Wall St.* (Jan. 14, 2015), http://247wallst.com/special-report/2015/01/14/americas-most-hated-companies/4.
5. Nick Russo, Danielle Kehl, Robert Morgus, & Sarah Morris, "The Cost of Connectivity 2014," New America Foundation, fig. 3 (Oct. 30, 2014), www.newamerica.org/oti/policy-papers/the-cost-of-connectivity-2014.
6. Executive Office of the President, "Community-Based Broadband Solutions" 14 (Jan. 2015), https://obamawhitehouse.archives.gov/sites/default/files/docs/community-based_broadband_report_by_executive_office_of_the_president.pdf.
7. Edward Wyatt, "Fast Internet Is Chattanooga's New Locomotive," *New York Times* (Feb. 3, 2014).
8. Dominic Rushe, "Chattanooga's Gig: How One City's Super Fast Internet Is Driving a Tech Boom," *Guardian* (Aug. 30, 2014).
9. *Tennessee v. FCC,* 832 F.3d 597, 601 (6th Cir. 2016).
10. Executive Office of the President, "Community-Based Broadband Solutions," at 14.
11. *Tennessee v. FCC,* 832 F.3d 597, 602 (6th Cir. 2016).
12. Executive Office of the President, "Community-Based Broadband Solutions," at 15.
13. *Tennessee v. FCC,* 832 F.3d 597, 601 (6th Cir. 2016).
14. Federal Communications Commission, "Memorandum Opinion and Order in the Matter of City of Wilson, North Carolina" (Feb. 26,

2015), https://apps.fcc.gov/edocs_public/attachmatch/FCC-15-25A1.pdf.

15. *Tennessee v. FCC,* 832 F.3d 597 (6th Cir. 2016).
16. Lauren C. Williams, "Rural Tennesseans Could Have Gotten Free Internet but Their Legislators Shut It Down," *ThinkProgress* (Apr. 17, 2017).
17. Tara Siegel Bernard et al., "Equifax Says Cyberattack May Have Affected 143 Million in the U.S.," *New York Times* (Sept. 7, 2017).
18. Ron Lieber, "Finally, Some Answers from Equifax to Your Data Breach Questions," *New York Times* (Sept. 14, 2017).
19. Tara Siegel Bernard, "Credit Error? It Pays to Be a VIP," *New York Times* (May 14, 2011); Bobby Allyn, "How the Careless Errors of Credit Reporting Agencies Are Ruining People's Lives," *Washington Post* (Sept. 8, 2016).
20. Federal Trade Commission, Report to Congress Under Section 319 of the Fair and Accurate Credit Transactions Act of 2003, i (Dec. 2012), www.ftc.gov/sites/default/files/documents/reports/section-319-fair-and-accurate-credit-transactions-act-2003-fifth-interim-federal-trade-commission/130211factareport.pdf (finding that 5 percent of consumers had a major change in score after detecting and correcting an error; finding, too, that 26 percent of consumers had an error on at least one of the three credit reports).
21. Bryce Covert, "Get Rid of Equifax," *New York Times* (Sept. 21, 2017).
22. See, e.g., Pavlina R. Tcherneva, "The Job Guarantee: Design, Jobs, and Implementation," Levy Economics Institute Working Paper No. 902 (Apr. 2018); Mark Paul, William Darity Jr., & Darrick Hamilton, "The Federal Job Guarantee—A Policy to Achieve Permanent Full Employment," Center for Budget and Policy Priorities (Mar. 9, 2018); Neera Tanden et al., "Toward a Marshall Plan for America: Rebuilding Our Towns, Cities, and the Middle Class," Center for American Progress (May 16, 2017). Even centrists like former Clinton-era treasury secretary Robert Rubin

and Trump administration economist Kevin Hassett have registered support for the idea. See Robert E. Rubin, "Why the U.S. Needs a Federal Jobs Program, Not Payouts," *New York Times* (Nov. 8, 2017); Ben White, "Trump's Top Economist Offers Solution to Unemployment: More Government Jobs," *Politico Money* (Nov. 1, 2017).

23. 372 U.S. 335 (1963).
24. State of New Jersey, Office of the Public Defender, "History," www.state.nj.us/defender/history.
25. New York Civil Liberties Union, "A History of Public Defense in New York State," www.nyclu.org/en/history-public-defense-new-york-state.
26. Holly R. Stevens et al., "State, County, and Local Expenditures for Indigent Defense Services, FY2008," prepared for the American Bar Association (November 2010), www.americanbar.org/content/dam/aba/administrative/legal_aid_indigent_defendants/ls_sclaid_def_expenditures_fy08.authcheckdam.pdf.
27. Commission on the Future of Indigent Defense Services, "Final Report to the Chief Judge of the State of New York" (June 2006), http://nycourts.gov/ip/indigentdefense-commission/IndigentDefenseCommission_report06.pdf.
28. Yotam Shem-Tov, "Make-or-Buy? The Provision of Indigent Defense Services in the United States," Department of Economics, University of California, Berkeley (Dec. 5, 2017), https://papers.ssrn.com/sol3/papers.cfm?abstract_id=2816622.
29. See, e.g., Morris B. Hoffman et al., "An Empirical Study of Public Defender Effectiveness: Self-Selection by the 'Marginally Indigent,'" 3 *Ohio State Journal of Criminal Law* 223 (2005) (finding that measures of public defender effectiveness may be confounded if public defender clients have less defensible cases).
30. James Anderson & Paul Heaton, "How Much Difference Does the Lawyer Make? The Effect of Defense Counsel on Murder Case Outcomes," RAND Corporation and University of Pennsylvania Law School (Oct. 1, 2011), http://ssrn.com/abstract=1884379.

Acknowledgments

Our earliest conversations about public options began when Ganesh was visiting at Yale Law School, and they continued cross-country between Anne, at Yale, and Ganesh, at Vanderbilt University. We thank Deans Robert Post and Heather Gerken at Yale, Dean Chris Guthrie at Vanderbilt, and the Vanderbilt Program on Law and Government for their encouragement, support, and resources. In the later stages of this project, the Carnegie Corporation of New York offered generous and important backing through an Andrew Carnegie Fellowship.

A great thanks must also go out to the many people who read drafts of part or all of the book or who provided helpful comments during (sometimes very long) conversations: Bruce Ackerman, Rebecca Allensworth, Ian Ayres, Mehrsa Baradan, William Boyd, Paul Dempsey, Dan Epps, Franklin Foer, Ethan Gurwitz, Richard John, Jonathan Kanter, Lina Khan, Mike Konczal, Andy Koppelman, Matt Kozlov, Barry Lynn, Martha Minow, Julie Morgan, Sabeel Rahman, Morgan Ricks, Chris Serkin, Marshall Steinbaum, Maurice Stucke, Ramsi Woodcock, Tim Wu, Luigi Zingales, and participants in workshops at the law schools at Northwestern and Washington University. Quenna Stewart was invaluable in helping organize a roundtable at Vanderbilt, and Katie Choi, Ariel Dobkin, Laura Dolbow, Will Hudson, Brain Moore, Jeesoo Nam, Nathan Nash, Anderson Tuggle, and Elena Zarabozo provided research help.

The intrepid Chris Parris-Lamb championed our work, and Thomas LeBien was a pleasure to work with, as were Kathi Drummy, Louise Robbins, and Colleen Lanick at Harvard University Press. Finally, we thank our family and friends, who put up with hearing incessantly about the wonders of the Postal Service and public libraries.

Index